CHAUCER AT WORK

Chaucer at Work: The Making of the Canterbury Tales

Peter Brown

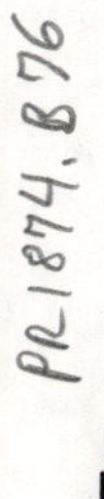

Longman
London and New York

Longman Group UK Limited,
Longman House, Burnt Mill,
Harlow, Essex CM20 2JE, England
and Associated Companies throughout the world.

Published in the United States of America
by Longman Publishing New York

First published 1994

ISBN 0 582 01319 4 PPR

British Library Cataloguing-in-Publication Data

A catalogue record for this book is available from the British Library

Library of Congress Cataloging-in-Publication Data

Brown, Peter, 1948-
Chauncer at work: the making of the Canterbury tales/Peter Brown.
p. cm.
Includes bibliographical references and index.
ISBN 0-582-01319-4
1. Chaucer, Geoffrey, d. 1400. Canterbury tales. 2. Christian pilgrims and pilgrimages—In literature. I. Title.
PR1874.B76 1994
821'.1—dc20 93-39019
CIP

Set by 13B in 10/12pt Bembo

Produced by Longman Singapore Publishers (Pte) Ltd.
Printed in Singapore

Contents

List of Illustrations

Author's Preface

The roots of this book lie in difficulty and ignorance. Any attempt to understand the *Canterbury Tales,* whether the reader be a novice or an advanced teacher, sooner or later runs into problems. Characteristically those problems concern lack of information: the words, and the ideas expressed, are alien or unfamiliar.

Much of the difficulty of the *Canterbury Tales,* and of medieval English literature in general, derives from its remoteness in time. It does not follow that more recent works are instantly intelligible. *The Waste Land* and *Ulysses* are not models of accessibility. For difficulty is a general feature of reading and interpretation which serious students of literature must face and overcome. But how are those ends to be achieved in the case of Chaucer?

Chaucer at Work rehearses some of the remedies customarily applied, but is chiefly concerned to advance a method founded in the experience of teaching Chaucer's poetry over a period of a dozen years. The method's mode of operation is fully explained in the Introduction. Its underlying objective is a shared experience of reading, and of trying to understand, the *Canterbury Tales.* Of course, a book can never replace the spontaneous and dynamic interaction of teaching and learning, but it can at least open up possibilities for future discussion, rather than pretend to be the last word.

My greatest debt is to the sixth-formers, undergraduates and graduates who have participated in the bewilderment, struggle, laughter, elation and sense of discovery which have marked our discussions of Chaucer's poetry. I have learnt much from teaching at the universities of York, Exeter, Kent, Connecticut and California (in Los Angeles), and from talking to sixth-formers and their teachers at conferences organised in Birmingham (University of Birmingham Department of Extramural Studies), Canterbury (Kent Education

Committee), Eltham (Avery Hill College), Folkestone (Eversley College), London (University of London Department of Extramural Studies; and the Museum of London); Manchester (Manchester Association for the Teaching of English); Rye (Syskon College); Sheffield (Department of English Language); Stratford-upon-Avon (University of Birmingham Department of Extramural Studies); and Thurmaston (Leicestershire Education Committee). I have also benefited from addressing individual schools, especially in the Canterbury area (Geoffrey Chaucer School, Kent College, King's School, Simon Langton Girls' School), but also further afield (Collyer's Sixth Form College, Horsham; Millfield School, Street). On a number of these pleasant excursions I have been accompanied as a co-teacher by my colleague in History, Andrew Butcher, from whom I have learnt more than I care to admit about Chaucer, fourteenth-century society and the art of teaching.

My dues to others who 'work on Chaucer' are extensive, and are all too apparent in the annotated booklists which conclude each chapter. The following pages also bear painful testimony to my own abiding ignorance and failure to overcome many of the difficulties raised by Chaucer's poetry.

The time in which to complete this book was generously provided by the University of Kent in the form of a study term; and the task of picture research was much eased by an award from the Colyer-Fergusson Charitable Trust, administered by the Faculty of Humanities at Kent. *Chaucer at Work* could not have been realised without the interest, help and encouragement of my family, friends, professional associates and students, particularly Helen, Oliver and Louisa Brown, Andrew Butcher, Gill Hogarth, Jim Styles, John West, the editorial staff at Longman and the Winter Quarter 1993 members of section 3, course 141A, at UCLA.

Darwin College
University of Kent at Canterbury
September 1993

Acknowledgements

We are grateful to the following for permission to reproduce illustrations and photographs:

The Bodleian Library, Oxford, pages 20, 124 and 149; Musée Condé, Chantilly, page 96; Corpus Christi College, Oxford, page 104; Pierpoint Morgan Library, New York, page 160; The British Library, page 174.

We have been unable to trace the copyright holder for the illustration on page 73 and would appreciate any information that would enable us to do so.

List of Abbreviations

Bo.	*Boece*
EETS	Early English Text Society
FrankT	Franklin's Tale
GP	General Prologue
HF	*House of Fame*
KnT	Knight's Tale
MerchT	Merchant's Tale
MillP	Miller's Prologue
MillT	Miller's Tale
MkT	Monk's Tale
NPP	Nun's Priest's Prologue
NPT	Nun's Priest's Tale
ns	new series
os	original series
PardP	Pardoner's Prologue
PardT	Pardoner's Tale
ParsP	Parson's Prologue
ProlTh	Prologue to Sir Thopas
PMLA	*Publications of the Modern Language Association of America*
Rom.	*Romaunt of the Rose*
Tes.	*Teseida*
WBP	Wife of Bath's Prologue
WBT	Wife of Bath's Tale

Note: line glosses are not provided for extensive quotations from the *Canterbury Tales*. Readers are referred to the *Riverside Chaucer*, ed. Benson, detailed on page 11. All quotations from Chaucer's works are from this edition.

Biblical quotations are from the Douay-Rheims translation of the Latin vulgate, detailed on page 135.

In memoriam

Leonard Brown
1906–1993

Introduction

Geoffrey Chaucer's work was of two kinds. The surviving records provide evidence of his busy public career as a court official, diplomat and civil servant. Its origins may be traced to 1357, when he was about seventeen and an attendant first to the countess of Ulster and then to her husband Lionel, duke of Clarence, one of Edward III's sons. Such an occupation was not without its adventures and dangers. In 1359–60, the duke of Clarence led a company of some seventy knights, esquires and archers to fight in the French wars. It is likely that Chaucer was among them, if only in the lowly capacity of valet, because he was serving in France at the time: he was ransomed by the king in 1360, showing that he had been captured, perhaps at the siege of Reims. One way or another, Chaucer caught the king's eye. By 1367 he was a member of Edward III's household and subsequently made many journeys overseas (to France, Italy and Spain) on diplomatic missions. Under both Edward and Richard II, who became king in 1376, Chaucer was also entrusted with a number of important commissions at home. His most significant was that of controller of the wool custom for the Port of London, a post he held for twelve years (1374–86). Throughout the reign of Richard, he continued to enjoy royal appointments, notably as clerk of the works (1389–91), with responsibility for maintaining and overseeing the king's buildings. Towards the end of his career, Chaucer became prominent in legal and political activities, both as a justice of the peace for Kent and as a knight of the shire for Kent (which entailed his attending parliament).

For all of this work Chaucer was indebted to the royal court: directly or indirectly he was, throughout his professional life, dependent upon the king for his annuities and other material benefits. Since Chaucer worked within a patronage system his prosperity depended upon the stability of his relationship with the court. Courts, though, are notoriously unstable places, not least when one dynasty replaces another (as happened on the accession of Henry IV in 1399, the year before Chaucer's death). Nevertheless, Chaucer's career indicates that he had remarkable staying power, and while there might have been periods when it was difficult for him to find favour, by and large he survived the fluctuations in court politics and continued to uphold his position as a distinguished royal official.

Chaucer's other work was the one for which he is chiefly remembered: writing. Success in this field also depended upon a secure arrangement with a patron, and there can be no doubt that, in this work too, Chaucer enjoyed considerable acclaim. He was admired and valued, both at court and by his professional associates, for his skill as a translator and poet. But writing was not his 'real work'. Except for one or two possibly lucrative commissions, it did not earn him a living. For that he depended upon his other, official, activities. His writing therefore had to be undertaken when other duties were less pressing. While it would be wrong to think of him as 'moonlighting', the effect was sometimes similar. Chaucer records, in the prologue to the *House of Fame,* the state of exhaustion he would reach in pursuing literary work after a day among his accounts:

For when thy labour doon al ys,
And hast mad alle thy rekenynges,
In stede of reste and newe thynges
Thou goost hom to thy hous anoon, 655
And, also domb as any stoon,
Thou sittest at another book
Tyl fully daswed ys thy look ... *dazed*

(*HF,* 652–8)

For a man of Chaucer's background and social position, work of any kind had two particular values. First there was its value as an instrument of social advancement. Many of the traditional demarcations between social categories were being eroded during his lifetime by the devastating effects of recurrent plague. That situation was aggravated by a protracted war with France, and by a revolt – the uprising of 1381 – which specifically targeted social inequality. In these circumstances it was becoming easier for people of skill and versatility to fill the gaps left by depopulation and social upheaval, and in the process to create new categories of work or, as we might say, niches for themselves. Chaucer's career is a case in point. As the son of a prosperous wine merchant who himself had connections with the court, Chaucer bettered his original mercantile status by dint of natural talent, hard work, the help of powerful patrons, and an advantageous marriage: his wife, Philippa de Roet, was the daughter of a nobleman, a member of the queen's household and sister-in-law to John of Gaunt, the father of Richard II.

Work also had a less immediate, more traditional, significance. Its theological value – which no one within Chaucer's Christian culture could escape – was as a punishment for sin. Work was the consequence of Adam and Eve's disobedience in the garden of Eden. God had forbidden them to eat from the tree of knowledge, but Eve was tempted to do so by Satan, in the form of a serpent. Adam in turn listened to the blandishments of his wife, and ate the forbidden fruit. As a result, they were both banished from the garden, and God pronounced: 'cursed is the earth in thy work; with labour and toil shalt thou eat thereof all the days of thy life ... In the sweat of thy face shalt thou eat bread' (Genesis 3:17 and 19). Salvation lay in the conscientious fulfilment of God's command: only through arduous work could man hope to regain paradise (Plates 4 and 8, pp. 104 and 174).

The focus of this book is on Chaucer's work as a writer (or, as we usually say, on his works) and in particular on a number of the Canterbury tales, although it will be impossible to ignore either their social or theological aspects. If Chaucer has left only a shadowy portrait of himself as a writer, it is possible nevertheless to reconstruct some of his habits and processes of work through a detailed examination of the poetry. But such an approach does not entail a merely mechanical analysis or dismantling into component parts. It has the advantage of bringing the reader close to the crucial thought patterns and priorities which shaped Chaucer's compositions, and therefore of leading to a fuller understanding of what his works mean. What becomes clear is that, while writing may not have been Chaucer's 'real work', neither was it just therapeutic recreation. He expected his compositions to work, both in the sense of causing pleasure and entertainment to others, and in promoting debate on serious matters – in short, in providing a combination of 'sentence' (serious, substantive meaning) and 'solaas' (comfort and diversion), to use Chaucer's own terms.

For modern readers, though, the title of this book may have quite different connotations, in that their encounter with the *Canterbury Tales* takes place at work, within the context of a school or college curriculum. *Chaucer at Work* is indeed intended to function in part as a tool with which teachers and students can work. It may be thought that there are sufficient of these ancillary works already, and indeed the production of aids for interpreting the *Canterbury Tales* has, in recent years, reached a high level of sophistication. The Penguin Critical

Studies series (formerly called Masterstudies), which devotes a book to a single tale, provides a comprehensive introduction to the ideas, literary procedures and verbal dexterity which inform Chaucer's writing, together with a line-by-line commentary. So conscientious is the undertaking that the tale itself (which forms part of the book) seems somewhat dwarfed and insignificant by comparison with the surrounding apparatus. The accent throughout – for example in Coote's *Nun's Priest's Tale* (1985) – is on thorough explanation in order to make the text as accessible and comprehensible as possible. Compiled with much erudition, enthusiasm and eloquence, such books run the danger of being over-informative in their drive to be all-inclusive. For the reader of Chaucer takes away two, not necessarily helpful, impressions: that in order for the poetry to be understood the issues raised in the introduction and commentary must first be fully absorbed; and that all of the issues which the poetry raises are set out in the critical framework. The effects of such Masterstudies (the original series title itself implying dominance) is to induce dependence on the part of their users when, for the sake of the individual's 'possession' of what Chaucer wrote, a more reciprocal attitude is needed.

A more oblique approach is made in *The Cambridge Chaucer Companion* (1986), a collection of new critical essays by leading specialists, covering all of Chaucer's works. The focus may be the *Canterbury Tales* (as in Derek Pearsall's discussion of comedy) or topics which cover an even wider range of material (as in Barry Windeatt's chapter on literary structures) but the intention remains the same: to provoke critical debate through exemplary readings. To this end, the authors leave a considerable amount of space for the student approaching Chaucer for the first time to develop his or her own ideas. The editors, Piero Boitani and Jill Mann, write: 'We feel the student is best served by a clearly pursued line of argument, which may set off his or her own thinking, rather than an exhaustive survey of the field' (p. viii). Consequently, the critical interpretations are not presented as definitive but in order to suggest that Chaucer's poetry is susceptible to a wide variety of different approaches. The book surely fulfils its function of making the reader of Chaucer want to read more, and more attentively; of suggesting ideas which can be taken away and worked with; of being an appetiser for the main course. The extraordinarily intelligent level of its engagement with Chaucer's works is intellectually stimulating, rather than overbearing. And yet a reader may be left wondering precisely what to do with the excitement generated by such a book. Wide in its scope, thematic in orientation, an individual chapter can cover individual tales only in general terms, with a scattering of brilliant *aperçus*. In these circumstances the section on further reading (a vital part of any introductory book) is particularly important, even though a student will look in vain for precise linkage between points made in individual chapters and items in the bibliography.

Helen Cooper's *The Canterbury Tales* (1989), one in a series of Oxford Guides to Chaucer, deals with the tales in the manner of an introduction to an edition. For each there is a careful discussion of the received wisdom concerning date of composition, textual matters, genre, sources and themes. It is a scholarly compilation, meticulously weighing the pros and cons of various theories and interpretations, and also advancing arguments of its own. Its highly rational and repetitive structure enables the guide to be used readily as a reference work, and indeed any of its chapters would form an excellent starting place for anyone wishing to make a serious and systematic study of a Canterbury tale. At the same time Cooper, like Boitani and Mann, recognises that it is impossible to provide a definitive account of Chaucer's poetry: the *Canterbury Tales* is, after all, unfinished; that, and the inherent open-ended nature of Chaucer's narratives, make the possibilities for interpretation virtually limitless. Or do they? What Cooper has in fact provided are the parameters within which new interpretations might be advanced. It is not the case (as she would concede) that all interpretations are equally valid, but, in order for a new interpretation to win acceptance, it must first take account of the terms and limits of existing debates. The apprentice critic has a lot to learn.

Other recent examples of introductory studies are listed at the end of this Introduction. It is difficult to imagine that readers of Chaucer, of various levels of competence, have ever been better served by professional critics and scholars. Each of the works mentioned above has an air of authority as well as an infectious desire to share their authors' central enthusiasms. For all that, they share a common failing, one that is generic among introductions to Chaucer's works. It is a failing to which Chaucer himself might have been sensitive: in their drive to be authoritative, and bolstered by the publishers' blurbs, the books leave precious little room for the learning experience of the stumbling student, in spite of their well intentioned gestures in that direction.

The Chaucer guide, companion, or masterstudy, is based on the assumption that information and approaches relevant to, say, a Canterbury tale are there to be learnt, applied, imitated and reproduced, probably in the context of a school or higher education curriculum. Reasonable though the assumption may be, it excludes specific reference to the ways in which a student might duplicate the processes whereby respected scholars and critics themselves reach their wise conclusions. The Chaucer guidebook tends to be a compendium of conclusions. Except in the matter of developing an argument (a skill necessary to all literary study) it does not exemplify those other methods of literary enquiry which are no less basic to developing a reader's sense of confidence and independence in interpreting a Chaucerian text. Boitani and Mann, introducing *The Cambridge Chaucer Companion,* hope that the explanations, contexts and criticisms which it provides will enable students to 'test their own responses' to Chaucer's works (p. viii). But a student's response, unless it eventually attains specialist status, will almost always be, and feel, inferior to that of the published expert. In what ways, then, can a testing of response in such circumstances be a productive and genuinely enlarging educational transaction? The student is as much likely to feel overwhelmed and intimidated by expertise, and doubtful about the possibility of producing authentic readings of his or her own, as confident in arguing an individually developed viewpoint.

It is instructive at this point to give some consideration both to the kind of literary guide or companion with which Chaucer was familiar, and to the kind of guide which he favoured within his own compositions. Here the term 'guide' is taken to mean just that: not a book, but an individual who offers help and direction. A work which Chaucer translated from Latin, and which exerted a profound influence on his writing, was the *Consolation of Philosophy* by Boethius (*c.* AD 475–525). It is structured by a dialogue between the imprisoned author and Lady Philosophy, who appears to him in a vision. Before her appearance, Boethius has been seeking some comfort from the rigours of imprisonment in the art of poetry, a mainstay of his previous life. The *Consolation* begins with an acknowledgement that the poetry he will now write will, of necessity, be less joyful than hitherto. Chaucer's version, *Boece,* reads: 'Allas! I wepynge, am constreyned to bygynnen vers of sorwful matere, that whilom [*once*] in florysschyng study made delitable ditees' (I, metrum 1, 1–3). But with the arrival of Lady Philosophy, the consolations of poetry are rejected. Seeing 'poetical muses' attending Boethius she is angry and dismisses them as 'comune strompettis' who encourage self-indulgent introversion (I, prosa 1, 43–53). For the remainder of the treatise – which is nevertheless of the highest literary quality – she introduces Boethius to the more austere, but more enduring and spiritually beneficial, solace of philosophical speculation.

Poetry is given a more positive role by Dante (1265–1321), whom

Chaucer calls the 'wise poete of Florence' (WBT, 1125). In his *Divine Comedy* it is none other than the great poet of Roman antiquity, Virgil, who acts as Dante's guide to hell and purgatory. Kindred spirits and fellow practitioners they may be, but the fictional Virgil, no less than Lady Philosophy, is quick to correct the error of the author's ways. Faltering at the thought of his long, tortuous and dangerous journey, Dante attempts to avoid it in a show of fear and false humility: he is not Aeneas, who visited the underworld, nor St Paul, who is supposed to have entered hell, but someone less heroic and more prone to folly. Virgil stiffens Dante's resolve, torn as it is by indecision, by declaring that his soul is 'smitten with cowardice' before going on to explain that it was no less a person than Beatrice, Dante's dead love, who asked Virgil to bring him to her (*Inferno,* canto II, lines 31–54; trans. Sinclair).

Through figures such as Lady Philosophy and Virgil, Chaucer was acquainted with authoritative fictional guides who explained bewilderment, corrected error and prevented hesitation by providing a superior knowledge and sense of direction. And yet, when he introduces such figures into his own poetry, Chaucer shuns the models he knew. Instead, he shifts the focus to the problem of internalising knowledge, of making it personally meaningful. The *House of Fame,* quoted above, is an early poem presented in the form of a dream. It draws some of its inspiration from the *Divine Comedy*. But it gives short shrift to informative companions. In one incident derived from Dante's poem (*Purgatorio,* canto IX), an eagle seizes the lost narrator ('Geffrey') and carries him away. As they fly ever higher above the receding earth the eagle, not unlike Virgil, offers detailed explanations of what has happened, and what they see: how he was sent by Jupiter to take Geffrey to a place (the House of Fame) where he might have some news about love, a subject on which he is well read but of which he has no direct experience. Having broached the subjects of news, fame, rumour and reputation, the eagle advances at length a theory about the transmission of sound. By the time that this is over, the earth is little more than a speck and so Geffrey's loquacious teacher turns his attention to the stars and constellations now clearly visible. Geffrey, dangling like a lark in the talons of the great bird, absorbs little of this information: he is too scared. Fear, not a calm absorption of intellectual matters, dominates his response. At first he faints, only to be roused by the eagle with a loud 'Awake!'. The best he can manage in response to his captor's lengthy orations is tight-lipped, trembling monosyllables. Only towards the end of his flight does he have the presence of mind to marvel at what he can see: the galaxy, the Milky Way, and 'ayerissh bestes, / Cloudes, mystes, and tempestes' (965–6). The lasting impressions are not of information absorbed but of emotions experienced; of a guide or teacher who is actually an obstacle to the personal possession of knowledge; and of the direct and affecting impact of marvellous sights, stirring that curiosity and wonder which are the roots of genuine learning, once the eagle falls silent. In the end it is by showing, not by telling, that the eagle succeeds.

Another example demonstrates how, again through comedy, Chaucer deflates the pretensions of an over-authoritative guide. Even in the early stages of the pilgrimage to Canterbury, Harry Bailly, the pilgrims' host and guide, finds that his control of the tale-telling game is not entirely secure. Once the Knight has finished his contribution, the Host invites the Monk to begin his. In a hierarchical scheme of things it would be appropriate that he should: a prominent member of the clerical establishment would thereby follow a prominent member of the secular one. But Harry Bailly has counted without the presence of a drunken miller who insists that he, not the Monk, should tell the next tale. The Host protests, but the Miller is not in a state to be argued with. The Reeve then voices his disapproval of the 'lewed dronken harlotrye' (MillP, 3145) which is likely to follow, only to be silenced by personal abuse from the Miller. Again, it is the logic of emotion, rather than the logic of preconceived structures, which wins the day. For, in spite of appearances to the contrary, there is method in the Miller's madness. He has heard certain views expressed in the Knight's Tale with which he does not agree and so he wants to cap it or 'quite' it from the opposite end of the social spectrum. So he offers a churl's tale in opposition to the tale of a noble knight, in which the high-flown principles which inform the Knight's world (both real and fictional) are debunked in favour of more basic human drives. At the same time, his tale acts as a vehicle for attacking the Reeve, who is a carpenter like John, the old fool who is duped in the Miller's Oxford tale.

If a guide to the *Canterbury Tales* is to reflect as faithfully as possible Chaucer's own ambivalence towards authority figures and the wisdom at their disposal, it must pay as much attention to the process by which relevant knowledge is acquired (the learning experience) as it does to the intrinsic importance of sanctioned information. That is an objective much more difficult to achieve in print than in the classroom or seminar room, where the interchange between teacher and student can readily foster co-operative learning and the making of discoveries. A book, on the other hand, is always in danger of itself being taken as the last word (since it can't be questioned, or answer back), however much its author might resist that role. But a book can offer something more radical than exemplary argument and an acknowledgement that the interpretation of Chaucer's works is still open to debate. It can also provide access to methods of analysis which scholars and critics use but which usually remain hidden from the reader of introductory studies. Those learning processes, like the ones experienced by 'Geffrey', are characterised by feelings of hesitancy, tentativeness and doubt, although little of that is evident in the confident assertions of published research. Most importantly, those processes are ones which map the internalising of the imaginative and intellectual life, the possessing for oneself, of a given text. That, together with the confidence and security in interpretation which inevitably follow, must surely be desirable ends for all readers.

But how can readers of Chaucer, at a relatively elementary level of study, become involved in the kinds of research procedures normally reserved for 'Chaucerians'? By becoming acquainted with some of the raw materials with which Chaucer worked to fashion his literary creations. (One Middle English word for 'poet' was *makar* or 'maker'.) The visual images which Chaucer manipulated, and the compositions of other medieval writers, both fascinate in their own right and supply crucial data by the side of which Chaucer's distinctive practices become clearer. From such a basis, students are indeed well placed to undertake their own critical projects, to evaluate the interpretations of established specialists and, from a well-informed viewpoint, to define for themselves the horizon of meaning which a particular tale holds in prospect.

Chaucer at Work, therefore, approaches the *Canterbury Tales* through its sources and contexts. That phrase is here taken to mean not merely the directly influential origins of Chaucer's narratives, but the broad relationship of his literary activities to, say, rhetorical handbooks, the Bible and its commentaries, pictorial images and the work of contemporary and earlier poets and writers. The concern is as much with his imaginative roots and affiliations as with the works from which he borrowed material outright. The advantages of the approach are manifold. First, it introduces students to a cross-section of medieval cultural products – symbols and images, ideas and modes of expression, stylistic and narrative models – which fed the imagination of Chaucer and his contemporaries, forming vital reference points for an understanding of his poetry, whether by a medieval audience or by a modern one. Second, it highlights one of the most distinctive features of medieval poetry: that it was not created from nothing out of the genius of a poet, but that it is highly derivative – each Canterbury tale, for example, being a carefully worked compilation of borrowings.

Understanding the extent of that borrowing is a prerequisite to evaluating the nature of its transformation and its originality: it is a way of watching Chaucer at work as he made choices and decisions on the basis of the material available to him and in accordance with certain thematic imperatives. Finally, source and context study fosters the essential but too often neglected critical techniques of attentive reading, close observation, comparison and contrast. Such practices are useful in studying all Chaucerian texts, but they are also basic to literary study in general. Their practical appeal, in offering the prospect of results on the basis of carefully evaluated evidence, is matched by the intellectual stimulus they provide.

Each chapter is devoted to a single work or tale, and divided into two or more linked parts. Within each part a passage from the tale is subjected to close analysis and examined in the light of a particular source or context. Care is taken to select a passage and context which are crucial to an understanding of the tale as a whole. The accent in the first instance is on detail, on particularities, rather than on general statements. The detail is then built into a single line of interpretive argument which connects with those developed along similar principles in the rest of the chapter. As each chapter progresses, matters of more general interest gradually come into focus. Beyond this, the end-point of each chapter is not so much a ticking off of targets reached as the identification of further subjects worthy of debate. The intention throughout is to make observations and to raise questions, rather than to provide ready answers, to show rather than to tell. Concluding sections, of questions for further discussion, and of further reading, provide some direction. Many sources and analogues exist in translation, many medieval paintings exist in reproduction, and some of the major compilations are referred to at the end of this Introduction. They are a mine of information for the teacher or student who wishes to develop an independent approach to Chaucer's works. Direction may also be found in the book as a whole. Although the chapters may be read as free-standing, there is some cross-referencing among them, and the book does develop an overarching argument.

That argument concerns literary conventions, the construction of character, the representation of women, the use of symbolic images, key themes such as *gentillesse* and patience, and the modes and genres which Chaucer uses, as well as his preference for open-ended debate rather than conclusive moral teaching. But that is to anticipate the larger plan. First come detailed observation and the plotting of local arguments. No two readers will map the same route through Chaucer's works, and on the way they should enjoy some lively differences of tendency and opinion. If so, *Chaucer at Work* will have succeeded in its task.

FURTHER READING

Editions

Benson, Larry D. (ed.), *The Riverside Chaucer,* based on *The Works of Geoffrey Chaucer* edited by F. N. Robinson (Boston, MA: Houghton Mifflin, 1987).
All line references are to this standard edition.

Kolve, V. A., and Olson Glending, (eds), *The Canterbury Tales: Nine Tales and the General Prologue: Authoritative Text; Sources and Backgrounds; Criticism,* Norton Critical Edition (New York and London: Norton, 1989).
An extremely useful compendium, containing the prologues and tales of the Knight, Miller, Reeve, Wife of Bath, Clerk, Franklin, Pardoner, Prioress and Nun's Priest. Over 200 pages of carefully chosen sources and backgrounds follow, then some selected criticism (chiefly on the General Prologue and narrative framework of the tales).

Sinclair, John D. (trans.), *The Divine Comedy of Dante Alighieri,* rev. edn, 3 vols (London: Oxford University Press, 1948).

Introductory studies mentioned in this chapter

Boitani, Piero, and Jill Mann, (eds), *The Cambridge Chaucer Companion* (Cambridge and London: Cambridge University Press, 1986).

Cooper, Helen, *The Canterbury Tales,* Oxford Guides to Chaucer (Oxford: Clarendon Press, 1989).

Coote, Stephen, *Chaucer: The Nun's Priest's Tale,* Penguin Critical Studies, formerly Masterstudies, (Harmondsworth: Penguin, 1985).

Other introductions

Aers, David, *Chaucer,* Harvester New Readings (Brighton: Harvester, 1986).
Ranges over the major works, looking at three key themes – society; religion; and marriage and sexual relations – arguing that Chaucer

typically represents orthodox views in a critical if not subversive way.

Blamires, Alcuin, *The Canterbury Tales,* The Critics Debate (London: Macmillan, 1987).

A lively introduction to some of the main themes of modern criticism. See especially pp. 6–15 on source study.

Brewer, Derek, *An Introduction to Chaucer* (London: Longman, 1984).

Updated and rewritten version of his *Chaucer* and *Chaucer in his Times,* combined in a new book providing introductory historical and cultural contexts, biography and criticism (on all of Chaucer's works).

Kane, George, *Chaucer,* Past Masters (Oxford: Oxford University Press, 1984).

A literary biography, stressing Chaucer's originality and achievement, with some reference to the documented events of his life.

Knight, Stephen, *Geoffrey Chaucer,* Rereading Literature (Oxford: Blackwell, 1986).

Revisionary attempt at a radical reappraisal in order to demonstrate how Chaucer's writing is necessarily a response to his social and political conditions. Half of the book is on the *Canterbury Tales.*

Pope, Rob, *How to Study Chaucer* (London: Macmillan, 1988).

A user-friendly guide aimed at the beginner.

Stone, Brian, *Chaucer,* Penguin Critical Studies (Harmondsworth: Penguin, 1989).

Provides introductory commentary on all of Chaucer's verse narratives.

Williams, David, *The Canterbury Tales: A Literary Pilgrimage,* Twayne's Masterwork Studies, no. 4. (Boston: Twayne, 1987).

Sets the *Canterbury Tales* in their historical context, with an emphasis on philosophical themes.

Chaucer's life

Brewer, Derek, *Chaucer and his World* (London: Eyre Methuen, 1978).

Vivid and lavishly illustrated biography, using social history as well as literature to reconstruct Chaucer's formative experiences.

Crow, Martin M., and Clair C. Olson, (eds), *Chaucer Life-Records* (Oxford: Clarendon Press, 1966).

Standard scholarly collection of edited documents (in Latin and French) with a bearing on Chaucer's professional career. Extensive commentaries evaluate the significance of individual items.

Du Boulay, F.R. H., 'The Historical Chaucer', in *Geoffrey Chaucer,* ed. Derek Brewer (London: Bell 1974), pp. 33–57; repr. in Kolve and Olson, pp. 441–59.
Sets Chaucer's life in the context of his family, professional associates, the court and society.

Howard, Donald R., *Chaucer and the Medieval World* (London: Weidenfeld and Nicolson, 1987).
A lengthy but highly readable account of Chaucer's life, integrated with studies of medieval culture and of Chaucer's works.

Pearsall, Derek, *The Life of Geoffrey Chaucer: A Critical Biography,* Blackwell Critical Biographies, 1 (Oxford and Cambridge, MA: Blackwell, 1992).
Breathes life into the *Chaucer Life-Records* by providing historical contexts for Chaucer's career as a court official and poet, as well as by tracking the elusive connections between Chaucer's life and his works. Set to become the standard biography: both readable and scholarly.

Literary sources

Benson, Larry D., and Theodore M. Andersson, (eds), *The Literary Context of Chaucer's Fabliaux: Texts and Translations* (Indianapolis and New York: Bobbs-Merrill, 1971).
Versions of the Miller's Tale, Reeve's Tale, Merchant's Tale and Shipman's Tale, from a wide variety of periods and countries.

Bryan, W. F., and Germaine Dempster, (eds), *Sources and Analogues of Chaucer's Canterbury Tales* (Chicago, IL: University of Chicago Press, 1941).
The standard collection: marginal summaries give a guide to content, and each chapter includes a short critical introduction.

Miller, Robert P. (ed.), *Chaucer: Sources and Backgrounds* (New York: Oxford University Press, 1977).
Wide-ranging and illuminating collection, carefully keyed in to Chaucer's works, and arranged by theme, e.g. Creation and Fall, Modes of Love, The Antifeminist Tradition.

Rickert, Edith (comp.), *Chaucer's World,* ed. Clair C. Olson and Martin M. Crow (New York and London: Columbia University Press, 1948).
Anthology of vivid historical documents and excerpts (in modern English) providing such contexts as London Life; The Home, Training and Education; Travel; War; Religion.

Chaucer at Work: The Making of the Canterbury Tales

Pictorial contexts

Hussey, Maurice, *Chaucer's World: A Pictorial Companion* (London and New York: Cambridge University Press, 1967).
Illustrations with commentary, designed to enlarge the reader's understanding of people, places, buildings, objects, events and images in the *Canterbury Tales.*

Kolve, V. A., 'Chaucer and the Visual Arts', in *Geoffrey Chaucer,* ed. Derek Brewer (London: Bell 1974), pp. 290–320.
Explores different ways of using medieval art in the interpretation of Chaucer's writing, stressing the primacy of symbolic images, and their function in the imaginations of Chaucer and his audience.

Loomis, Roger Sherman, *A Mirror of Chaucer's World* (Princeton, NJ: Princeton University Press, 1965).
Compendium of illustrations of medieval buildings, pictures, sculptures and other objects to provide readers of Chaucer with better informed imaginations.

Special topics

Burlin, Robert S., *Chaucerian Fiction* (Princeton, NJ: Princeton University Press, 1977).
See ch. 1 on Chaucer's elusive attitude towards authority.

Justman, Stewart, 'Medieval Monism and Abuse of Authority in Chaucer', *Chaucer Review,* 11 (1976-7), 95-111.
The multiplicity, abuse and recession of authorities in Chaucer's compositions result in (at best) a relative truth; for this there are antecedents in formal academic debates and medieval scholarship.

Sklute, Larry, *Virtue of Necessity: Inconclusiveness and Narrative Form in Chaucer's Poetry* (Columbus: Ohio State University Press, 1984.)
Considers the unfinished nature of many of Chaucer's poems, with a special emphasis on the *Canterbury Tales* ('an early model for modern fiction'). Argues that inconclusiveness is a way of accommodating the opposing views of a debate without resolving them, and of promoting multiple meanings instead of certainty.

Bibliography

For a survey to the early 1970s see:

Benson, L. D. 'Chaucer: A Select Bibliography', in *Geoffrey Chaucer,* ed. D. S. Brewer, Writers and Their Background (London: Bell, 1974), pp. 352–72.

For the mid 1970s to the early 1980s consult:

Baird-Lange, Lorrayne Y., and Hildegard Schnuttgen, *A Bibliography of Chaucer 1974–1985* (Hamden, CT: Shoe String/Archon; Woodbridge: Boydell and Brewer, 1988).

The introduction by Baird-Lange, 'Chaucer Studies: Continuations, Developments, and Prognostications', provides an excellent account of major trends.

For 1985 on, refer to the annual listings of:

Heffernan, Thomas J. (ed.), *Studies in the Age of Chaucer,* vol. 8–. (Knoxville: University of Tennessee, 1986–).

Two recent surveys, each with the added advantage of short summaries of the contents of each items, are:

Allen, Mark, and John H. Fisher, *The Essential Chaucer: An Annotated Bibliography of Major Modern Studies,* A Reference Publication in Literature (Boston, MA: Hall; London: Mansell, 1987).

Leyerle, John, and Anne Quick, *Chaucer: A Bibliographical Introduction,* Toronto Medieval Bibliographies, 10 (Toronto: University of Toronto Press, 1986).

Still useful for its chapter length thematic surveys of criticism and scholarship, with appended bibliographies, is:

Rowland, Beryl, *Companion to Chaucer Studies,* rev. edn (New York and Oxford: Oxford University Press, 1979).

CHAPTER ONE

The General Prologue

This chapter, like the ones which follow, is organised around a series of exercises in analysis and comparison. In each case the onus is put on you to assess each passage or picture in turn, on its own merits, as well as to consider it in relation to other material. The point of this type of exercise should now be clear but it is worth reiterating. First, it will introduce you to a particular source or context important for a fuller understanding of Chaucer's tale. And second, you will be enabled by means of comparison to interrogate Chaucer's poetry in order to discover something of Chaucer's working methods, what meaning he was trying to express, and why. The exercises are linked in two ways: by introductory material that provides relevant information; and by a line of argument which builds on your responses. That argument does, of course, betray the intentions and values of the present author but, it is to be hoped, not in a way that predetermines the outcome of your own thinking. The intention is to maintain a dialogue, an interactive relation, between author and reader as far as is possible within the confines of a book. If the end result is a questioning of my own points of view, so much the better.

i. THE PILGRIMAGE CONTROVERSY

Pilgrimage was a controversial topic when Chaucer wrote the *Canterbury Tales*. It had become a subject of heated debate between the orthodox and reforming wings of the church. In order to understand the terms of those different positions, and their relevance to the General Prologue, it is necessary first to understand what pilgrimage meant in later fourteenth-century England. As we might expect, the Bible provides the basis for the medieval idea of pilgrimage. Adam and Eve, expelled from paradise, were the first exiles who wandered through the world because of their own sinfulness. The Israelites, led by Moses and Aaron, journeyed in search of the promised land. Most influential of all was the homeless travelling back and forth of Christ, a condition imitated in the deliberate homelessness of the early Christian ascetics. The church fathers were acutely aware of the importance of pilgrimage both as a devotional practice and as a metaphor for the human condition. St Ambrose described the Christian life as a three-stage pilgrimage which involves man's perception of the world as a desert, his determination to wander in search of redemption, and his final acceptance into paradise by Christ. St Augustine viewed human life as a journey either towards the sinful, man-made city of Babylon, or towards Jerusalem, the city of God.

What pilgrimage figures is alienation: alienation from God, caused in the first instance by Lucifer's act of rebellion, then by Adam and Eve's, and individually through sin, especially that of pride. Pilgrimage, whether understood literally or figuratively, was a means of signifying and enacting the individual's desire to return to the lost heavenly paradise. That desire springs from a sense of homelessness and strangeness in this world, a sense that one's true home is elsewhere, at the end of the 'journey'. Pilgrimage is therefore an expression of a double alienation: from God and the world. Ideally it is a search for a lost order and integrity.

What, in practice, did pilgrimage entail? At one extreme, it might mean withdrawal from the world to the rigours of a hermetic or monastic life. Here, the idea of pilgrimage is turned wholly inwards to signify the journey of the human soul towards salvation. At the other extreme it could involve an actual journey (the outer performance of the inner need) to sacred places. Those places were usually identified by their association with the life and suffering of Christ or of the saints and martyrs. At the pilgrim's destination, he or she would find tangible evidence of its sanctity in the form of relics – material remains such as the bones, skin or clothes of the saint, or of associated buildings and objects. Since churches were founded on the basis of the relics they possessed, pilgrimage in practice usually had as its objective a church, within which there would be a shrine housing a relic or relics. The shrine could be quite small and portable, in the form of a reliquary; or it might be large, like the shrine at Canterbury cathedral which contained the bones of St Thomas, martyred in 1170. At the shrine the pilgrim would make an offering and pray, in the hope and expectation that the spiritual supercharge of the place would ensure the efficacy of the prayer. Prayers might also be directed towards healing purposes, the healing of physical ailments being one of the prerogatives of Christ and his canonised disciples. So a pilgrimage was, in theory, an extremely pious act, designed to display devotion and perhaps to secure healing. It could also be an act of penitence, publicly or privately enjoined on an individual to make amends for sin. In order to show his remorse for the death of Thomas Becket, Henry II made a pilgrimage to Canterbury cathedral in 1174. At Harbledown (a mile from the city) he dismounted from his horse and in humble clothes began to walk, pausing half-way to remove his shoes. On reaching the tomb of St Thomas he prostrated himself and was flagellated by the monks.

The modernised excerpt below conveniently sets out in straightforward terms the ideology of pilgrimage. It dates from about 1400, the year of Chaucer's death, and is from an anonymous treatise, *A Mirror to Ignorant Men and Women,* of the sort that was to be produced in increasing variety and quantity to cater for the growing numbers of literate lay persons with a taste for private piety and for instruction in the essential components of the Christian faith. Deriving from a French Dominican work of the thirteenth century, it contains a series of expositions on such topics as the Creed, and the vices and virtues, linked by a commentary on the Pater Noster. The roots of the book are in long established traditions of spiritual guidance which urged a close consideration of both the literal and metaphoric implications of the Bible, buttressed with appropriate allusions to the church fathers. The *Mirror* opens as follows:

> It is true that all people in this world are in exile and live in wilderness outside their true country; everyone is a pilgrim or traveller in a foreign country where he may in no way live, but must every hour and minute of the day be passing on his way, as the Bible says: 'For here have we no continuing city, but we seek one to come' [Hebrews 13:14]. And the place to come is one of two cities, of which one may be called the city of Jerusalem, that is the city of peace, and the other the city of Babylon, or confusion. By the city of Jerusalem, or peace, should be understood the endless bliss of heaven, where there is endless peace, joy and rest without interruption. And by the city of Babylon, or confusion, you should understand the endless pain of hell, where all kinds of confusion, shame and destruction, sorrow and misery, shall be without end.
>
> And since all of man's life in this world is like a movement or journey or path to one of these two cities, that is to say to endless bliss or endless pain, the holy doctor saint Augustine in his meditations teaches us and says: with awareness, taking careful thought, superior effort and continual care, we are required to learn and find out by what means and by what way we may shun the pain of hell and obtain the bliss of heaven. For that pain, Augustine says, may not be shunned nor that joy bought

unless the way is known. And as we can see that these two cities are opposites, so are the ways that lead to them contrary to each other – which ways be none other but that the one leading to endless bliss is virtues and virtuous living, and the other leading to endless pain is sin and sinful living.

(*A Myrour to Lewde Men and Wymmen,* ed. Nelson, p. 71)

Now answer the following questions.

1. *How does the author of the* Mirror *express the idea of alienation?*
2. *What is the nature of reality as expressed in this passage?*
3. *What is the significance of pilgrimage in the author's scheme of things?*
4. *What are the respective attributes of Jerusalem and Babylon?*

The writer begins by stating that the basis of the human condition is exile and alienation. Like it or not, we are pilgrims, foreigners, strangers, and our true home is elsewhere. And not only our home, but also reality: the underlying assumption is that the world in which we find ourselves is, in spite of appearances, insubstantial, illusory and fleeting, and that truth and stability are elsewhere. For this view the Bible provides unimpeachable authority, as in the quotation from Hebrews. Having rehearsed, or established, a bifocal perspective on human experience, the unknown author goes on to use duality, binary opposition, as a way both of structuring the argument and of developing its content. Thus a distinction is drawn between Jerusalem – associated with the desirable peace, bliss, heaven, joy, rest – and Babylon – associated with pain, hell, confusion, shame, destruction, sorrow and misery. These then are alternative destinations of the human soul, which may be reached by alternative routes.

Now the writer, at the beginning of the second paragraph, returns to the metaphor of pilgrimage. Since life is a pilgrimage (goes the reasoning) and since our ultimate destination is one of two cities (Jerusalem or Babylon), then we ought to take care to map out the road by which such places are reached. Here another kind of authority, of the patristic variety (the reference to Augustine), is introduced to provide further support. Awareness, careful thought, superior effort – in a word, virtuous living – form the path to endless bliss, sinful living the path to endless pain. The emphasis then is not on pilgrimage as act but on pilgrimage as a way of figuring an internal reality. This metaphorical way of discoursing is an expression of an outlook which sees reality lying beyond or beneath the surface of sense impressions. Practical pilgrimage is of course not ruled out in this scheme of things, but pilgrimage is seen as essentially an inward movement of the soul to God.

An image from a contemporary manuscript (Plate 1) will help to capture the doubleness of pilgrimage. (The writing beneath reads: 'When these words I heard, of joy I was fulfilled; much liked me the abridging of my way and the shorting, and nothing misliked me ... ').
Look carefully at the picture and answer the following questions:

1. *What does the figure on the left represent?*
2. *What associations does the sea have?*
3. *What is the significance of the ship?*
4. *What is the narrative content of the picture?*
5. *How does the picture illuminate the passage from the* Mirror?

Ostensibly, this is a picture of a pilgrim, staff in hand, about to embark on a ship in order to continue with the next stage of his journey. We might also note that he is tonsured, and dressed in a habit, signifying that he is a monk; and that the ship's mast is topped by a crucifix (an emblem of which also appears on the sail), surrounded by spears. Perhaps they are associated with the crucifixion image as instruments of Christ's death.

Thus a close examination of the picture indicates that it is enigmatic, that it has a symbolic dimension, one that is suggested by the title of the

Plate 1: Pilgrim's progress.

text in which it appears, *The Pilgrimage of the Life of the Manhode,* an English translation made in the early 1400s of Guillaume de Deguileville's *Pèlerinage de la vie humaine* (1330–31), part of which was translated by Chaucer as his *ABC,* a prayer to the Virgin. In it the author, presenting himself as a monk, describes how he had a dream of a pilgrimage to Jerusalem. It turns out to be a medieval *Pilgrim's Progress:* en route, the dreamer encounters temptations and setbacks, as well as help and encouragement. Towards the end of his journey, a figure called Tribulation hurls him into the sea and, although he cannot swim, he keeps afloat by holding on to his pilgrim staff, the pommels of which signify Christ and the Virgin. Eventually he is rescued by Grace-Dieu (grace of God) who tells him that his progress to Jerusalem (or heaven) will be much helped if he boards the ship (the words beneath the picture express his gratitude). The ship is called 'To Bind Again' because those who enter must submit to its rules, which are of a monastic kind. Grace-Dieu explains that the vessel is the ship of religion: she is its mistress, the mast is the cross, and the wind which blows it is the Holy Ghost. Once on board, the dreamer learns how the shedding of Christ's blood makes his own salvation possible. He awakes much disturbed by his imaginings and prays that good pilgrims will be vouchsafed a good haven in heaven.

The dream framework of the *Pilgrimage* is important in identifying what subsequently happens as mental events. In other words, it is about pilgrimage as a metaphor for spiritual progress towards salvation. Although there are practical implications – as in Grace-Dieu's insistence that the good pilgrim must be bound by the rules and regulations of the church – the emphasis throughout is on the concrete realisation of the abstract, the inward. A rather different impression is created by the second, contemporary, extract, which is part of an attack on pilgrimage by an anonymous Lollard (the name disparagingly given to followers of the Oxford reformer, John Wyclif).

> These pilgrimages and offerings seem to be caused by the deceitfulness of the fiend and by his covetous and worldly clerics, for commonly such pilgrimages maintain lechery, gluttony, drunkenness, extortions, wrongs and worldly vanities. For men who may not practise their lechery at home as they would for fear of lords, masters, and the outcry of neighbours, make plans many days in advance and collect what funds and supplies they can, pinching and scraping to do so, to go out of the country on pilgrimage to distant images. On the way they live in lechery, in gluttony, in drunkenness, and maintain the falseness of landlords, cooks and taverners, and vainly spend their wealth, and leave behind the real work they should do at home to help themselves and their neighbours. They boast of their gluttony when they return home, saying

> that they drank nothing but wine during the entire journey, by which misspending a greater part of the people fares the worse in their household for half a year afterwards, and they are perhaps led into debts that they never pay off. Men guilty of extortion and of acquiring goods under false pretences are easily absolved and charged in confession to make such pilgrimages and offerings. And some men go because they desire to see fair countries rather than because of any sweet devotion in their souls to God or the saint that they seek. And thus is true penance prevented, and foul wrongs and extortions wickedly maintained, and the poor people wickedly robbed ...
> (Modernised from *English Wycliffite Writings,* ed. Hudson, pp. 86-7)

Now answer the following questions.

1. *Identify the major differences of emphasis between the* Mirror *and the Lollard tract.*
2. *Describe and discuss the economics of pilgrimage as they are presented by the author.*
3. *What are the negative effects of pilgrimage on society?*
4. *Do the authors of the* Mirror *and the tract share any opinions and attitudes?*
5. *Compare and contrast the representation of pilgrimage in the tract and in Guillaume's* Pilgrimage.

The emphasis here is not on theory but on practice: it is a polemical analysis of what the institution of pilgrimage has become – it has become, it seems (paradoxically), not the expression of an individual's desire to reach heavenly Jerusalem, but the fast lane to Babylon. We are sure that we are in the material world when the author begins by linking pilgrimage with offerings (the money and gifts offered by pilgrims at shrines), to which the church authorities looked for a source of income. This is the world of cash and economics, and the Lollard author has a shrewd idea of how pilgrimage – whatever else it may be – is a moneyspinner. There is expense implied in excessive indulgence, the 'maintenance' of lechery, gluttony, drunkenness; a sense of criminal exploitation in the word 'extortions'; a picture of getting and spending beyond the pilgrim's means, as he pinches and scrapes to collect funds and supplies; an insight into the black economy which was part of the infrastructure of pilgrimage, with its false landlords, cooks and taverners; an observation that mis-spending on pilgrimage has consequences for the household of the pilgrim, which is impoverished as a result, and perhaps led into debts that are never cleared; and perhaps most startling of all, that membership of the pilgrimage mafia extends even to the clergy themselves, who use pilgrimage as an easy way of absolving those criminals found guilty of extortion and of acquiring goods under false pretences.

At bottom, the corruption of 'covetous and worldly' clerics in league with the fiend is held responsible for the abuse of pilgrimage. It has become, to the Lollard's eyes, materialised, something undertaken or promoted for reasons of avarice or self-indulgence, or out of mere curiosity to see distant places. The superficialising of what should be a pious act, the outer expression of an inner, spiritual movement, is caught in the word 'images'. These are held to be the lures which make people leave home – in other words the marvellous shrines and reliquaries, often encrusted with jewels, and visual representations of the saint. The implication is that worship in front of such objects falls not far short of idolatry.

The first excerpt, from the *Mirror,* was deferential in its use of authority; the Lollard author is certainly not, at least in his attitude towards the authorities of the church. His lack of respect is fuelled in part by the connivance of priests in the abuse of pilgrimage, but also by deeply held convictions about how the corruption of this institution affects the whole community. We have already noted the adverse consequences of pilgrimage upon a household, but the consequences are felt more widely than individual domestic units. Pilgrimage, it is said, allows those who are unable to practise lechery at home for fear of the pressures and taboos and authority of their community (lords, masters, outcry of neighbours) to escape to a mini-society (that of the pilgrimage) in which such rules of conduct are in abeyance, where controls are relaxed. Thus immorality is fostered rather than cured. And there is in particular a class of society which suffers as a result of what pilgrimage has become – the exploited, the ignorant, the 'poor people' who are wickedly robbed. The Lollard author is their champion, making a radical criticism which is attempting not to abolish pilgrimage but to prevent its misuse and ensure that true penance can prevail. The author of the *Mirror* and the Lollard writer are perhaps not so far apart in their sympathies as may at first sight appear. If the Lollard author is a radical, he is one in the sense of wanting to return to the roots of the institution of pilgrimage, and of the church itself, to re-establish them on just principles, rather than in the sense of being a revolutionary who wants destruction and abolition in favour of a new order.

ii. CHAUCER'S PILGRIMAGE

We are now in a position to gauge the extent to which the General Prologue is informed by some current ideas about pilgrimage. We can begin to do that by looking in detail first at its opening lines and then at two portraits.

> Whan that Aprill with his shoures soote
> The droghte of Marche hath perced to the roote,
> And bathed every veyne in swich licour
> Of which vertu engendred is the flour;
> Whan Zephirus eek with his sweete breeth 5
> Inspired hath in every holt and heeth
> The tendre croppes, and the yonge sonne
> Hath in the Ram his half cours yronne,
> And smale foweles maken melodye,
> That slepen al the nyght with open ye 10
> (So priketh hem nature in his corages),
> Thanne longen folk to goon on pilgrimages,
> And palmeres for to seken straunge strondes,
> To ferne halwes, kowthe in sondry londes;
> And specially from every shires ende 15
> Of Engelond to Caunterbury they wende,
> The hooly blisful martir for to seke,
> That hem hath holpen whan that they were seeke.
>
> (GP, 1–18)

Now answer the following questions.

1. *What aspects of the 'pilgrimage controversy' can you detect in these lines, and what prominence is given to it?*
2. *In Chaucer's account, what is it that prompts people to go on pilgrimage?*
3. *Comment on the way in which Chaucer presents the idea of regeneration.*

The first feature to note is the general sense of stirring, movement, restlessness. Birds are prompted to sing, people long to travel, fuelled by curiosity about foreign shores and distant, famous shrines. There is a hint that a part of those restless desires may be sexual in origin: 'corages' carries that implication and suggests that 'smale foweles' sleep with their eyes open because they are not sleeping at all, but mating. 'Maken melodye' is also a euphemism for sexual activity. But the pious objectives of pilgrimage are not forgotten. Canterbury is a destination because it had the relics of St Thomas, the 'holy blisful martyr', who has helped when prayed to in times of sickness; and spring is the time of Easter, and Christ's crucifixion and resurrection, which made possible the redemption of mankind from sin.

So it is possible to detect traces of orthodox ideas about pilgrimage, and of less conventional attitudes of the sort which the Lollard writer deplored. But neither is prominent. They are introduced indirectly, allusively, and mostly towards the end of the passage. And they are subordinate to, and predicated upon, a quite different idea that we have not so far encountered: that pilgrimage is primarily prompted neither by piety nor by sinfulness, but by Nature, an irresistible force not necessarily subject to the man-made structures of morality or religion. The extent to which Chaucer scrupulously avoids the expected account of pilgrimage is quite extraordinary. The question of whether the pilgrimage is bound for Jerusalem or Babylon simply does not arise. In fact, it is only at the twelfth line that pilgrimage is mentioned at all, as if to suggest that it is merely a form taken by the human response to Nature, not a motive force on its own account.

Prior to this, the prelude to pilgrimage is represented entirely in seasonal, astronomical and classical terms. By these means Chaucer creates a sense of the inevitability and independence of natural (if God-given) processes. The human desire and longing to go on pilgrimage follow as a consequence of certain natural preconditions which co-exist at a particular time within a seasonal cycle: 'Whan that Aprill ... Whan Zephirus ... and the yonge sonne ... And smale foweles ... Thanne [but only then] longen folk ...' The autonomy of the energetic forces which generate this longing is suggested by the personifying of month and wind. 'Aprill' it is who actively pierces the drought of March with *his* sweet showers and who bathes plants in moisture; Zephirus, the west wind, who breathes life into the budding vegetation. The processes described are wonderful, cosmic, elemental: the sun, half-way through Aries, the Ram, is propitious; the elements – water with earth, air with the sun's fire – are recombining as if at the first creation. It is a time of natural regeneration, renewal, awakening and joy. The world is again 'tendre' and 'yonge', and involved in the whole exhilarating business are human beings who, no less than the plants and birds, must express their own response: they are stimulated and inspired, they desire and long, to go on pilgrimage.

Pilgrimage is a strange and unexpected outcome of the opening lines, not least because it suddenly replaces the simple, uncomplicated world of Nature with the world of civilisation, country with city, and with one of civilisation's conventional forms which, as we have seen, expresses an extremely complex response to the problem of human existence – a complexity increased by the controversy which surrounded its practice. That Chaucer was aware of these orders of complexity is clear from his portraits of the Parson and the Pardoner, to which we must now turn.

To get the measure of the Parson we must examine both the portrait of him in the General Prologue and the impression he creates elsewhere in the *Canterbury Tales.* At the end of the Man of Law's Tale, the Host is sufficiently impressed by what one example of 'lerned men' has done to invite another, the Parson, to tell his tale. In doing so, he blasphemes twice, and this earns him a rebuke from the Parson. Harry Bailly's riposte is to accuse him of being a 'Lollere' – Lollards being well known for their strictures on swearing. They were also well known for their preaching, and so the Host invites the Parson to deliver a sermon (unrepentantly delivering himself of another curse as he does so). But the Shipman protests, fearing that the Parson will do something else for which the Lollards, translators of the Bible into English, and commentators thereon, were famous: the 'gospel glosen' – that is, interpret scripture in plain but challenging terms. The Shipman's argument is that they all believe in one God, and that a suspected Lollard is likely to sow the seeds of difficulty and dissent among the company (Lollardy was condemned as heretical in 1401).

On this occasion, the Parson does not tell his tale and the question of his Lollardy remains a moot point. But his behaviour on the occasion when he does tell his tale indicates that he has allied himself with the reformist wing of the church. Invited by the Host to tell a 'fable' the Parson declines, quoting St Paul's epistle to Timothy as his authority, much as if he were making a point within a sermon. He goes on to assert that he prefers to avoid the trivialising and distracting effects of telling tales in verse, and intends to concentrate instead upon the unadorned truth – 'Moralitee and vertuous mateere' (ParsP, 38) – so that it might have maximum impact. He therefore proposes to speak his tale in prose rather than as poetry, and expresses his intentions in terms that have great resonance for the meaning of pilgrimage as he sees it:

> And Jhesu, for his grace, wit me sende
> To shewe yow the wey, in this viage,
> Of thilke parfit glorious pilgrymage
> That highte Jerusalem celestial.
>
> (ParsP, 48–51)

His opening plea for Christ's help is anything but the blasphemy which the Host might have used. Instead, this is the kind of language we encountered in the *Mirror,* and suggests that the Parson's radicalism is of the sort that seeks to return to first principles. He is reminding his fellow travellers of the true purpose of pilgrimage: rightly seen, the 'viage' (the journey to Canterbury, or life's journey itself) is a figurative expression of the true ('parfit glorious') pilgrimage which every human soul should make towards salvation ('Jerusalem celestial').

The General Prologue portrait of the Parson confirms that this is a man who believes in and practises the essentials of the Christian faith: he emulates Christ and the apostles; preaches the gospel in a straightforward manner, and teaches it by example; shows inexhaustible concern for the spiritual well-being of the community; deplores the pursuit of greed, especially by clerics; sympathises with and extends practical help to the poor and ignorant; and is indifferent to conventional structures of social authority.

A good man was ther of religioun,
And was a povre Persoun of a Toun,
But riche he was of hooly thoght and werk.
He was also a lerned man, a clerk, 480
That Cristes gospel trewely wolde preche;
His parisshens devoutly wolde he teche.
Benygne he was, and wonder diligent,
And in adversitee ful pacient,
And swich he was ypreved ofte sithes.
Ful looth were hym to cursen for his tithes, 496
But rather wolde he yeven, out of doute,
Unto his povre parisshens aboute
Of his offryng and eek of his substaunce.
He koude in litel thyng have suffisaunce. 490
Wyd was his parisshe, and houses fer asonder,
But he ne lefte nat, for reyn ne thonder,
In siknesse nor in meschief to visite
The ferreste in his parisshe, muche and lite,
Upon his feet, and in his hand a staf. 495
This noble ensample to his sheep he yaf,
That first he wroghte, and afterward he taughte.
Out of the gospel he tho wordes caughte,
And this figure he added eek therto,
That if gold ruste, what shal iren do? 500
For if a preest be foul, on whom we truste,
No wonder is a lewed man to ruste;
And shame it is, if a prest take keep,
A shiten shepherde and a clene sheep.
Wel oghte a preest ensample for to yive, 505
By his clennesse, how that his sheep sholde lyve.
He sette nat his benefice to hyre
And leet his sheep encombred in the myre
And ran to Londoun unto Seinte Poules
To seken hym a chaunterie for soules, 510
Or with a bretherhed to been withholde;
But dwelte at hoom, and kepte wel his folde,

So that the wolf ne made it nat myscarie;
He was a shepherde and noghte a mercenarie.
And though he hooly were and vertuous, 515
He was to synful men nat despitous,
Ne of his speche daungerous ne digne,
But in his techyng discreet and benygne.
To drawen folk to hevene by fairnesse,
By good ensample, this was his bisynesse. 520
But it were any persone obstinat,
What so he were, of heigh or lough estat,
Hym wolde he snybben sharply for the nonys.
A bettre preest I trowe that nowher noon ys.
He waited after no pompe and reverence, 525
Ne maked him a spiced conscience,
But Cristes loore and his apostles twelve
He taughte; but first he folwed it hymselve.

(GP, 477–528)

Chaucer's description falls into three sections. They all describe the Parson's relationship with his parishioners, but the emphasis of each is different. The first section (to line 490) stresses the Parson's values; the second (lines 491–514) develops the idea of the Parson as a guardian; and the third concentrates upon his role as a teacher. Now answer the following questions.

1. *What is the attitude of the narrator towards the Parson?*
2. *Comment on the relationship developed in this passage between poverty and riches.*
3. *How significant and revealing is the glimpse of the Parson at work among his parishioners?*
4. *Discuss the use and implications of the sheep and wolf imagery.*
5. *What does the portrait suggest about* general *standards of clerical knowledge and behaviour?*
6. *What teaching techniques does the Parson deploy, and with what end in view?*
7. *How radical is Chaucer's portrait?*
8. *Is the Parson's outlook closer to that of the author of the* Mirror, *of the author of the Lollard tract, or of Deguileville? Consider such matters as his practicality, his attitude towards authority, his use of metaphor, his views on money.*

By comparison with many other of the pilgrim portraits, that of the Parson is an exercise in plain speaking. Chaucer is unequivocal in his praise, in stating that the Parson possesses those attributes expected of a Christian pastor but (if the other clerics on the pilgrimage are anything to go by) all too rarely found. And the terms of approbation come thick, fast and unstintingly: the Parson is 'good', 'lerned', 'Benygne', 'diligent', 'pacient'. The ironies and other indirections by which the true nature of many another pilgrim must be inferred have here been abandoned – appropriately for a man who practises no guile but who teaches the gospel 'trewely'. But the Parson's admirable qualities do not follow inevitably from his calling. Good and poor he may be, but it comes as some surprise to learn that he also has a vigorous intellectual life, is energetic, learned, and an effective preacher: '*But* riche he was of hooly thoght and werk' (479). By any stretch of the imagination, the Parson is an unusual individual.

Poverty and riches are recurrent and interlinked topics. Poverty is represented as a fact of existence, but it is the Parson's attitude towards it, both in himself and in others, which is of crucial importance. He himself is poor, but he accepts that condition with patience and forbearance, knowing how to be content with little: 'He koude in litel thyng have suffisaunce' (490). More than this, he has a compassionate and generous attitude towards the poverty of others. He does not readily impose the letter of the law, and curse those unable to pay their tithes, preferring instead to practise the spirit of Christ's teaching by giving to the needy both from the money ('offryng') paid to the church by the better-off parishioners and from his own, limited, wealth ('substaunce'). The consequence of this considerate generosity and practical charity is that the Parson, though materially poor, is spiritually affluent: 'riche ... of hooly thoght and werk'.

The fluctuation between inner and outer qualities, the spiritual and the material, the metaphoric and the literal, gives these lines their integrity. Because value is put on inner riches, rather than outer wealth, it is appropriate that the Parson's physical appearance is left out of account. The one exception comes in the following lines, but even then the detail does not relate directly to the Parson's appearance on the road to Canterbury. Instead, Chaucer provides a glimpse of him at work in his far-flung parish, steadfastly visiting the scattered houses, regardless of rain, thunder, illness, mishap, distance or status ('muche and lite'). This he does on foot, 'and in his hand a staf'. Given the context of the portrait, it is difficult not to see the Parson's staff as emblematic of the staff customarily carried by pilgrims, as in the illustration of Deguileville's *Pilgrimage*. In keeping with the tendency of the previous lines, Chaucer's vignette would therefore show us 'the Parson as pilgrim' in the figurative sense: by conscientiously and devoutly pursuing his work as a parish priest he is engaged upon his own personal pilgrimage towards salvation. The staff has another significance. It also suggests the shepherd's crook, still carried by bishops today to indicate the cleric's role as pastor, as shepherd. The glimpse of the Parson in his parish therefore acts as a transition between the first and second sections of the portrait: sustaining the oscillation of inner and outer reality, it introduces an image – the shepherd with his sheep – which runs through the whole of the next section.

Not that the earlier order of imagery is forgotten. The Parson himself incorporates it in a figure of speech – 'if gold ruste, what shal iren do?' – and goes on to gloss it in terms of the good example which a priest must set his parishioners, and the implications of not doing so. He frames one kind of imagery with another that has a similar meaning: in order to set an example to their flock, their sheep, the souls in their charge, priests should themselves be clean, free from sin. Otherwise a parishioner may outshine his or her priest, to his disgrace: 'shame it is .../A shiten shepherde and a clene sheep' (503-4). What gives the shepherd/sheep imagery its air of quiet authority is its derivation – familiar enough to Chaucer's audience – from the New Testament, in which Christ described himself as the Good Shepherd, and framed a number of parables around the care of shepherds for their sheep. The devaluing of material wealth, the positive qualities of poverty and the idea of teaching by example – 'Out of the gospel he tho wordes caughte' (498) – all have the same foundations. The biblical authority which underpins the portrait of the Parson is all the more impressive because it is left unspecific, shared, assumed.

There follows a parable of the bad shepherd, a moral narrative example of the sort which a preacher like the Parson might well have included in a sermon. The villain is a bad priest who hires out his living. The victims are his neglected sheep, who become encumbered in the mire of sin. The temptation of the bad priest takes the form of material wealth and comforts: the rewards to be won from singing masses for the dead in London chantries (small endowed chapels or altars, such as were to be found at St Paul's, at which one or more priests sang daily masses for the souls of the founders and others specified by them), or from becoming a chaplain to a guild of prosperous townsmen. The fatal outcome is the devouring of the sheep by a wolf (the devil). All this is by way of showing what the Parson is not (but what many others are): instead, he stays at home, guards his fold, and is a proper shepherd, 'noghte a mercenarie'. In that last word is a reprise of the idea developed in the first section, and threading through the second, of the corrupting power of material wealth.

It is often said that the Parson is idealised, too good to be true. That impression derives in part from Chaucer's technique of defining him against a familiar background of the inadequacies and outright corruption of clerical life, in which he does not participate: he is their negation. The Parson is *not* merely a poor parson; he is *not* quick to curse for tithes; he does *not* fail to practise what he preaches; he does *not* abandon his flock for rich pickings in London; and so on. Against such a background, comprising some of the accusations often levelled against the contemporary priesthood, the Parson stands out in sharp relief as a paragon: 'A bettre preest I trowe that nowher noon ys' (524). But it does not follow that he is depersonalised, aloof, the unconvincing representative of admirable but abstract ideas. On the contrary, Chaucer insists on the extent to which the Parson is directly involved in the fabric of life (as he is involved in the pilgrimage, taking issue with some of the preconceptions on which it is based), challenging others by word and example, and embodying his beliefs in strenuous, dedicated practice.

The final section of the portrait, which shifts the focus to the Parson's effectiveness as a teacher, corroborates this interpretation. However holy and virtuous he might be, in his dealings with other people the Parson is *not* 'holier than thou' – hypocritical and self-righteous – disdainful, standoffish ('daungerous'), standing on his dignity ('digne'), but quiet, gracious, kindly, approachable ('discreet and benygne'), devoting his energies to others, persuading them by fair means, and particularly by the eloquence of his own example, to set their sights on heaven. ('Ensample' is indeed an insistent word which occurs at regular intervals throughout the portrait.) But he is no milk-and-water Christian. He meets obstinacy with sharp rebuke, and is no respecter of social status ('heigh or lough estat'). If need arises, he will 'snybben sharply for the nonys', as Harry Bailly has already discovered.

There is a hint here of the radical and uncomfortable implications of Christianity both for the individual and for society. Following the gospel entails both a fundamental re-ordering of the individual's priorities (away from material riches, towards spiritual values), and the recognition that social position and ambition are irrelevant – all men being equal in the sight of God. The Parson therefore has little time for 'pompe and reverence', and while there can be no doubt that he himself has opted for the path of radical Christianity, his internalising of Christ's gospel has not turned him inwards to the point where he is forever picking over his own moral scruples ('spiced conscience') and making subjective assessments of them. The whole point of his version of the gospel is that, while founded on a profound sense of inner, spiritual values, it is also outward looking, robust, dedicated to the reform both of the individual and of society. His credo is summed up in the closing lines: 'Cristes loore and his apostles twelve / He taughte; but first he folwed it hymselve.'

There could hardly be a greater contrast than that between the Parson and the Pardoner, who accompanies the Summoner:

> With hym ther rood a gentil Pardoner
> Of Rouncivale, his freend and his compeer, 670
> That streight was comen fro the court of Rome.
> Ful loude he soong 'Com hider, love, to me!'
> This Somonour bar to hym a stif burdoun;
> Was nevere trompe of half so greet a soun.
> This Pardoner hadde heer as yelow as wex, 675
> But smothe it heeng as dooth a strike of flex;
> By ounces henge his lokkes that he hadde,
> And therwith he his shuldres overspradde;
> But thynne it lay, by colpons oon and oon.
> But hood, for jolitee, wered he noon, 680
> For it was trussed up in his walet.
> Hym thoughte he rood al of the newe jet;
> Dischevelee, save his cappe, he rood al bare.
> Swiche glarynge eyen hadde he as an hare.
> A vernycle hadde he sowed upon his cappe. 685
> His walet, biforn hym in his lappe,
> Bretful of pardoun comen from Rome al hoot.
> A voys he hadde as smal as hath a goot.
> No berd hadde he, ne nevere sholde have;
> As smothe it was as it were late shave. 690
> I trowe he were a geldyng or a mare.
> But of his craft, fro Berwyk into Ware
> Ne was ther swich another pardoner.
> For in his male he hadde a pilwe-beer,
> Which that he seyde was Oure Lady veyl; 695
> He seyde he hadde a gobet of the seyl
> That Seint Peter hadde, whan that he wente
> Upon the see, til Jhesu Crist hym hente.
> He hadde a croys of latoun ful of stones,
> And in a glas he hadde pigges bones. 700
> But with thise relikes, whan that he fond
> A povre person dwellynge upon lond,
> Upon a day he gat hym moore moneye
> Than that the person gat in monthes tweye;
> And thus, with feyned flaterye and japes, 705
> He made the person and the peple his apes.
> But trewely to tellen atte laste,
> He was in chirche a noble ecclesiaste.
> Wel koude he rede a lessoun or a storie,
> But alderbest he song an offertorie; 710
> For wel he wiste, whan that song was songe,
> He moste preche and wel affile his tonge
> To wynne silver, as he ful wel koude;
> Therefore he song the murierly and loude. (GP, 669–714)

Now answer the following questions.

1. *Refer to the Lollard tract, and discuss ways in which the Pardoner exemplifies abuses of the institution of pilgrimage.*
2. *What is implied about the Pardoner's sexuality, how, and to what end?*
3. *How does Chaucer express the Pardoner's materialism?*
4. *What enables the Pardoner to manipulate his audiences?*
5. *What grounds of comparison and contrast exist between the Pardoner and the Parson?*
6. *What significance do you attach to the Pardoner's hair?*
7. *What are the portrait's principles of organisation and form?*
8. *Does the narrator disapprove of the Pardoner?*

The anonymous author of the Lollard tract would have recognised the Pardoner instantly for what he is. For he represents one consequence of pushing the abuse of pilgrimage to its logical conclusion. First, there is the question of his sexual behaviour. If the Pardoner is on the road to Babylon, he is going there by way of Sodom. The pilgrimage enables him to travel in the company of the unsavoury Summoner (himself a church official expert in detecting, while participating in, sexual offences). Their intimacy is expressed through the singing (perhaps to each other) of erotic love songs such as 'Com hider, love, to me', in which the Summoner sings the sexually suggestive 'stif burdoun', or bass (but also 'pilgrim staff'). The nature of the Pardoner's own voice is a further indicator of his sexual preferences: it is effeminate, high pitched, a voice 'as smal as hath a goot' (an animal associated with lechery). And to drive the point home, in a manner of speaking, Chaucer notes that he has glaring eyes like a hare which, with the goat, was a noted hermaphrodite of medieval animal lore; and he is not only without a beard, as if freshly shaved, but incapable of growing one. The pilgrim narrator speculates: 'I trowe he were a geldyng or a mare' (691) – the latter word implying homosexuality. The use of animal comparisons to define the Pardoner's sexual ambiguity helps to frame it as subhuman, bestial: animal imagery was often used (as it still is) to represent particular sins. It is all the more demeaning and distasteful, therefore, when he makes 'apes' of his dupes: he reduces them to his level.

Again, the Pardoner is an example of one of those covetous and worldly clerics who exploit the idea of pilgrimage to satisfy their own avarice, using extortion and the collusion of the church to perpetuate an immoral economy. For the Pardoner operates with the sanction of and under the authority of the Pope. We are told that he has come straight from the papal court with a wallet crammed full of freshly minted pardons. Also from Rome is his 'vernycle', a pilgrim badge representing Christ's face as it appeared on St Veronica's veil. The Pardoner plans to convert his pardons into cash (whether for himself or the discredited community at Rouncevale is not clear) by exchanging them for offerings from people impressed by his 'relics' and by his liturgical skills. He is in effect a mobile shrine, fabricating wherever he sets up his wares an artificial substitute for the experience in which Chaucer's pilgrims are engaged: seeing powerful relics; making an offering; receiving forgiveness.

Ideally, as we have seen, such activities should be the expression of a spiritual transaction between priest and believer. But in the hands of the Pardoner they are a travesty, as deviant as his sexuality. He is driven not by holiness but by avarice and, however official, authentic and impressive his paper pardons may be, they are worthless when conjoined with his motivation and the worthless rubbish which passes for relics: pigs' bones (pigs being notoriously greedy) and a torn pillow cover masquerading as Mary's veil. But, on his own terms, the Pardoner is a great success. The money pours in as people, too ignorant to know any better, are impressed by his presence in church, his elocutionary and rhetorical skills as he reads from the Bible, and especially by the sweet singing of that part of the service associated with the offertory – a task at which he excels, knowing full well that the better he preaches, the more pleasant and entertaining his speaking, and the more merry and loud his songs, the greater will be his takings. It is just that, in the process, as the Lollard writer puts it, true penance is prevented and the poor people wickedly robbed. Nor is there any attempt to preach, as the Parson does, the more challenging aspects of the gospel.

What has happened? With the Pardoner we seem to have entered a world in which the ideal of pilgrimage has been turned back to front, with the Pardoner and his paraphernalia – bogus shrine and sham officiating priest – travelling to the faithful, rather than the faithful going on their own pilgrimage. The Pardoner's success in sustaining this inversion derives from the simple-minded nature of his targeted audiences, and the extent to which he deploys showmanship, what the congregation sees and hears, as a foil for his true activities. As we saw in the case of the Parson, the symbolic nature of Christianity is a source of its strength: it insists that ultimate reality lies beneath the surface of things – not in the getting of riches (say) but in the acquiring of spiritual treasure; not in the mere performance of pilgrimage, but in what that action signifies for the spiritual progress of the individual pilgrim. Such an outlook is open to exploitation by the unscrupulous. For it has the effect of imbuing things, and especially those things associated with the divine service, with a mystical aura and power. In the hands of an unscrupulous operator, such as the Pardoner, the symbolic significance of traditionally revered objects, actions and words can be manipulated to conceal ulterior motives and the gulling of the credulous, to the point at which idolatry (belief in the power of the things themselves) replaces true worship. Not that Chaucer's audience, or a modern reader, is in the category of 'apes'. The pilgrim reporter leaves us in no doubt about the worthlessness of the Pardoner's relics, whether in spiritual or material terms: the cross itself is made from alloy – latten – encrusted with cheap stones to make it look impressive, like the real thing. The Pardoner's best efforts are, through Chaucer's steady eye, nothing but 'feyned flaterye and japes'.

It is as if the Pardoner has been deliberately created as the antithesis of the Parson. Where one lives by duplicity, the other has complete integrity. There is a virtual invitation to make comparisons and contrasts between them when we learn that the Pardoner was especially effective in gulling 'A povre person dwellynge upon lond' (702) and his parishioners or 'peple'. Clearly the Pardoner has not previously encountered the pilgrim Parson on his travels, for he would have met some determined resistance, and a stout defence of the congregation. The difficulty in imagining Chaucer's Parson as the Pardoner's dupe only emphasises the extent to which he is exceptional among 'povre persons' who, in the Pardoner's portrait, are synonymous with ignorance, naiveté, and weakness. At the same time, the juxtapositions within the Pardoner's portrait of country priest and urban pardoner (the hospital of Rouncevale was near Charing Cross in London), the inept and the sophisticated, the exploitative and the defenceless, abject poverty and avaricious ambition, provide Chaucer with an opportunity to measure the distance between them. They live in different worlds, with different values and expectations. The money that would sustain such a parson for two months is a day's takings for the Pardoner. After his rapacious, predatory, wolf-like visit, he leaves the community, glutted with offerings, in a worse state than it was before. We remember that the pilgrim Parson was prone to apportion some of the money which *he* received from his flock to benefit the needy.

Their contrasting attitudes towards money are, of course, one of the ways in which the nature of the gulf separating Pardoner from Parson is defined. If the Parson has rejected worldly riches, the Pardoner has dedicated his life to them. His values are reflected in the form which his portrait takes, just as the Parson's values are mirrored in the form of his portrait. Just as we know almost nothing about the spiritual Parson's appearance, so the Pardoner is all too physical. His hair, for example, is both fascinating and repellent. Like it or not, we see it in detail, at close quarters, and register its yellow, waxy appearance, its smooth, flaxen texture, its matting together, its sparseness, the way in which it lies long on his shoulders. Once imagined, the Pardoner's hair is never forgotten. Like the image of the Parson, staff in hand, striding over his parish, it is a detail designed to be memorable because we can attach to it crucial components of the Pardoner's character. It expresses his materialism, his self-conscious attention to bodily appearances, his vanity, the underlying tawdriness of his outlook and activities. Some of this is also conveyed in his attempt at being a fashionable layman (he is in fact a cleric) by riding without a hood, even though he seems to be wrong here, as he is fundamentally wrong on more serious matters: 'Hym *thoughte* he rood al of the newe jet' (682). Appropriately enough for someone who lives by the manipulation of images, and of others' interpretations of what they see, he is bound up, stultifyingly, in his own self-image.

The hood which the Pardoner does not wear is trussed up in his wallet, and it might be argued that his entire portrait is focused upon, and organised around, his head and his wallet (that other emblem of the pilgrim), his scheming and his avarice, one being linked to the other by sexual connotations: the head for the supposed attractiveness of his hair; the wallet because it lies in his lap. The wallet is full both of pardons and of relics, indicating that the debased and devalued kind of religion which the Pardoner peddles is one which is thoroughly materialised, one which puts its faith in the semi-magical power of things – things which, to an unprejudiced eye, are so much worthless and ludicrous trash.

The profusion of physical detail with which the Pardoner and his activities are represented is itself expressive of the nature of the man: relentless, unavoidable, oppressive. Whereas the Parson was exemplary, discreet, quiet, self-effacing, at the service of others, the Pardoner is deceptive, overbearing, a public performer, drawing attention to himself all to his own self-aggrandisement and profit. He is a loud person, and something of that is conveyed in the actual volume of his voice. He sings his love-song with the Summoner taking the bass line – 'As nevere trompe of half so greet a soun' (674) – 'Ful loude', and also sings the offertorie 'murierly and loude'.

Both on account of his overbearing presence, and his moral degeneracy, the reader does not want to identify too closely with the Pardoner. As we want more detail about the Parson, so we have too much about the Pardoner. And yet responses to the Pardoner are complicated by a note of approbation on Chaucer's part, of the sort which also informed his portrait of the Parson. The Pardoner is also a nonpareil: 'of his craft, fro Berwyk into Ware / Ne was ther swich another pardoner' (692-3). It is as if Chaucer admires the Pardoner's professionalism, even though it is the expertise of an out-and-out and despicable rogue: 'trewely to tellen atte laste, / He was in chirche a noble ecclesiaste' (707-8). This cannot be the truth-telling of the Parson. It is instead the truth-telling of Chaucer the pilgrim, whose priorities are different from either Parson, or Pardoner.

Later in the pilgrimage, the Host is rebuked by the Pardoner, just as he is by the Parson. It is a moment of great comedy, almost of self-parody, with the Pardoner in the role of jester, or licensed fool, imitating what the Parson does but without a shred of authority or a hope of success. The uproarious outcome is that he, in his turn, is rebuked in no uncertain terms by the Host. Before their exchange takes place, the Pardoner provides a demonstration of his salesmanship. He has just told a compelling tale about the fatal consequences of avarice and now steps forward to exemplify the same vice in himself. He does so by attempting to turn the pilgrimage to Canterbury into a marketing opportunity for his pardons. It is an acutely self-conscious moment for the pilgrims as the Pardoner brings them face to face with their motivations for going on the journey. Were they to accept his blandishments at face value, there would hardly be any point in continuing it. For the Pardoner reminds them that he has relics, and pardons with the seal of papal authority, in his wallet. If any of the pilgrims, out of piety ('devocion') cares to make an offering and receive absolution, or have a pardon 'Al newe and fressh at every miles ende' (PardT, 928) – as long as they offer 'Nobles or pence' – then the Pardoner will be happy to oblige. He reminds them that they are honoured to have a pardoner in their company who can provide such a service. For – so the patter goes – pilgrimages are notoriously dangerous undertakings, and a pardon can provide an insurance policy against an unexpected accident or sudden death. As the Pardoner casually says: 'Paraventure ther may fallen oon or two / Doun of his hors and breke his nekke atwo' (935-6). What a comfort it will be to have the reassurance and safeguard ('seuretee') of a pardoner's presence, since he will be able to perform the last rites 'Whan that the soule shal fro the body passe' (940).

The Pardoner is blatantly and provocatively usurping the role of a priest, and especially that of a priest charged with the care of holy relics. He now invites the Host, as the pilgrim 'moost envoluped in synne', to begin the devotional activity by kissing all his relics, and at a bargain price: 'Ye, for a grote! Unbokele anon thy purs' (945). But the Host appears not to take kindly to this suggestion. He appears to take the Pardoner's remarks seriously and points out that his proposal will imperil, rather than save, his soul '"Nay, nay!" quod he, "thanne have I Cristes curs!"' (946), a much more solemn matter than the curses which Harry Bailly customarily heaps upon Christ. The Host vilifies the Pardoner's relics and his use of them, saying that he would make him kiss his soiled underwear and swear it was a saint's relic. It is not that he rejects relics as such, for he swears by a true one: Christ's cross as found by St Helen. But the attack turns more personal:

> But, by the croys which that Seint Eleyne fond,
> I wolde I hadde thy coillons in myn hond
> In stide of relikes or of seintuarie.
> Lat kutte hem of, I wol thee helpe hem carie;
> They shul be shryned in an hogges toord!
>
> (PardT, 951–5)

The Pardoner is rendered speechless with anger; the Host resolves to 'pley' no more with the Pardoner on account of his wrath; and the Knight, seeing all the pilgrims laughing, persuades Pardoner and Host to make up their quarrel with a kiss.

This is a complex incident. It foregrounds the nature and value of pilgrimage and the motivation of the participants; and raises questions about the nature of comedy. As long as the Pardoner is allowed to be in his adopted role as chaplain to the pilgrims, he can tease them. But there is seriousness behind his play because he is, after all, providing a demonstration of how he profits by bogus means from the impetus which drives pilgrims. Once the Host exposes that inner core of irredeemable avarice, and in a way that links it forcibly to the Pardoner's sexuality, then the role collapses, the Pardoner freezes, and the play is ended. The pilgrimage game, however, continues unabated.

iii. TWO MIDDLEMEN

Of course, most of the Canterbury pilgrims are neither as virtuous as the Parson nor as reprehensible as the Pardoner. Their moral existence is somewhere in the middle. Thus extreme cases such as the Parson and the Pardoner act as yardsticks not only for each other but also for other pilgrims. For instance, it is revealing that the Prioress is all 'conscience and tendre herte' when it comes to caring for her dogs when we know that the Parson has no room for a 'spiced conscience' about himself, let alone animals.

The gap between ideal and reality, between what might be expected of a pilgrim by virtue of his or her calling or profession, and what they are in fact (fostered, as here, by comparisons between pilgrims), is one of the ways in which Chaucer creates a sense of character and a sense of irony in representing character. As in the case of our day-to-day acquaintances, appearances do not always match reality. It is from the way in which individuals fall short of an ideal role, or accommodate themselves to the occupation or social position in which they find themselves, that distinctive qualities emerge.

However, in the case of the General Prologue it would be wrongheaded to embark on a purely psychological account of the individual pilgrims. Similarly, it would be inadequate merely to give an account of those pilgrims in relation to the internal dynamics, or drama, of the pilgrimage. They are both viable contexts, but they are not the whole picture. A further, crucial, context, is the tradition of representation which such figures enjoyed before Chaucer wrote about them. For example, the hypocritical cleric is a cliché who appears in the works of other writers, sometimes in the form of a pardoner. So we should be careful not to detect too much 'social reality' behind Chaucer's portrait. And so it is for the majority of his pilgrims, who have been invented from models found in a broad range of writing, and particularly in writing which satirises representatives of the estates, or classes, of medieval society.

A full account of one of Chaucer's pilgrim portraits must therefore pay due attention to the model on which it is based. For the purposes of demonstration we may consider a 'middleman' who has already been the subject of discussion – Harry Bailly. As the Host of the Tabard Inn he is a key enabler and encourager of the pilgrimage, an entrepreneur and, as it later emerges, the inventor of the idea that the pilgrims should tell stories with himself in the role of organising go-between. He introduces a new dimension into the idea of pilgrimage. Hardly as idealistic as the Parson, but able to better the Pardoner, he expresses the vitality of commercial enterprise and wins the consent of all in regarding pilgrimage as an occasion for a game.

> Greet chiere made oure Hoost us everichon,
> And to the soper sette he us anon.
> He served us with vitaille at the beste;
> Strong was the wyn, and wel to drynke us leste. 750
> A semely man Oure Hooste was withalle
> For to been a marchal in an halle.
> A large man he was with eyen stepe –
> A fairer burgeys was ther noon in Chepe –
> Boold of his speche, and wys, and wel ytaught, 755

And of manhod hym lakkede right naught.
Eek therto he was right a myrie man;
And after soper pleyen he bigan,
And spak of myrthe amonges othere thynges,
Whan that we hadde maad oure rekenynges, 760
And seyde thus: 'Now, lordynges, trewely,
Ye been to me right welcome, hertely;
For by my trouthe, if that I shal nat lye,
I saugh nat this yeer so myrie a compaignye
Atones in this herberwe as is now. 765
Fayn wolde I doon yow myrthe, wiste I how.
And of a myrthe I am right now bythoght,
To doon yow ese, and it shal cost noght.
'Ye goon to Caunterbury – God yow speede,
The blisful martir quite yow youre meede! 770
And wel I woot, as ye goon by the weye,
Ye shapen yow to talen and to pleye;
For trewely, confort ne myrthe is noon
To ride by the weye doumb as a stoon;
And therfore wol I maken yow disport, 775
As I seyde erst, and doon yow som confort.
And if yow liketh alle by oon assent
For to stonden at my juggement,
And for to werken as I shal yow seye,
Tomorwe, whan ye riden by the weye, 780
Now, by my fader soule that is deed,
But ye be myrie, I wol yeve yow myn heed!
Hoold up youre hondes, withouten moore speche.'
Oure conseil was nat longe for to seche.

(GP, 747–84)

Now answer the following questions.

1. *What functions does the Host have, and how do these help to define his character?*
2. *What significance does pilgrimage have in his eyes?*
3. *Comment on the meaning and implication of the idea of 'mirth' as it appears in this passage.*

The Host is defined in the first instance by his function as a provider of good cheer, good food, good wine and hospitality. He is attractive ('semely') and has an imposing figure. The memorable detail of his prominent eyes ('eyen stepe') suggests that he exerts a benevolent, social power over those who fall under his gaze. (How different from the significant gaze of that other pilgrim with remarkable eyes, the Pardoner, whom Harry Bailly outfaces.) He has authority and control over the guests whom he welcomes to the Tabard. Being under his jurisdiction is evidently not uncomfortable, for although he may be assertive ('Boold of his speche') he is also judicious and well informed ('wys, and wel ytaught'). It hardly comes as a surprise to learn that, like so many of Chaucer's pilgrims, he is the best of his kind: 'A fairer burgeys was ther noon in Chepe' (754).

The Host gives the pious motivation for pilgrimage its due – 'Ye goon to Caunterbury – God yow speede, / The blisful martir quite yow youre meed!' (769-70) – but that is not his primary concern. Instead, he recognises that pilgrims – as indeed was their reputation – habitually tell stories and 'pleye' to beguile the long hours and tedium of the journey: 'confort ne myrthe is noon / To ride by the weye doumb as a stoon' (773-4). As a 'myrie man' himself who enjoys to 'pleyen', as we know also from his exchange with the Pardoner, the Host is well placed to recognise the recreational needs of pilgrims, and to develop them.

He does so by stressing the importance of 'myrthe' or 'disport' and being 'myrie' (words which appear no fewer than eight times in this short passage) and the 'confort' or solace which mirth brings. Harry Bailly himself embodies mirth and generates it: it is one of his infectious qualities. It comes to the fore after the meal and the strong wine, with the feeling of well-being which they produce, and the settling of accounts. Unlike the other fare for which Harry Bailly acts as the middleman, this commodity is not tangible, but it is beneficial as well as free of charge: 'of a myrthe I am right now bythoght, / To doon yow ese, and it shal cost noght' (767-8).

Mirth is a socially binding force. And it cannot function in a divided group. The companionable circumstances of the pilgrimage provide fertile ground. But it can only become a driving force of the journey when there is unanimous agreement ('by oon assent') that the Host should extend his role within the Tabard and assume control of the subsequent proceedings. The Host does not reveal until the morning the scheme for mirth he has in mind, but the idea is greeted with enthusiasm. All the pilgrims hold up their hands and vote for the mirth that will give them, as a 'compaignye', 'confort' and 'ese' on their journey.

There an account of the Host might rest, but another dimension would have been visible to Chaucer and his audience. The extraordinary emphasis on 'myrthe' and its variants, which continues in the following lines, signals the model on which Chaucer's portrait is based. For a figure called 'Myrthe' (Mirth) has a central role in a widespread and well-known French love allegory composed in the 1230s by Guillaume de Lorris, and continued some forty years later by Jean de Meun, the *Roman de la rose (Romance of the Rose),* the earlier parts of which Chaucer translated. Chaucer's *Romaunt* relates in the first person the experience of a young man who falls asleep to dream that he is walking in a spring landscape, beside a stream, when he encounters a walled garden. The outside of the garden is adorned with sculptures of figures – such as 'Elde' (Old Age) and 'Povert' (Poverty) – representing human conditions excluded from the experience of erotic love. On reaching a small door, the dreamer knocks, and it is opened by a fetching young girl who introduces herself as 'Ydelnesse' (Idleness). She informs the dreamer that the lord and maker of the garden is Mirth, who frequently visits it in order to find solace, bringing with him his 'meynee' or followers. Mirth, she says, is at present making one such visit and deriving particular pleasure from the singing of the birds, while the people accompanying him are the finest in the world. The dreamer wishes to join their 'companye'.

On entering the garden, the dreamer is affected by a feeling of gladness. With its profusion of birds, and their exquisite, melodious songs, the place seems paradisal. Its beneficial effect makes the dreamer 'wondir gay', more 'joyful' and 'merye in herte' than he has ever been before. He resolves to report as accurately as possible his experience, his impressions, the activities of Mirth, what people were with him, and the appearance of the garden, all in due order and to the best of his ability. Above all he longs to see the appearance and demeanour ('countenance' and 'manere') of Mirth. Walking down a narrow path, he finds Mirth and his followers enjoying their 'solace', as Idleness had promised. He is amazed at the angelic beauty of the people. Their recreational activity takes the form of a carol. A lady called 'Gladnesse' sings with a clear, sweet voice, accompanied by flute players and minstrels, while two other women dance amorously. Another lady, 'Curtesie', invites the dreamer to join them, and he is eager to do so, but not before he has told of the 'shap ... bodies ... cheres,/countenance and ... maneres' (*Rom.*, 814–15) of all the people there, beginning with Mirth:

Ful fair was Myrthe, ful long and high;
A fairer man I nevere sigh.
As round as appil was his face,
Ful rody and whit in every place. 820
Fetys he was and wel beseye, *handsome*
With metely mouth and yen greye; *well-proportioned*
His nose by mesure wrought ful right;
Crisp was his heer, and eek ful bright; *curly*
His shuldris of a large brede, 825
And smalish in the girdilstede. *waist*
He semed lyk a portreiture,
So noble he was of his stature,

So fair, so joly, and so fetys,
With lymes wrought at poynt devys, *to perfection* 830
Delyver, smert, and of gret myght; *agile*
Ne sawe thou nevere man so lyght.
Of berd unnethe hadde he nothyng,
For it was in the firste spryng.
Ful yong he was, and mery of thought, 835
And in samet, with briddis wrought, *samite*
And with gold beten ful fetysly,
His body was clad ful richely.
Wrought was his robe in straunge gise, *manner*
And al toslytered for queyntise *slashed, elegance* 840
In many a place, lowe and hie.
And shod he was with gret maistrie *skill*
With shoon decoped, and with laas. *open-cut*
By druery and by solas *affection*
His leef a rosyn chapelet *love* 845
Hadde mad, and on his heed it set.

(*Rom.*, 817–46)

Now answer the following questions.

1. *In what respects does Guillaume's Mirth contrast with Harry Bailly?*
2. *What similarities of role can you detect?*
3. *What are the implications of considering Harry Bailly and Mirth within the same frame of reference?*
4. *Are there any similarities between Chaucer's narrator and Guillaume's dreamer?*

It would be something of an understatement to say that a figure of this sort is not exactly what we have in mind when Chaucer describes Harry Bailly. On the other hand, he does encourage his audience to imagine the Host in an aristocratic setting (such as Mirth inhabits) where he would not be out of context: 'A semely man Oure Hooste was withalle / For to been a marchal in an halle' (GP, 751-2). Were Mirth and Harry Bailly ever to find themselves in the same great hall, it would be Mirth who would have the place of honour at the high dais, while Harry would have a relatively menial role. Nevertheless, as an official in charge of ceremonies within a large noble household, the marshall occupied a position of considerable status. Of unblemished handsomeness, tall, straight, with a fair and fresh complexion, Mirth has all the customary hallmarks of noble birth: a well proportioned mouth, grey eyes, a straight but not immoderately long nose. With his curly, shining hair, broad shoulders, slim waist, well formed limbs, agility and clean-shaven youth, he is more like the pilgrim Squire (or the dreamer as he would like to be) than the Host. He is conspicuously dressed in rich, expensive material – samite, embroidered with birds, and gold – while his robe is slit in many places in accordance with fashionable elegance. For the same reason his shoes are cut in openwork patterns. And his lady love has adorned his head with a chaplet of roses. In a word, he is as perfect as a picture ('semed lyk a portreiture').

The juxtaposition of Host and Mirth brings out the contrasts between an artificial ideal and a common-sense pragmatist; between a representative of aristocratic leisure and an active member of commercial enterprise; between youth and (so we imagine) middle age; between a perfect physical specimen and someone whose body and face are lived in; between the personification of a particular quality and a man whose character includes that quality along with other attributes. And yet, on further reflection, Harry Bailly and Mirth (mirth being a quality with which the Host is well acquainted) have much in common. In their different spheres, they are both presiding spirits; each promotes in his own way the comforting and solacing virtues of communal recreation; both have a commanding presence and a controlling function in relation to their immediate social group; each is inventive or innovative: Mirth in building the garden and encouraging its festivities and rituals, Harry Bailly in deploying the arts of hospitality and in devising the story-telling game.

We must ask why Chaucer found it necessary and desirable to invoke the picture of Mirth in the course of his portrait of Harry Bailly. One answer might be that it has the effect of making the Host seem vital and complex by comparison, grounded securely in a recognisable and more widely accessible social reality. This suggests in turn that another of Chaucer's motives was to debunk a work like the *Rose,* intended for an aristocratic audience, which identifies certain experiences (like mirth) as the preserve of an élite. This would be characteristic of his attitude towards much of the courtly literature which he inherited. If Chaucer did not exactly bite the hand that fed him, he enjoyed giving it a playful nip. While not denying the *Rose* its force as a source of his inspiration, he transforms it to the point of burlesque (for Harry Bailly displaces Mirth), and uses it to focus attention upon his own, broader representation of society. But the playfulness may not be only at the expense of his source. It might be argued that to refer so deliberately to a classic definition of mirth has the effect of rendering the pilgrimage version itself ludicrous (Harry Bailly can never be Mirth). The *Rose* would therefore act as a satirical scanner of contemporary life, introducing a further twist to the satire of social status and aspiration which threads through the General Prologue.

In looking at the *Romaunt* we have identified another model which Chaucer used in the General Prologue for the most important middleman of all: the narrator. For Chaucer's fictional persona shares some striking similarities with Guillaume's dreamer. It is spring, nature is in full throat and everything (and everyone) is of the best when, in a spirit of mirth, celebration and festivity each narrator joins a company of other people engaged in seasonal activities. Both remain to some extent outsiders and adopt the role of reporters and expositors of a novel experience. To do this they focus initially on the individuals they meet and so produce a series of formal portraits – Chaucer the pilgrim matching the dreamer's 'countenance' and 'manere' with 'estaat' and 'array'. Both narrators, willy-nilly, become involved in the activities which they describe: Guillaume falls in love, and Chaucer the pilgrim is called upon to tell a story.

The existence of such a model, which must have been extremely influential upon Chaucer as a translator of the *Roman de la rose,* goes a little way towards providing us with a firmer outline for the one portrait that is conspicuously missing from the General Prologue. Some other details can be provided on the basis of Chaucer the pilgrim's interactions with the individuals he describes. For example, we have already inferred, through the absence of any irony, his approval of the Parson's moral rectitude and spiritual vigour. And we have noted that, while he represents the Pardoner's villainy with an unprejudiced eye, he nevertheless admires the professionalism and gusto with which that villainy is practised. It would be possible to scour the other portraits for similar clues about the outlook and values of 'Chaucer the pilgrim'. Most promising seem to be the direct and apparently revealing remarks he occasionally makes. For instance, his reaction to the Monk's zest for life outside of the cloister is 'And I seyde his opinion was good' (GP, 183). But one is left wondering if the endorsement is entirely genuine, or tongue in cheek, or produced under the social pressure of the moment. If genuine, the pilgrim narrator is condoning a clerical abuse, which is not consistent with his attitude towards the Parson. Or he may simply be acknowledging the validity of the Monk's *opinion,* while not necessarily endorsing it. There is no way of being certain.

But the elusive, mercurial nature of Chaucer the pilgrim is something of which we can be sure. He is to be detected, if at all, through the figures he animates, the way in which he describes them, his teasing remarks in the first person. But as often as not it is impossible to see behind the mask. The desire for self-concealment, for being marginal to the proceedings, is caught in the few details of his physical bearing which the narrator lets slip when Harry Bailly invites him to tell a tale.

The Host invites him to identify himself, as if he were a complete unknown – 'What man artow?' – and remarks on the self-absorbed and detached impression which he creates:

> Thou lookest as thou woldest fynde an hare,
> For evere upon the ground I se thee stare.
> Approche neere, and looke up murily.
>
> (ProlTh, 696–8)

Addressing the pilgrim company, the Host draws attention to Chaucer's portly girth – 'He in the waast is shape as wel as I' (700) – small build (he is like a 'popet', or small doll, for a woman to cuddle) and face which is, significantly, 'elvyssh .../For unto no wight dooth he daliaunce' (703-4). He is with the pilgrims, but not of them.

Chaucer seems to have enjoyed disguising himself, and to have derived benefit from it. For it left him free to engage sympathetically with a wide range of people and experiences. So much is implied in the General Prologue when he announces that he has completed his prelude to pilgrimage and proceeds to apologise for what will follow:

> Now have I toold you soothly, in a clause, 715
> Th'estaat, th'array, the nombre, and eek the cause
> Why that assembled was this compaignye
> In Southwerk at this gentil hostelrye
> That highte the Tabard, faste by the Belle.
> But now is tyme to yow for to telle 720
> How that we baren us that ilke nyght,
> Whan we were in that hostelrie alyght;
> And after wol I telle of our viage
> And al the remenaunt of oure pilgrimage.
> But first I pray yow, of youre curteisye, 725
> That ye n'arette it nat my vileynye,
> Thogh that I pleynly speke in this mateere,
> To telle yow hir wordes and hir cheere,
> Ne thogh I speke hir wordes proprely.
> For this ye knowen al so wel as I: 730
> Whoso shal telle a tale after a man,
> He moot reherce as ny as evere he kan
> Everich a word, if it be in his charge,
> Al speke he never so rudeliche and large,
> Or ellis he moot telle his tale untrewe, 735
> Or feyne thyng, or fynde wordes newe.
> He may nat spare, althogh he were his brother;
> He moot as wel seye o word as another.
> Crist spak hymself ful brode in hooly writ,
> And wel ye woot no vileynye is it. 740
> Eek Plato seith, whoso kan him rede,
> The wordes moote be cosyn to the dede.
> Also I prey yow to foryeve it me,

Al have I nat set folk in hir degree
Heere in this tale, as that they sholde stonde. 745
My wit is short, ye may wel understonde.

(GP, 715–46)

Now answer the following questions.

1. *What qualities does the narrator possess for dealing with his material?*
2. *Describe and discuss the narrator's attitude towards his audience.*
3. *On what grounds does the narrator defend 'plain speaking', and to what effect?*
4. *Do you accept the narrator's words at face value? If not, why not? What are the consequences of not doing so?*

The narrator begins in a business-like way, reminding his audience of the scope of the work. This, it seems, is an individual we can trust to control and organise the necessary information and to fulfil his function of reporter. But first there is an item of business to settle, and here the tone changes from being brisk and self-assured to being deferential – no bad thing if the speaker wishes to gain the audience's support. He appeals to his listeners that they should not misinterpret his plain speaking. He does so in supplicatory manner ('I pray yow'), thereby putting himself in an inferior position. He bolsters the audience's sense of superiority by attributing to them an estimable and desirable quality. It is because of their inherent courtesy stretching a point, in view of the high number of churls that they are likely to construe the narrator's plain speaking as a sign of courtesy's opposite, 'vileynye' – in other words, that he is not one of them. Evidently he does not want to be placed in an invidious position, or role that is not of his own devising.

His defence of plain speaking is on grounds of veracity, but it is also involved with questions of style: he is concerned to explain *why* he will 'pleynly speke' the tales and mood of the pilgrims ('hir wordes and hir cheere') even if he is not really adequate to the task – 'Ne thogh I speke hir wordes proprely' (729). It is a consequence of his role as reporter, and here he appeals to the sense of logic, obligation and common sense of his listeners: if he is to make a true record of the tales the pilgrims told, then to discharge his responsibility he must imitate their forms of speech, however crass, as best he can. The alternative is something removed from truth, a fiction, 'feyne thing', rendered in different words. The narrator's persuasiveness is inescapable: if the audience wish him to be an accurate informant (and who wouldn't?) they must tolerate the indiscretions and rudeness which are the stuff of pilgrimage. For telling the truth about what happened, and who said what, can know no favouritism, even towards close kindred (a sentiment of which the Parson would have approved): 'He may nat spare, althogh he were his brother' (737). Truth must therefore have priority over sensibility. The meaning matters much more than the form of the words: 'He moot as wel seye o word as another' (738). To clinch the argument, the narrator appeals to revered authorities. Christ spoke in plain language, but 'vileynye' cannot be attributed to him, and Plato, if understood properly, maintained that there must be stylistic congruence between the kind of words used and the kind of actions described. In view of the advantageous position which the narrator has conferred upon the audience, they are unlikely to demur – the more so when he goes on to pray for their forgiveness because, ineptly, he has not put the pilgrims in order of social status. He pleads inadequacy of 'wit', or intelligence, as his excuse.

Lines such as these go a considerable way towards establishing the key characteristics of Chaucer the pilgrim. He is organised; common-sensical; self-deprecating; learned in a bookish sort of way; naive; apprised of his own inadequacies; ignorant about social niceties; concerned not to be regarded as churlish; worried about the conscientious fulfilment of his obligations; now confident, now not. But it is impossible to remain solemn about him for long. For, peeping out occasionally from behind the mask, we can see all too clearly the elfish face of its creator, Chaucer the poet. Then it is that the pilgrim narrator seems outrageous. Almost without realising it, we had been drawn into accepting his suppositions, namely that there really was a pilgrimage in which he participated, listening to and recording information about twenty-nine pilgrims, and then relaying verbatim their doings and stories. We know full well that the whole edifice of the *Canterbury Tales* is a fiction, that – whatever its narrator may say – it was composed by Geoffrey Chaucer out of 'feyne thyng' and 'wordes newe'. The passiveness of his narrative persona is a sham. In practice, he is an active intermediary, or middleman, within a pilgrimage which is a pretext for writing and linking stories, a pretext which enabled Chaucer to lever himself into the fiction and mediate between narrative and listeners (or reader), using not only his pilgrim alter ego but also all the other pilgrims into whom, like a ventriloquist, he projects his many voices.

iv. DISCUSSION POINTS

Read the description of the Knight (General Prologue, lines 43–78) and then answer the following questions.

1. *What importance do you attach to the lack of emphasis upon the Knight's physical appearance?*
2. *How significant are the details of the Knight's appearance?*
3. *By what other means is the Knight's character established?*
4. *What evidence is there (if any) for reading the Knight's portrait as ironic?*
5. *Compare and contrast the arguments about the Knight put forward by Jones, Keen and Pratt (see below, pages 55–7).*

The following questions relate more generally to the General Prologue:

6. *What other information about 'Chaucer the pilgrim' can be gleaned from the portraits of the General Prologue?*
7. *Consider the portrait of the Prioress as one in which character is built from the disparity between reality and the ideal.*
8. *What is the narrator's attitude towards the Monk?*
9. *How, if at all, is the 'pilgrimage controversy' a revealing context for the portrait of the Wife of Bath?*
10. *Which pilgrims, other than the Pardoner and Host, are predominantly described by reference to their physical appearance, and why? Discuss two pilgrims in detail.*
11. *How important is 'professionalism' as a criterion by which the pilgrims are judged?*
12. *Compare and contrast the voice used by Chaucer in the concluding phases of the General Prologue with that used at its opening.*
13. *To what extent is 'attitude to material wealth' a guiding principle of Chaucer's portraiture?*

v. FURTHER READING

a. *Sources and contexts*

Chaucer, Geoffrey, *The Romaunt of the Rose*, ed. Larry D. Benson in *The Riverside Chaucer*, ed. Benson, pp. 685–767.

Henry, Avril (ed.), *The Pilgrimage of the Lyfe of the Manhode: Translated*

Anonymously into Prose from The First Recension of Guillaume de Deguileville's Poem 'Le Pèlerinage de la vie humaine', 2 vols, EETS, os 291 (1985) and os 292 (1988).

Hudson, Anne (ed.), *Selections from English Wycliffite Writings* (Cambridge: Cambridge University Press, 1978).

Nelson, Venetia (ed.), *A Myrour to Lewde Men and Wymmen: A Prose Version of the 'Speculum Vitae'*, ed. from B. L. MS. Harley 45, Middle English Texts, 14 (Heidelberg: Winter, 1981).

b. Becket and pilgrimage

Adair, John, *The Pilgrims' Way: Shrines and Saints in Britain and Ireland* (London: Thames and Hudson, 1978).
Lavishly illustrated for the armchair pilgrim, with an introductory chapter on the idea of pilgrimage, followed by accounts of over thirty pilgrimage centres, with an emphasis on legend, places to visit, and local atmosphere. Prominence given to the Canterbury pilgrimage (pp. 35–73).

Barlow, Frank, *Thomas Becket* (London: Weidenfeld and Nicolson, 1986).
Authoritative and readable modern biography, with a final chapter which covers the origins of the cult of St Thomas and the pilgrimage to Canterbury. Illustrated.

Finucane, Ronald C., *Miracles and Pilgrims: Popular Beliefs in Medieval England* (London: Dent, 1977).
On the miracle-working reputation and effectiveness of saints whose popular cults emerged between 1066 and 1300, with an emphasis on English examples, including Becket. Framed by an account of the origins of miracles and relics, and the eventual neglect and destruction of shrines. Based on a study of 3,000 medieval people who claimed to have experienced a miracle at the shrine of a 'new' saint. Illustrated.

Hall, D. J., *English Mediaeval Pilgrimage* (London: Routledge and Kegan Paul, 1965).
Introductory chapter on 'Pilgrimage and the Mediaeval Mind' followed by seven chapters on English shrines. Chapter 6 is a study of Becket the man, his dispute with Henry II, martyrdom, spread and demise of the cult of St Thomas. Line illustrations.

Sumption, Jonathan, *Pilgrimage: An Image of Mediaeval Religion* (London: Faber, 1975).
Authoritative, interesting and full of vivid examples and anecdotes. European in scope (with an emphasis on France) from the eleventh to

fifteenth centuries. Coverage includes the pilgrimage ideal; relics; healing; penitence; travel. Periodic references to Becket and Canterbury.

c. Collections of critical essays

Anderson, J. J. (ed.), *Chaucer, The Canterbury Tales: A Casebook*, Casebook series (London: Macmillan, 1974).

Andrew, Malcolm (ed.), *Critical Essays on Chaucer's Canterbury Tales* (Milton Keynes: Open University Press, 1991).

Bloom, Harold (ed.), *Geoffrey Chaucer's The General Prologue to the Canterbury Tales*, Modern Critical Interpretations (New York and Philadelphia: Chelsea House, 1988).

Schoeck, Richard J., and Jerome Taylor (eds), *Chaucer Criticism*, vol. 1, *The Canterbury Tales* (Notre Dame and London: University of Notre Dame Press, 1960).

d. Pilgrimage as narrative structure

Baldwin, Ralph, *The Unity of the Canterbury Tales*, Anglistica, 5 (Copenhagen: Rosenkilde and Bagger, 1955); repr. Norwood Editions, 1977). Excerpts repr. in Schoeck and Taylor, pp. 14–51. Specialised, scholarly and influential study. The pilgrimage is not a static frame, but a dynamic entity. Ch. 1: detailed analysis of opening lines of the General Prologue; ch. 2: on the principles of characterisation and representation of space and time; ch. 3: on Chaucer's apology for his work and on the Host; ch. 4: on the narrative voices of Chaucer the pilgrim and Chaucer the poet; and on audience; ch. 5: Parson's Prologue, Tale and its application to the pilgrims.

Cooper, Helen, *The Structure of The Canterbury Tales* (London: Duckworth, 1983).
A major and important study: measures the novelty of Chaucer's story-telling collection against other medieval examples of the genre, stressing the brilliant handling of convention, poetic self-consciousness, embedding of tales within tales, use of pilgrimage as narrative structure, interrelation of tales, principles (especially generic ones) for grouping pilgrims and tales, links between tales, thematic interrelationships.

Howard, Donald R., *The Idea of the Canterbury Tales* (Berkeley, Los Angeles and London: University of California Press, 1976). Part of ch. 4, 'Memory and Form', repr. in Bloom, pp. 37–50.

In ch. 4, Howard stresses the importance of memory in Chaucer's structuring of the General Prologue and *Canterbury Tales,* as well as in the reader's experience of them, and the absence of circumstantial detail about the pilgrimage. Instead, the pilgrims skirt the edges of towns and time is represented unrealistically. The pilgrimage is an outer form, best thought of in terms of a rose-window design, which makes possible the inner forms of the individual tales.

Howard, Donald R., *Writers and Pilgrims: Medieval Pilgrimage Narratives and Their Posterity* (Berkeley, Los Angeles and London: University of California Press, 1980).

On the idea and image of pilgrimage, informed by a study of writings about actual pilgrimages to Jerusalem, with a chapter (ch. 4) on the *Canterbury Tales* as a story about pilgrimage, Chaucer as pilgrim, pilgrimage as game.

Tuve, Rosemond, *Allegorical Imagery: Some Mediaeval Books and Their Posterity* (Princeton, NJ: Princeton University Press, 1966).

Ch. 3 for a detailed study of the imagery of Deguileville's *Pèlerinage,* the content of which is summarised. Tuve argues for the work's importance and influence in the seventeenth century as well as in the fourteenth. Many illustrations.

Zacher, Christian K., *Curiosity and Pilgrimage: The Literature of Discovery in Fourteenth-Century England* (Baltimore and London: Johns Hopkins University Press, 1976).

Curiosity and pilgrimage are themes which inform chapters on Richard of Bury's *Philobiblon,* Mandeville's *Travels* and the *Canterbury Tales.* In ch. 5 Zacher rejects a wholesale allegorical interpretation of pilgrimage as it applies to Chaucer, emphasising instead the extent to which pilgrimage is associated with contest, disorder, social instability, *compaignye, felaweshipe* and restlessness.

e. General principles of composition, and overviews

Bowden, Muriel, *A Commentary on the General Prologue to the Canterbury Tales,* 2nd edn (New York: Macmillan, 1967. Repr. London: Souvenir Press, 1973).

Originally written in 1948, but still useful. Provides illuminating contextual information, e.g. on pilgrimage (ch. 2), the Knight (ch. 3), the Parson (ch. 15), the Pardoner (ch. 18) and Host (ch. 19). Should be used alongside Mann (see below).

Brewer, D. S., 'Class Distinction in Chaucer'. *Speculum,* 43 (1968), 290-305.

On three overlapping systems of social division which operate throughout Chaucer's work (with special reference to the General Prologue): the 'binary' system, i.e. the difference between being or not being *gentil;* the system of *degree,* i.e. place within the social hierarchy; and the functional system of three *estates,* i.e. those who fight, those who work and those who pray.

Eberle, Patricia J., 'Commercial Language and the Commercial Outlook in the General Prologue', *Chaucer Review*, 18 (1983–84), 161–74. Repr. in Bloom, pp. 113–23.

The getting and spending of money is a theme which informs all of the portraits, breaking down the traditional separation of court and commerce. Thus Chaucer credits his implied audience with an awareness of commercial realities. Among the pilgrims, Harry Bailly, unlike his aristocratic counterpart in the *Roman de la rose,* is 'the most obvious spokesman for the commercial outlook'.

Hoffman, Arthur W., 'Chaucer's Prologue to Pilgrimage: The Two Voices', *English Literary History,* 21 (1954), 1–16. Repr. in Anderson, pp. 105–20.

The unity of the Prologue derives from the vision of pilgrimage as prompted both by nature and by God – a doubleness which also runs through the pilgrim portraits, in which sacred, secular and profane motives mix: they are 'affected by a variety of destructive and restorative kinds of love'.

Hughes, Geoffrey, 'Gold and Iron: Semantic Change and Social Change in Chaucer's Prologue', *Standpunte,* 137 (1978), 1–11. Repr. in Bloom, pp. 73–84.

On the role of linguistic style in creating a sense of character. *Bisynesse, profit* and *winne* are keywords. Economic competition and materialism are motivating forces, but their effects are spiritually, psychologically and socially destructive.

Huppé, Bernard F., *A Reading of the Canterbury Tales* (Albany, NY: State University of New York, 1964).

Ch. 2 on the spring opening, ideal and reality of pilgrimage, Chaucer as pilgrim and author, analysis of a selection of pilgrim portraits, and the incipient drama of the journey.

Josipovici, G. D., 'Fiction and Game in *The Canterbury Tales*', *Critical Quarterly,* 7 (1965), 185–97.

Covers Chaucer's apology, his narrative persona, the story-telling game, the Host's exchanges with the Parson and Pardoner.

Lenaghan, R. T., 'Chaucer's General Prologue as History and Literature', *Comparative Studies in Society and History,* 12 (1970), 73–82.

An economic analysis of the pilgrims which divides them into three categories of occupation and sources of livelihood: land, the church and trade.

Mann, Jill, *Chaucer and Medieval Estates Satire: The Literature of Social Classes and the General Prologue to the 'Canterbury Tales'* (Cambridge: Cambridge University Press, 1973). Ch. 9, 'Conclusions', repr. in Bloom, pp. 21–36.

A detailed analysis of each pilgrim portrait, relating it to the medieval tradition of satirising representatives of the different estates or ranks of society. One feature of the tradition, as it surfaces in the General Prologue, is an emphasis upon the work and everyday activities associated with the particular estate. This helps to differentiate and characterise individual pilgrims. See also the penultimate chapter on three further types of traditional portrait – the rhetorical, moral/allegorical and physiological – which also fed Chaucer's imagination. The final chapter makes some general remarks about the relation of individual to type, the 'lack of systematically expressed values' and Chaucerian irony.

Martin, Loy D., 'History and Form in the General Prologue to the *Canterbury Tales*', *English Literary History,* 45 (1978), 1–17. Repr. in Bloom, pp. 51–65.

The series of portraits is based on rhetorical catalogues of professions, moral qualities, physical locations and geographical origins. Pilgrimage provides a sense both of separation from normal life and of social competition and conflict.

Nevo, Ruth, 'Chaucer: Motive and Mask in the General Prologue', *Modern Language Review,* 58 (1963), 1–9. Repr. in Bloom, pp. 9–20.

The General Prologue has 'its own internal system of contrasts, similarities and recurrences', which includes a moral analysis of social rank in terms of economic behaviour.

Owen, Charles A., Jr, 'Development of the Art of Portraiture in Chaucer's *General Prologue*', *Leeds Studies in English,* ns 14 (1983), 116–33.

Thought-provoking study on a variety of important topics, e.g. the means whereby Chaucer builds up the identity of individual pilgrims; the implications of the narrator's informal, conversational tone; the different values to which the pilgrims aspire.

Sklute, Larry, 'Catalogue Form and Catalogue Style in the General Prologue of the *Canterbury Tales*', *Studia Neophilologica,* 52 (1980), 35–46.

Chaucer bases his portraits on a traditional type of catalogue description which he makes dynamic and complex: indicators of moral evaluation are mixed with ones which point to historical and psychological complexity.

f. Studies of separate pilgrims and passages

Chance, Jane, 'Creation in Genesis and Nature in Chaucer's General Prologue 1–18', *Papers in Language and Literature,* 14 (1978), 459–64. Repr. in Bloom, pp. 67–71.
The General Prologue has a Genesis-like opening, with Nature (God's agent) recreating a fallen world.

Cunningham, J. V., 'The Literary Form of the Prologue to the *Canterbury Tales*', *Modern Philology,* 49 (1951–52), 172–81.
The form of the General Prologue derives from the dream vision tradition, of which the *Roman de la rose* is the prominent example: detailed comparisons follow.

Donaldson, E. Talbot, 'Chaucer the Pilgrim', *PMLA,* 69 (1954), 928-36. Repr. in Schoeck and Taylor, pp. 1–13; Donaldson, *Speaking of Chaucer* (London: University of London Athlone Press, 1970), pp. 1–12; Anderson, pp. 93–104; and Andrew, pp. 67–75.
Influential article which identifies the distinctions between the related figures of Chaucer the man, Chaucer the poet and Chaucer the pilgrim, emphasising the latter and with particular attention to the function of Chaucer's narrative persona.

Hamilton, Marie P., 'The Credentials of Chaucer's Pardoner', *Journal of English and Germanic Philology,* 40 (1941), 48–72.
Historical evidence for the activities and abuses of *quaestors* (pardoners licensed by the church), arguing that Chaucer's Pardoner is a member of the regular order of Austin canons rather than a layman or a clerk in minor orders. The Pardoner's attitude to his calling is indicated in part by his long hair, and by his not wearing a hood. Further information follows on the Pardoner's home base, the priory of Rouncival.

Jones, Terry, *Chaucer's Knight: The Portrait of a Medieval Mercenary* (London: Weidenfeld and Nicolson, 1980).
Disproportionately influential. Ch. 3 argues that the portrait of the Knight in the General Prologue is ironic: he is in fact a proud and efficient killer, an habitué of notorious pillaging raids and of battles and campaigns in which he fought fellow Christians to feed his own greed, vanity and self-advancement. As antidotes, see Keen and Pratt (below).

Keen, Maurice, 'Chaucer's Knight, the English Aristocracy and the Crusade', in *English Court Culture in the Later Middle Ages,* ed. V. J. Scattergood and J. W. Sherborne (New York: St Martin's Press, 1983), pp. 45–61.
To crusade against the heathen, as the Knight does, was an

experience not uncommon among the English nobles and knights whom Chaucer knew.

Kellogg, Alfred L., and Louis A. Haselmayer, 'Chaucer's Satire of the Pardoner', *PMLA*, 66 (1951), 251–77.

Chaucer's satire is directed not so much at the Pardoner as at the church which makes his existence possible: a historical account of the licensing and authorising of pardoners by the church, their functions as fund-raisers, attempts to control their abuses and the implications of these contexts for interpreting Chaucer's Pardoner.

Leicester, H. Marshall, Jr, 'The Art of Impersonation: A General Prologue to the *Canterbury Tales', PMLA,* 95 (1980), 213-24. Repr. in Bloom, pp. 85–100; and Andrew, pp. 138–54.

See especially the concluding paragraphs on the indeterminacy of the identity of 'Chaucer the pilgrim' and the extent to which he exists through impersonating other pilgrims.

McAlpine, Monica E., 'The Pardoner's Homosexuality and How It Matters', *PMLA,* 95 (1980), 8–22.

On the evidence for the Pardoner's homosexuality; its customary confusion with effeminacy, hermaphroditism and eunuchry; the Pardoner's preoccupation with the human body; how his sexual ambivalence relates to his spiritual condition as an alienated individual unable to name or confess his sin.

Nolan, Barbara, '"A Poet Ther Was": Chaucer's Voices in the General Prologue to the *Canterbury Tales', PMLA,* 101 (1986), 154–69. Repr. in Bloom, pp. 125–47.

On the elusiveness of Chaucer's authority as pilgrim-poet, which takes the form of a series of impersonations: learned clerk, tavern keeper, pilgrim. Chaucer thus juxtaposes images of himself as three possible kinds of poet and this 'multiple voicing' is provided with a context in later medieval theories of narrative, in which the voice is subservient to and articulates the argument, rather than a character. At the end of the prologue the dominant voice of the Host, who has other ideas about poetry as mirth, assumes control.

Page, Barbara, 'Concerning the Host', *Chaucer Review,* 4 (1969–70), 1–13.

On the appearance of the Host throughout the pilgrimage, concluding that his extravagant mirth, bravado and impatience add up to a satire of the prosperous townsman.

Pratt, John H., 'Was Chaucer's Knight Really a Mercenary?' *Chaucer Review,* 22 (1987–8), 8–27.

On the basis of contemporary chronicles and other documents, questions Jones's thesis that Chaucer's audience would have perceived the Knight as a mercenary in the pejorative sense. The impression he creates is a positive one, since he took part in crusades against enemies of the church.

Storm, Melvin, 'The Pardoner's Invitation: Quaestor's Bag or Becket's Shrine', *PMLA,* 97 (1982), 810–18.

The Pardoner threatens to destroy the pilgrimage by acting as a 'meretricious surrogate for what the other pilgrims seek at Becket's shrine'; in so doing he tempts them to avarice.

Wenzel, Siegfried, 'Chaucer's Pardoner and His Relics', *Studies in the Age of Chaucer,* 11 (1989), 37–41.

On the association of Pardoners with false relics.

Wurtele, Douglas J., 'The Anti-Lollardry of Chaucer's Parson', *Mediaevalia,* 11 (1985), 151–68.

Points out that the Parson's radicalism is of a conservative kind, i.e. it is directed at returning to the roots of the Christian faith, and denies that he is a card-carrying Wycliffite, although there is 'congruence of attitude'. The Parson is a 'conformist', for the abuses to which he is opposed (e.g. blaspheming and cursing those who had not paid their tithes) were the target of orthodox churchmen, as well as being the concern of Lollards.

CHAPTER TWO

The Knight's Tale

i. A QUESTION OF CONTEXT

If we wish to identify what is distinctive about the Knight's Tale we must pay some attention to Chaucer's major narrative source, the *Teseida* of Giovanni Boccaccio. It provides a point of contrast and comparison, as well as a context, for Chaucer's poem. But it is not a sufficient context, and should not be taken as a means to a complete interpretation of the poem. Other factors influenced the composition of the Knight's Tale, such as its place within the sequence of Canterbury tales, or the condition of chivalry within Chaucer's society. Again, we should not regard the *Teseida* as in some way an inferior version of the Knight's Tale, merely because it was Chaucer's source. It is an independent and earlier creation, written according to different imperatives. If a comparison between it and the Knight's Tale is to be meaningful, then some attention must also be paid to the circumstances in which it was written.

An important feature of that context, though by no means the only one, is the literary ancestry of the *Teseida* itself. No less than Chaucer, Boccaccio derived his story from an earlier version by another author, in this case the Roman poet Statius, who wrote the *Thebaid*. Thus there is a mirroring of one text by another: the Knight's Tale reflects the *Teseida* which reflects the *Thebaid*. To some extent, each new version of the story provides a commentary on the one that precedes it so that, in a sense, texts 'talk' to each other. Actually, as we shall see, the situation is much more complex. Chaucer makes independent, if limited, use of Statius, but also adds to a narrative borrowed from Boccaccio material derived from other compositions with which he was acquainted. Books breed more books and, as in the best of families, there is a good deal of whispering among its members. This elaborate process of cross-pollination and mutual dependence of one text upon another we call *intertextuality*. An understanding of its mechanisms, as well as an understanding of the broader issue of context, is an important outcome of the comparative method.

Like Chaucer, Boccaccio had more than one source. In addition to the *Thebaid* he also made use of writings by Virgil, Lucan and Ovid. Identifying his sources only begs other questions: why did he choose these authors and not others? What was he setting out to do? What Statius and the other authors have in common is that they are all Latin poets who wrote at a time when the Roman empire was in its heyday. They all to a greater or lesser extent reflected and celebrated Roman civilisation, and particularly its marked emphasis on military life. They did this by writing epic, that is a type of composition which records the progress of a soldier-hero, such as Ulysses or Aeneas or Theseus, in his attempts to overcome the worst of what fate, the gods and his enemies can do to prevent his eventual success. Not infrequently, the epic hero (with his companions) represents and defends a particular cultural identity. Thus Virgil's hero, Aeneas, is at once a survivor of Troy and the founder of Rome. Such stories are by their very nature full of battles, duels, ceremonies, lists and addresses to the gods. Their values are male, pagan ones, and their sense of reality is of a world which can be explained through events, deeds and words. Women play important roles within epic, but their influence is generally restricted, and confined to single episodes.

Epic survived as a vital literary mode for a thousand years after the fall of Rome. But when Boccaccio completed the *Teseida* in 1341 the dominant narrative mode had been, for the best part of two centuries, not epic but romance. Now romance also enshrines the values of heroic conduct, but they are those of the Christian ethic of chivalry. That ethic stressed not so much the primacy of heroic deeds as service: service to God, to king, and to lady. In many ways it was an impossible ideal, since service to lady (say) might well conflict with service to God, to king, or to both. Thus one of the main obstacles in the path of a romance hero is not so much the physical trials of combat and survival in a hostile world as the impossibility of living up to the ideal. So its sense of reality is displaced from the objective world to the subjective, and a tension builds up between the two, between the expectations of the public world and the drives of the private world. The subject of romance is therefore the values it seeks to express, which are forever being tried and tested. Epic is not self-questioning. And one symptom of the difference of romance is the central role given to women.

Through them, as much as by any other means, is the hero tested.

So when Boccaccio wrote the *Teseida* he was going against the grain: rejecting the obvious choice of genre (romance) and opting instead for one which was all but defunct (epic). In this he was being progressive and avant-garde. Quite deliberately he wanted to write the first epic in the vernacular, that is his own language of Italian, rather than in Latin. The association of epic with Latin literature is itself significant. Boccaccio is an early figure in that cultural shift we call the Renaissance. One of its dominant features was the enthusiastic revival of the artistic forms of classical Greece and Rome. Living in Italy, surrounded by the architectural heritage of the Roman empire, Italian writers and artists were in a particularly advantageous position to spearhead that moment.

As an example of epic in the classical tradition the *Teseida* fails. Boccaccio could not escape his other, more immediate, medieval inheritance. Intermingled with his accounts of battles and funerals, his descriptive lists and reference to the gods, is the tale of two knights, Palemone and Arcita, who become rivals for the love of Emilia. In other words, romance competes with epic to produce a hybrid. That may have been part of Boccaccio's intention from the outset. *Teseida* is subtitled *le nozze di Emilia,* the nuptials of Emilia. An examination of a short excerpt from the *Teseida,* describing the first appearance of Emilia, will now help to clarify the nature of Boccaccio's writing. A comparison between it and the equivalent scene in the Knight's Tale will then highlight some of the distinctive characteristics of Chaucer's composition. Once you have read the passage by Boccaccio, try to answer the following questions.

1. *What are the epic qualities of this episode? Consider both its content and its 'sense of reality'.*
2. *What characteristics of this episode define it as romance?*
3. *Before you go on to read the parallel passage from the Knight's Tale, consider what influences were at work on Chaucer which might have made his approach different from Boccaccio's.*

> One fine morning, when she had risen and bound up her golden hair, she went down into the garden as usual, and singing gaily she was joyfully and deftly making herself a garland of many flowers as she sat there upon the grass – all the while singing love-songs with an angelic voice and a glad heart.
>
> At the sound of that charming voice Arcita, who was in the prison beside the lovely garden, rose without saying anything to Palemone and eagerly opened a small window in order to hear the song better. And in order to see who could be singing it he put his head out some way between the bars.

The day was still somewhat dark, for the sun shone upon only part of the horizon. But nonetheless by straining his eyes he could glimpse what that as yet unknown young girl was doing there with such extreme delight. And gazing fixedly upon her face he declared to himself: 'She is from Heaven!'

And drawing back within he said softly: 'Palemone, come and see: Venus herself has descended here! Do you not hear her singing? Ah, if you care for me at all come here quickly! I know you will be delighted to see what a celestial beauty has come down here below from the highest heavens.'

Palemone, whose joy in listening to her was already greater than he would have thought possible, arose and went with him towards the window, so that they might both silently behold the goddess. And when he saw he declared fervently: 'This must indeed be Cytherea, for I have never before seen any creature so lovely, charming or graceful.'

(*Tes.*, III, 10-14; trans. Havely)

Yclothed was she fresshe, for to devyse:
Hir yelow heer was broyded in a tresse
Bihynde hir bak, a yerde long, I gesse, 1050
And in the gardyn, at the sonne upriste,
She walketh up and doun, and as hire liste
She gadereth floures, party white and rede,
To make a subtil gerland for hire hede;
And as an aungel hevenysshly she soong. 1055
The grete tour, that was so thikke and stroong,
Which of the castel was the chief dongeoun
(Ther as the knyghtes weren in prisoun
Of which I tolde yow and tellen shal),
Was evene joynant to the gardyn wal 1060
Ther as this Emelye hadde hir pleyynge.
Bright was the sonne and cleer that morwenynge,
And Palamoun, this woful prisoner,
As was his wone, by leve of his gayler,
Was risen and romed in a chambre an heigh, 1065
In which he al the noble citee seigh,
And eek the gardyn, ful of braunches grene,
Ther as this fresshe Emelye the shene
Was in hire walk, and romed up and doun.
This sorweful prisoner, this Palamoun, 1070
Goth in the chambre romynge to and fro
And to hymself compleynynge of his wo.
That he was born, ful ofte he seyde, 'allas!'
And so bifel, by aventure or cas,
That thurgh a wyndow, thikke of many a barre 1075
Of iren greet and square as any sparre,
He cast his eye upon Emelya,
And therwithal he bleynte and cride 'A!'
As though he stongen were unto the herte.

(KnT, 1048-79)

We are now in a position to make detailed comparisons between these two passages. Ask yourself:

1. *What differences are there in the descriptions of the two settings?*
2. *What details of the action are different?*
3. *How does Palamon's mood and response differ from Arcita's (his counterpart in the* Teseida*).*
4. *Which passage is the more tense and dramatic, and why?*

Superficially, Chaucer's lines read as a reasonably approximate translation of Boccaccio's scene. A number of details recur: the dawn setting; Emelye's braided, blonde hair; her angelic singing; her gathering of flowers to make a garland; and so on. But a closer reading shows that Chaucer has systematically altered his Italian source. For example, where Emilia sits, Emelye 'walketh up and doun' gathering flowers as the fancy takes her, 'as hire liste' (1052). The change may seem insignificant, but it is repeated later (at line 1069), and Emelye is not the only person who 'romed up and doun'. Palamon also is roaming about his high prison chamber, going 'to and fro', as Chaucer twice informs us (1065 and 1071). In fact, the references to 'roaming' alternate so that the reader sees first Emelye, then Palamon, then Emelye again, then Palamon again.

Such an arrangement encourages comparisons between the two figures, and it soon becomes clear that the activities of Emelye and Palamon, apparently so similar, are actually expressions of fundamentally different states of existence. Emelye is free, wandering in the garden because she wishes to. She may walk at her ease, where she pleases, and with a sense of purpose and fulfilment. Palamon may 'roam' only with his gaoler's permission (1064), and then no further than the severely restricted confines of a prison chamber. His walking, such as it is, is aimless, frustrated, restless. That being said, at the end of the passage Palamon's attention and direction, initially so listless and general, suddenly become concentrated and focused. His roaming abruptly ceases. It is as if the trajectories of two randomly orbiting planets coincide, and one is drawn into the gravitational field of the other.

The principle of contrast which Chaucer here employs is one which informs the entire passage. Reference to Boccaccio's scene indicates the extent to which Chaucer further accentuated the harsh circumstances of imprisonment, so different from Emelye's situation. Their Italian counterparts are subjected to a relatively lax form of house arrest, and occupy a room close to the garden. But Palamon and Arcite are incarcerated in a high prison tower, 'thikke and stroong', the chief dungeon of Theseus' castle (1056–7). Although their tower also is adjacent to the garden where Emelye walks (1060) they are removed from the garden's immediate proximity: Palamon looks down on to the garden rather than into it. Such is the distance between the prisoners and Emelye that they, unlike Palemone and Arcita, do not hear her singing. And at the moment when Palamon sees Emelye the prison bars, far from allowing him to put his head between them for a better view, emphatically intervene, being 'thikke of many a barre / Of iren greet and square as any sparre' (1075–6). In such ways, Chaucer redesigns Boccaccio's prison in order to underline the extreme differences in physical circumstances of the knights and Emelye. Emelye's setting is among the coloured flowers, in the bright, clear morning, within the open green garden, she herself being fresh and radiant. By contrast, the knights' prison is enclosed, excluding the natural world and is monochrome, gloomy, isolated, its inhabitants pallid.

Chaucer's manipulation of his source also increases the poignancy of the knights' predicament. Palamon is so near and yet so far from the object of his desire. Of course, even before seeing Emelye, he is in a state of anguish at the condition of his life. He is, as a prisoner, 'woful' (1063) and 'sorweful' (1070), given to utterances of despair (1073). How unlike the joyful and serene Emelye: while she sings and enjoys her 'playyinge' (1061) in the garden, Palamon is 'compleynynge of his wo' (1072). His emotions, then, are already activated and he is sensitised to inner suffering when the sight of Emelye adds a new dimension to his torment. Boccaccio's heroes are altogether more placid, Emilia altogether more accessible.

So the moment at which Palamon sees Emelye has a dramatic intensity absent from Chaucer's source. There is a careful build up of expectation as the climax approaches. The contrast between prison and garden, and the state of Palamon's emotions, play their part, but so does the sense that he was fated to see Emelye. It was on that particular morning (1062) at that particular time, when Emelye was in that particular place and Palamon was in that particular room looking through that particular window 'by aventure or cas' (1074), by chance or accident. What further contributes to the dramatic quality of the scene is Chaucer's transference of the impact of Emelye's presence from sound to sight. In the *Teseida* it is Emilia's sweet singing which gradually attracts the imprisoned knights. In the Knight's Tale it is the sudden sight of her which forcibly activates Palamon's love, a sight so overwhelming that, unlike his Italian counterpart, he has no thought of sharing it with his brother knight. The experience of seeing her is therefore made particular to him (and subsequently particular to Arcite). Each sees Emelye in his own way, and their different, separate experiences have an isolating and divisive effect. Boccaccio's heroes share the pleasure first of hearing, then of gazing at, Emilia. They already know what they are looking for – the source of the music – when they move to the window. But Chaucer's Palamon is entirely unaware of the shock that awaits him on the other side of the prison bars. His glance is at first general, panoramic: he sees the entire city (1066). Then his gaze settles on the colourful garden, 'ful of branches grene' (1067). Finally, his eye is caught by a moving figure and he remains transfixed, mesmerised, devastated, the victim of a sudden heart-wound.

ii. THE IDEA OF IMPRISONMENT

A comparison between similar passages in the *Teseida* and the Knight's Tale has shown that Chaucer deliberately accentuated the prison and made it a place altogether different – in design, in nature – from Boccaccio's model. At the same time he intensified, through Palamon, the experience of imprisonment. Why did he wish to draw attention to the prison and its effects, to make the scene so prominent? One obvious answer would be that the prison is an important, if not the most important, locus of action within the tale as a whole. The sighting of Emelye, and the resulting quarrel between Palamon and Arcite, provide the motive forces for the remainder of the narrative. But is that a sufficient explanation? The same might be said of the prison scene in the *Teseida,* but Boccaccio felt himself under no obligation to highlight it. Clearly, then, Chaucer's episode has additional functions. What might these be? One way of framing an answer is by looking at the representation of imprisonment within two texts which fed Chaucer's imagination, the *Romance of the Rose* and the *Consolation of Philosophy*. They are very different from each other in motivation and temper, and it is essential to understand their distinctive qualities before going on to consider what each may have contributed to the representation of imprisonment in the Knight's Tale itself.

The *Romance of the Rose,* which we have already encountered, had a formative effect on the imaginations of literate people throughout Europe for the best part of two centuries. Widely known, and often illustrated, it provided its audiences with a vocabulary of traditional images for different aspects of sexual desire and frustration. In Chapter One, we saw how it tells the story of a young man who falls asleep and dreams that, one May, he is walking joyfully through the spring countryside when he encounters a walled garden. Ushered in by a beautiful girl called Idleness, he discovers a kind of paradise, teeming with natural life and inhabited by attractive individuals, led by Mirth, who sing and dance and who are attended by the God of Love. Subsequently, the dreamer arrives at the Fountain of Narcissus and, looking into its pool, he sees in its depths a rosebud and longs to possess it. From this moment onwards, the romance catalogues his successes and setbacks – often with elaborate digressions – as he attempts to discover the place where the rose (the woman whom he desires) is, and seize it.

Once the dreamer has conceived his desire for the rosebud, the God of Love shoots five arrows at him, and captures him. The Lover (as the dreamer is called) willingly submits as Love's prisoner and allows his heart to be locked by Love with a small golden key. The god explains that to be in the service of love is harmful and dangerous: each man is afflicted by pain and would attempt to escape death, or give up the prospect of doing so, were it not for the hope which sustains him. The Middle English translation describes how the lover is

Glad, as man in prisoun sett,	2755
And may not geten for to et	
But barly breed and watir pure	
And lyeth in vermyn and in ordure;	*filth*
With all this yitt can he lyve,	
Good hope such comfort hath hym yive,	2760
Which maketh wene that he shall be	*think*
Delyvered, and come to liberte.	
In fortune is [his] fulle trust,	
Though he lye in strawe or dust;	
In hoope is all his susteynyng.	2765
And so for lovers, in her wenyng,	
Whiche Love hath shit in his prisoun,	
Good hope is her salvacioun.	

(*Rom.*, 2755–68)

Now consider the following questions.

1. *Is the writing literal or symbolic?*
2. *What central image is used to describe a man in love, and how is it elaborated?*
3. *Is love seen as a positive or negative and threatening force?*
4. *In spite of his conditions the lover is described as 'Glad'. Why?*

For Boethius, on the other hand, imprisonment was all too real. He had been a high-ranking government official who served the Gothic emperor, Theodoric. But he became a victim of factional politics and was exiled to Pavia where he was imprisoned. Under threats to his life he composed there the *Consolation of Philosophy*, an attempt to reconcile himself to the arbitrary twists and turns of his career. Though a Christian, he attempted to do so in entirely rational and philosophic terms: the *Consolation* is a triumph of reason over emotion. His work was destined to exert a profound influence over western thought not merely as an example of prison literature but as an attempt to give meaning, purpose and dignity to human life. Among its distinguished translators are King Alfred, Chaucer and Queen Elizabeth I. Its author, an early political prisoner, was tortured and bludgeoned to death in AD 524 or 525.

The author presents himself as being in a state of extreme anguish, one which contrasts with his former state of happiness. In Chaucer's translation *(Boece)*, he refers to his 'grevous' weeping (I, prosa 1, 87), the 'wawes [*waves*] of my wepynges' (I, prosa 2, 29–30), his 'sorwe and ire and wepynge' (I, prosa 5, 69–70), the heavy chains which oppress his neck (I, metrum 2, 29–32), and the 'litargye [*lethargy*], which that is a comune seknesse to hertes that been desceyved' (I, prosa 2, 20–1). In this condition, his thoughts turn to destiny, 'the sorwful wyerdes [*destiny*] of me, olde man' (I, metrum 1, 12–13), and to the power of Fortune, who seems to have determined his present condition. In his prison, bewailing his lot, Boethius experiences a vision of an aged woman of changing stature, dressed in beautifully woven clothes. It is Philosophy herself.

Philosophy offers an alternative perception of the prison which so oppresses Boethius. She acknowledges that philosophers are not immune to the vicissitudes of life, the 'tempestes blowynge aboute', such as the displeasure of wicked men. But whatever their power it is to be despised because it is not governed by the true leader, reason, 'but it es ravyssched oonly by fleetynge errour folyly and lyghtly' (I, prosa 3, 63–71). If an enemy, driven by error and passion, should make a trial of strength, reason withdraws his riches into a tower. There, reason's followers remain indifferent to the turmoil around them:

> But we that ben heghe above, syker [*safe*] fro alle tumolte and wood [*mad*] noyse, warnstoryd [*fortified*] and enclosed in swich a palys [*palisade*] whider as that chaterynge or anoyinge folye ne may nat atayne, we scorne swyche ravyneres [*plunderers*] and henteres [*takers*] of fouleste thynges.
>
> (*Bo.* I, prosa 3, 76–81)

Thus, by force of thought, Philosophy enables Boethius to 'escape' his immediate surroundings by transforming his perception of them.

Consider next the following questions, taking into account both the passage just quoted and the preceding commentary.

1. *For Boethius, is imprisonment literal, symbolic, or both?*
2. *What are the negative and positive forces governing Boethius' life?*
3. *How does Philosophy attempt to change Boethius' perceptions of his condition?*

We are now in a position to compare and contrast the *Romance of the Rose* and the *Consolation of Philosophy:*

1. *Compare the role played by the female in the two poems.*
2. *Is Fortune seen in the same light by both Boethius and Guillaume de Lorris?*
3. *Are the grounds for optimism the same in each case?*

An examination of the above passages shows how imprisonment could be represented as an idea as much as a fact. For Guillaume's lover it expresses the state of being in love. For Boethius it is at first an uncomfortable fact of existence, but with Philosophy's help his prison takes on positive connotations as an image for the protection which reason provides from the ups and downs of life. We now wish to determine whether Chaucer, influenced as he was by Boethius and Guillaume de Lorris, also represented the idea as well as the fact of imprisonment. If so, this would help to account for the relative prominence given to Theseus' prison. We can interrogate Chaucer's poem on the basis of what we have observed in the *Romance* and the *Consolation*. In the following questions, the emphasis is on the legacy of the *Romance*.

1. *Can you point to any evidence in the poem as a whole which suggests that Palamon and Arcite are 'imprisoned' by love?*
2. *Are there any additional forces generated by their sexual rivalry which produce in them a sense of constraint?*
3. *Compare the role of Emelye with that of Guillaume's 'rose' and Lady Philosophy.*

Not unlike the prison of Boethius, that of Theseus has a double status. It is at once a stage on which crucial events unfold and an embodiment of those non-material forces, like love, which hem in the lives of Palamon and Arcite. It is as much a focus of meaning as a locus of action, fluctuating between its two functions. What is more, the tower-prison's resonance as a symbol survives long after Palamon and Arcite leave its narrow confines. As an image which articulates the deeper significance of the Knight's Tale, the tower-prison has considerable importance.

One of the most remarkable examples of interplay between tower-prison as place, and imprisonment as idea, comes in the aftermath of Arcite's release. Far from feeling liberated by such an unexpected turn of events, Arcite's sense of imprisonment is actually worse than when he was behind bars. Exiled by Theseus, he suffers extreme sorrow and apprehensions of death. He weeps, wails, and cries piteously, entertaining thoughts of suicide, and exclaims 'Now is my prisoun worse than biforn' (1224). If Theseus' tower was purgatory, he is now consigned to hell. Being in Theseus' castle, even if 'Yfetered in his prisoun everemo' (1229), was a blissful state by comparison with the kind of existence he now faces, bereft of the sight of Emelye. By contrast, Palamon continues to dwell 'Ful blisfully in prison ... / In prison? Certes nay, but in paradys!' (1236–7).

What causes the renewed 'imprisoning' of Palamon? Desire for Emelye. Theseus has been replaced by another gaoler, erotic love, which is perhaps even harsher than the duke of Athens himself. From this perspective the prison tower becomes a potent image for the entrammelling power of sexual longing. Now the figurative possibilities of imprisonment, as expressing the emotional condition of the two knights, were not lost on Boccaccio. At one point Arcita says of love that 'his prison is already more oppressive to me than that of Theseus is' (*Tes.* III. 23). But the metaphor is never developed, as it is by Chaucer, to the point where the prison assumes a complex and enduring significance beyond its immediate material existence.

Should we therefore hail Chaucer as unusually ingenious, to the point of originality, in the extent to which he developed the idea of imprisonment? Perhaps. Certainly the complexity of meaning (as it will emerge in this chapter) generated by the prison of Theseus is a major achievement, for which he alone was responsible. But the principle of giving symbolic value to the material world was, as we have seen, deeply ingrained in the practices of many medieval writers, and in the responses of their audiences. It required no straining of their imaginations to read the prison of Theseus as in some measure an image for the constraining effects of love. In this respect Chaucer might again be seen as the more conservative poet by comparison with Boccaccio who, as earlier indicated, was attempting to shed traditional habits of composition in favour of an early encounter with the novelty of classical, pre-Christian writing.

iii. THE VAGARIES OF FORTUNE

The movement, in the *Consolation,* from prison as place to prison as an image of Fortune's effects, to prison as an image of reason's protective qualities, sharpens our perception of the prison of Theseus.

1. *In what ways are Palamon's conditions and experience of imprisonment similar to those of Guillaume's lover and to those of Boethius?*
2. *To what extent does Fortune, no less than love, constrain the lives of Palamon and Arcite?*
3. *Compare the attempts of Palamon and Arcite to reconcile themselves to their situation with those of Boethius.*

Extensively and systematically, the unpredictable nature of the knights' experiences is amplified through allusions to Fortune's influence. In the aftermath of Emelye's appearance Arcite counsels patience, describing the circumstances of Palamon and himself as follows:

> For Goddes love, taak al in pacience
> Oure prisoun, for it may noon oother be.
> Fortune hath yeven us this adversitee.
>
> (KnT, 1084–6)

But the influence of Fortune has been operative before Palamon and Arcite appear on the scene (912–26). It is by chance that Palamon and Arcite are discovered at Thebes (1009–19); by chance, 'by aventure or cas' (1074), that they see Emelye and fall in love. Arcite advises that each of them must take what comes in life, in terms which suggest that prison and the vagaries of experience have become synonymous: 'Heere in this prisoun moote we endure / And everich of us take his aventure' (1185–6). Arcite comes to believe that Fortune is favourable to Palamon – 'Wel hath Fortune yturned thee the dys' (1238) – while Palamon also realises that chance may give Emelye to his rival (1285–90). Arcite's fortunes do revive once he is made a page of Emelye's chamber, but they are soon to plunge again with Palamon's escape from prison: he 'litel wiste how ny that was his care, / Til that Fortune had broght him in the snare' (1489–90). Arcite approaches the grove where Palamon is hiding 'By aventure' (1506), where 'by aventure' Palamon is concealed in a bush (1516). The discovery by Theseus of the fighting knights is prefaced by the remark that 'somtyme it shal fallen on a day / That falleth nat eft withinne a thousand yeer' (1668–9). The ladies of the court pity the chance that brings Palamon and Arcite together in mortal combat (1751–2); Theseus decrees that the tournament, the outcome of which is in the hands of Fortune (1860–1), will be an 'aventure of love'

(2357); and it is by 'aventure' (2703 and 2722) that Arcite falls from his horse in the lists. By the time that Theseus, in his closing speech, refers to 'this foule prisoun of this lyf' (3061) his castle tower has gathered a tremendous significance. It is something more than a place where important events happen.

In the *Consolation,* Philosophy's argument urges a growing separation between the unpleasant experience of imprisonment and the prisoner's mental and emotional perception of his physical conditions. In the Knight's Tale we have observed a similar kind of separation (if less philosophical detachment!) between physical circumstances on the one hand and thoughts or feelings about them on the other. Clearly, then, imprisonment is a state of mind (and heart) as much as a physical condition. This separation of ideas and feelings about imprisonment from the place of imprisonment (however much they might initially be caused by actual incarceration) itself helps to explain how Theseus' tower cell continues to exert a strong influence within the Knight's Tale long after both Palamon and Arcite have left its confines. Important as it is to the plot of the tale, Chaucer uses the tower-prison of Theseus to activate the idea of imprisonment, exploring its figurative values in order to thicken the meaning of the narrative. As the Knight's Tale progresses the tower accumulates significance until, as we have seen, it comes to express in symbolic terms the restrictions imposed on man's life by abstract forces (such as that of Fortune) beyond his control, as well as the constraining effects of erotic love. In articulating such meanings through the image of the tower-prison, Chaucer drew on ideas which may be located in the *Romance of the Rose* and the *Consolation of Philosophy,* works which had a profound effect on both his intellectual outlook and that of his audience.

What we are witnessing here is an alchemy of the imagination, whereby one text (the *Teseida*) is blended with others (the *Rose,* the *Consolation*) to make a new, shimmering amalgam (the Knight's Tale). It is a procedure which Chaucer was to adopt time and again. Identifying it enables us to recognise that the tower-prison of Theseus has a complex, not a single, meaning. Important as the scene of a decisive event, it also articulates the experience of love and the power of Fortune. Having reached such a conclusion it is tempting to accentuate one of the meanings which Theseus' tower reflects, giving it precedence over the other. In fact they do not exist in a stable relationship: now love, now Fortune, is to the fore. That Chaucer makes it difficult to provide a definitive and enduring interpretation of the prison is itself significant, for it illustrates one of the fundamental principles of his story-telling. He rarely, if ever, promotes or enables a single, unifying meaning. In this respect he is, after all, more radical than Boccaccio in the *Teseida* whose predominant concern, as announced in the prologue to his work, is to present his estranged lover, 'Fiammetta', with a narrative which, while making covert reference to their own affair, may also win back her favour. Chaucer, however conservative he may be in dealing with other aspects of Boccaccio's narrative, is drawn rather to show how all interpretation must be relative, qualified, provisional. Thus his creative energies are directed towards identifying issues, and putting them in play as part of the text, but leaving their resolution to the audience. For all his learning, he is rarely authoritative, preferring rather to set up the conditions for a debate to be continued beyond the boundary of the narrative, rather than to close down options before the story is finished. The question which he asks, through the Knight, at the end of the first part of the tale, is very much in the spirit of his entire literary enterprise: 'Who hath the worse, Arcite or Palamoun?' (1348). It is a question which, without distorting its intention, applies to the present discussion. 'Who is in the worse prison, Arcite or Palamoun?' Chaucer provides a range of possible answers, and we must now consider another.

iv. THE BONDS OF LOVE

Love and Fortune are not the only forces which 'imprison' Palamon and Arcite. The two knights also feel that their actions are controlled by the gods, who reduce their scope for independent action. The idea is corroborated by Saturn, who declares: 'Myn is the prison in the derke cote [*cell*]' (2457), thereby claiming to be the god of imprisonment. His remark is part of a speech in which he lays claim to tremendous powers. They exceed those of the other gods who feature in the tale, enabling him to declare that he will end – if temporarily – the traditional hostility of Venus and Mars which lies behind the quarrel of Palamon and Arcite. Saturn illustrates his power by providing some examples of his many effects on earth. The occasion for Saturn's speech is an approach by his granddaughter, Venus, who is aggrieved by Mars' promise that Arcite will have victory in the tournament. The episode does not feature at all in the *Teseida* and indeed the precise nature of Chaucer's source (or sources) is unknown, although it is based on the traditional ideas that each planetary god is responsible for particular kinds of events and experiences on earth; and that each planet has 'children', that is types of people prone to be affected by that planet's influence. So Saturn's prominence in the Knight's Tale, which is one of Chaucer's major innovations, provides a valuable clue to some of the distinctive meanings which he wished his narrative to convey.

The kind of power to which Saturn lays claim is illustrated in Plate 2. It shows the planet-god in the zodiacal signs of Capricorn and Aquarius, dominating events on earth. The Italian caption says that Saturn is a masculine planet positioned in the seventh, or outermost, sphere of the universe; by nature cold and dry, causing lethargy (or slothfulness) and melancholy; and the controller of religious and agricultural activities. Before going on to read Saturn's speech, look closely at the detail of the illustration, and answer these questions.

1. *What features of the caption are exemplified in the picture itself?*
2. *What evidence is there that Saturn is the god of hard, physical labour?*
3. *What images of violence and constraint occur within the picture?*
4. *How would you describe the overall effect of Saturn's rule?*

'My deere doghter Venus,' quod Saturne,
'My cours, that hath so wyde for to turne,
Hath moore power than woot any man. 2455
Myn is the drenchyng in the see so wan;
Myn is the prison in the derke cote;
Myn is the stranglyng and hangyng by the throte,
The murmure and the cherles rebellyng,
The groynynge, and the pryvee empoysonyng; 2460
I do vengeance and pleyn correccioun,
Whil I dwelle in the signe of the leoun.
Myn is the ruyne of the hye halles,
The fallynge of the toures and of the walles
Upon the mynour or the carpenter. 2465
I slow Sampsoun, shakynge the piler;
And myne be the maladyes colde,
The derke tresons, and the castes olde;
My lookyng is the fader of pestilence.
Now weep namoore; I shal doon diligence 2470
That Palamon, that is thyn owene knyght,
Shal have his lady, as thou hast him hight.
Though Mars shal helpe his knyght, yet nathelees
Bitwixe yow ther moot be som tyme pees,
Al be ye noght of o compleccioun, 2475
That causeth al day swich divisioun.
I am thyn aiel, redy at thy wille;
Weep now namoore; I wol thy lust fulfille.'

(KnT, 2453–78)

Plate 2: Saturn and his children.

Now answer the following questions.

1. *What details of Saturn's rule are common to the picture and passage?*
2. *Which of Saturn's effects are described by Chaucer but omitted in the picture?*
3. *Taking into account both the illustration and the passage, how extensive is Saturn's influence within the Knight's Tale as a whole?*

Even if one looks no further than Saturn's speech, he is making a very considerable claim to be the wielder of power and the arbiter of justice in Athenian society, and to an extent unrealised by any of its members. This in itself identifies him as a rival to Theseus, who believes that he, as duke of Athens, wields justice and power. At the same time the reader is put in the privileged position of having access to both Saturn's domain and Theseus', and therefore of being able to evaluate the different principles according to which they each exercise power and justice.

It has often been remarked that Theseus rules Athenian society according to principles of order and restraint. These are reflected not only in the hierarchical arrangement of individuals within it, but also in his concern for custom, ceremony and procession. One of the great affronts to his sense of propriety is the discovery of Palamon and Arcite fighting in the grove like wild animals, 'Withouten juge or oother officere' (1712). Consequently, he arranges that they should resolve their differences according to the accepted forms of chivalry, in a tournament. The amphitheatre, or lists, which he has built for that tournament, stands as an emblem of his world view. Now look at the description of Theseus' amphitheatre (1881–1913) and consider the following questions.

1. *What details of its design suggest the principles of order and symmetry according to which Theseus views his world?*
2. *What attitude towards the gods does the design of the amphitheatre express?*
3. *To what extent are notions of symmetry and order sustained in subsequent preparations for the tournament?*
4. *Does order prevail in the eventual outcome of the tournament?*
5. *If not, how is it disrupted and by whom?*

In its circular design the building is an image of wholeness and perfection. Even the arrangement of the seating – raked in order to give a good view to all spectators – reflects Theseus' belief in the benefits of an interdependent, hierarchical society. The architectural features are also balanced: the east gate is matched by the west gate. And it pays due attention to the part which the gods play in human affairs, by including an oratory to Venus above the east gate, one to Mars above the west gate and, midway between them, one to Diana.

Within such an ideal space, it would seem that a true balance of justice might be struck. Initially, at least, Theseus' conceptions do hold sway. The rules, or ordinances, designed to prevent the shedding of blood, are proclaimed. The tournament will end once either Palamon or Arcite is captured. After processional entries into the lists at opposite gates, the numerically equivalent knights of Palamon and Arcite plunge into the fray. At length, Palamon is captured and taken to the stake. Victory (and Emelye) are Arcite's. But at the moment of victory, Arcite's horse rears, he is thrown on to the pommel of his saddle, and is fatally wounded in the chest. Soon he will die a lingering and disgusting death. In spite of Theseus' best efforts, therefore, his system of justice has not prevailed – it has been thwarted by an apparent accident. Once Arcite dies, there is an understandable note of despair in Athenian society, captured memorably by the female citizens, who cry: 'Why woldestow be deed ... / And haddest gold ynough, and Emelye?' (2835–6). It is a despair born not just of personal grief of the sort felt most intensely by Emelye and Palamon – 'Shrighte Emelye, and howleth Palamon' (2817) – but also of bewilderment that the man who, according to Theseus' scheme of things, proved that he merited Emelye, cannot have her. Arcite's death therefore challenges the adequacy of Theseus' vision.

What he cannot see, any more than the other members of his society, is the hand of Saturn. But the poem's audience knows that Arcite's horse rears because of the sudden appearance out of the ground of a 'furie infernal' (2684) sent by that god. And, between the triumph of Arcite and his unhorsing, the poem's audience sees Saturn in conference with Venus, assuring his 'doghter' that, in spite of appearances, events will turn out in her favour. These are clear indications that the power of Saturn transcends that of Theseus. The argument of the poem would therefore seem to lie in the direction of saying that might is greater than right. For the principles of order, restraint, balance and justice according to which Theseus governs are superseded and nullified by the arbitrary, vengeful, destructive power which Saturn wields.

Now look again at Saturn's descriptions of his effects on earth, printed above.

1. *How would you describe Saturn's principles of operation, and to what extent are they opposed to Theseus' ideals?*
2. *Are there any ways in which Saturn's words and actions promote justice and harmony?*
3. *What examples can you find in the Knight's Tale of the making and*

> *breaking of bonds of love, loyalty, friendship and devotion? Does any meaningful pattern emerge?*

Like Theseus, Saturn also claims to be exercising justice, to be striking a balance between Venus and Mars such that Mars' knight will have his victory and Venus' knight will have his lady. True, the effects on earth of Saturn's justice are horrendous, but it is justice nevertheless. It is exercised in response to a request from Venus, the granddaughter of Saturn. That blood relationship is kept constantly in mind, Saturn in one instance saying 'I am thyn aiel [*grandfather*], redy at thy wille' (2477). He puts himself, his power, his justice, at the service of a bond too sacred to violate.

Saturn's respect for a family tie is interesting because it identifies a mainspring for the exercise of justice and power which Theseus himself recognises. In his speech before the parliament at Athens, he offers a consolatory view of Arcite's death. To do so he alludes first to the creator of the universe, the 'First-Moevere' who made a 'cheyne of love' which bound together the elements of fire, air, water and earth, making them at once interdependent and having their own well-defined boundaries: 'In certeyn boundes, that they may nat flee' (2993). In a similar way, according to Theseus, the same deity has established that each form of life exists within a prescribed span of time. It is pointless therefore to lament a death which was inevitable; rather it is timely to celebrate Arcite's honour, excellence, reputation and indeed good fortune to die in his prime and escape the prison of this life, before old age should obscure his achievements (3041–66).

A pessimistic view of Theseus' argument might see in it a cynical attempt to 'maken vertu of necessitee' (3042), to provide a shallow philosophical rationalisation for the depressing fact of Arcite's death, one that does little to answer the anguish caused by Saturn's intervention in Athenian affairs. Nevertheless, Theseus' account of universal principles offers a glimmer of hope that, behind the appearance of arbitrary violence, there lies an order and meaning which he identifies as 'the bonds of love'. Saturn himself, in fulfilling his granddaughter's wishes and respecting a family bond, might not have objected to the idea. Theseus proceeds to put the principle into action by establishing between Palamon and Emelye 'the bond / That highte matrimoigne or mariage' (3094–5), a bond which is at the same time political since it unites representatives of the traditional enemies, Athens and Thebes.

Clearly, then, in the Knight's Tale, the identification and operation of the 'bonds of love' are fundamental concerns. They are of universal significance, and on the human plane they can take a variety of forms: through marriage (as between the Athenian widows and their dead husbands); through blood relationships (as between Palamon and Arcite); through chivalric obligations (such as initially exist between the two heroes); through friendship (such as Perotheus bears for Theseus); through religious devotion (of the sort practised towards Mars, Venus and Diana). Love in all its varieties is thus represented not only as the governing principle of the universe but also as the cohering factor in society as a whole.

What is remarkable about the Knight's Tale in this respect is its insistence, systematically expressed, on violating the bonds of love. Insofar as such bonds are conventionally expressed through solemn oaths, the tale is a saga of broken promises. Creon oversteps the bounds of chivalry in dishonouring the bodies of his victims (938–47); Arcite reneges on his 'cosyn' and brother knight when he exchanges one oath dedicated to mutual help for another 'gretter lawe of love' (1126–86), so becoming Palamon's rival; the gods give ambiguous undertakings; even those who (like Theseus) fully intend to keep their word find that, by force of circumstance, they are unable to do so. Only Saturn, it seems, is able to keep his word. Supreme power would appear to be a prerequisite of promise-keeping.

The bonds of love bring the discussion full circle, back to the prison of Theseus. The prison comes into play as an image of the constraining and oppressive effects of love, Fortune and other powers beyond human control. But the tale also offers an alternative, more positive view of bonds and boundaries. By exploring the devastating consequences of broken promises it points to the merits of a kind of self-imposed restraint (experienced through the obligations of friendship and duty) which, although they might seem to be entrammelling, paradoxically offer the best prospect for true liberation from the prison of human life.

v. DISCUSSION POINTS

Read the final speech of Theseus (lines 2987-3089) and answer the following questions.

1. *What preparation has there been for the prominence now given to Jupiter?*
2. *In what respects is the mood struck here different from that surrounding Arcite's death and its immediate aftermath?*
3. *To what extent is Theseus' speech politically motivated?*

4. *Does Theseus succeed or fail in answering the problems raised by the experiences of Palamon and Arcite?*
5. *Palamon marries Emelye. Has the better man won?*
6. *To what extent is Theseus' own conduct as a ruler based upon the philosophy he describes here?*
7. *Theseus counsels that we should 'maken vertu of necessitee' and avoid wilfulness. In what respects have Palamon and Arcite followed or flouted these precepts?*

The following questions are related more generally to the Knight's Tale.

8. *To the imprisoned knights, Emelye is an image of freedom, but to what extent is she really free?*
9. *According to what ideals do Palamon and Arcite live, and how are those ideals tested?*
10. *To what extent is Theseus susceptible to the influence of women, and what significance do you attach to his susceptibility?*
11. *By what means does the Knight's Tale explore conflict between public, outer experience and private, inner experience?*
12. *It has been said that, although Chaucer retains epic features in the Knight's Tale, they are there merely to provide decoration and a sense of the exotic. What are these epic features, and do you agree with this account of their use?*
13. *To what extent do the gods (other than Saturn) constrain the outlook and behaviour of Palamon, Arcite and Emelye?*
14. *Do you find the Knight's Tale optimistic or pessimistic as an account of human life? What is the basis for your point of view?*

vi. FURTHER READING

a. Sources and contexts

Boethius, *The Consolation of Philosophy*, trans. V. E. Watts (Harmondsworth: Penguin, 1969).

Guillaume de Lorris and Jean de Meun, *The Romance of the Rose*, trans. Charles Dahlberg (Princeton, NJ: Princeton University Press, 1971).

Havely, N. R. (ed. and trans.), *Chaucer's Boccaccio,* Chaucer Studies, 3 (Cambridge: Brewer, 1980).
Includes translations of all those sections of the *Teseida* used by

Chaucer (pp. 103–61).

b. *Selected studies*

Boitani, Piero, *Chaucer and Boccaccio,* Medium Aevum Monographs, ns 8 (Oxford: Society for the Study of Mediaeval Languages and Literature, 1977).
Provides a critical account of the *Teseida* and a detailed and sustained comparison with the Knight's Tale.

Boitani, Piero, 'Style, Iconography and Narrative: The Lesson of the *Teseida',* in *Chaucer and the Italian Trecento,* ed. Boitani (Cambridge: Cambridge University Press, 1983), pp. 185–99.
On the *Teseida*'s double allegiance to classical epic and medieval romance, and on Chaucer's various adaptations of Boccaccio's work.

Brooks, Douglas, and Alastair Fowler, 'The Meaning of Chaucer's Knight's Tale', *Medium Aevum,* 39 (1970), 123–46.
Explores the influence of Saturn and other deities over events, characters and the process of maturing, and argues that Theseus' amphitheatre is designed as a kind of horoscope.

Brown, Peter, and Andrew Butcher. *The Age of Saturn: Literature and History in the* Canterbury Tales (Oxford: Blackwell, 1991).
Ch. 5 covers the influence of Saturn in the Knight's Tale.

Burlin, Robert B., *Chaucerian Fiction,* Princeton, (NJ: Princeton University Press, 1977).
Ch. 5 explores Chaucer's general debt to Boccaccio before focusing both on the influence of the *Teseida* and the influence on it of the *Consolation of Philosophy*.

Curry, Walter Clyde, *Chaucer and the Mediaeval Sciences,* rev. edn (New York: Barnes and Noble; London: George Allen and Unwin, 1960).
Ch. 6, on the Knight's Tale, explains the effects of Saturn in planetary conflict, the portrait of Lycurgus, and the illness of Arcite.

Gaylord, Alan T., 'The Role of Saturn in the Knight's Tale', *Chaucer Review,* 8 (1973-4), 171–90.
Takes issue with interpretations which stress the negative aspects of Saturn's role, and argues instead for the dominion of Jupiter who brings reason, moderation and compassion.

Kean, P. M., *Chaucer and the Making of English Poetry* (2 vols) vol. 2, *The Art of Narrative* (London: Routledge and Kegan Paul, 1972).
In ch. 1, comparison with the writings of Boccaccio and Boethius includes accounts of Chaucer's use of Saturn and his effects, the role of Theseus, the function of Fortune, and Chaucer's treatment of the bonds of love.

Kolve, V. A., *Chaucer and the Imagery of Narrative: The First Five Canterbury Tales* (London: Arnold, 1984).
Ch. 3 explores extensively, with the help of illustrations, the literal and symbolic significance of key images within the Knight's Tale, especially the tower-prison.

Leyerle, John, 'The Heart and the Chain', in *The Learned and the Lewed: Studies in Chaucer and Medieval Literature,* ed. Larry D. Benson, Harvard English Studies, 5 (Cambridge, MA: Harvard University Press, 1974), pp. 113-45.
Pages 118–21 on the patterning of bonds and imprisonment affecting the lives of the characters.

Loomis, Dorothy Bethurum, 'Saturn in Chaucer's Knight's Tale', in *Chaucer und seine Zeit: Symposion für Walter F. Schirmer,* ed. Arno Esch, Buchreihe der Anglia, Zeitschrift für englische Philologie, no. 14 (Tübingen: Niemeyer, 1968), pp. 149-61.
Explores possible sources of Chaucer's interest in Saturn, emphasising Saturn's traditional double nature as god both of disaster and of justice.

Pearsall, Derek, *The Canterbury Tales,* Unwin Critical Library (London, Boston and Sydney: George Allen and Unwin, 1985).
Pages 114–38 for a general but stimulating introduction to the main themes of the Knight's Tale.

Salter, Elizabeth, *Fourteenth-Century English Poetry: Contexts and Readings* (Oxford: Clarendon Press, 1983).
Ch. 6 examines Chaucer's debt to Boccaccio and Boethius, as well as his distinctive variations on the subjects of Fortune, Saturn, the role of the gods in human affairs, and the ending of the poem.

Southern, R. W., *The Making of the Middle Ages* (London: Hutchinson, 1953).
Ch. 5, 'From Epic to Romance', shows how the transition from epic to romance reflects the growing importance of individuality, privacy, introspection, solitude and feeling across a wide range of cultural activities.

Van, Thomas A., 'Imprisoning and Ensnarement in *Troilus* and *The Knight's Tale*', *Papers in Language and Literature,* 7 (1971), 3–12.
Pages 9–12 for imprisonment as a metaphor for the human condition in the Knight's Tale.

Wilson, H. S., '*The Knight's Tale* and the *Teseida* Again', University of Toronto Quarterly, 18 (1948–49), 131–46.
Summarises plot of *Teseida* and demonstrates Chaucer's greater interest in the conflict between Palamon and Arcite and its reconciliation.

CHAPTER THREE
The Miller's Tale

i. THE PORTRAIT OF ALISOUN

By 1215, Geoffrey of Vinsauf (who was probably from Normandy, but who was educated in England) had put the finishing touches to a Latin manual on the art of writing poetry. Called *Poetria nova* ('the new poetics') it expressed in a medieval idiom the ideas for writers earlier put forward by such classical authors as Cicero and Horace. Following them, its intention was to provide poets with models for planning, developing, describing, and above all amplifying, the meaning of their compositions. *Poetria nova* is one of a number of similar treatises composed at the turn of the twelfth century, and would not merit special attention here were it not for the fact that Chaucer himself referred to it. In the Nun's Priest's Tale the narrator wishes for the 'sentence' (meaning) and 'loore' (technical expertise) of 'Gaufred, deere maister soverayn' (3347–51).

Chaucer should not be imagined writing the *Canterbury Tales* with a quill in one hand and an open copy of *Poetria nova* in the other. It is nevertheless useful to have some acquaintance with this handbook because, while it cannot be considered as one of Chaucer's narrative sources, it was one of his *re*sources: it provided (and provides) a point of reference for some of the literary strategies available to him and to other medieval poets. Geoffrey of Vinsauf exemplifies one such device when he provides a model for describing female beauty:

> Let the compass of Nature first fashion a sphere for her head; let the colour of gold give a glow to her hair, and lilies bloom high on her brow. Let her eyebrows resemble in dark beauty the blackberry, and a lovely and milk-white path separate their twin arches. Let her nose be straight, of moderate length, not too long nor too short for perfection. Let her eyes, those watch-fires of her brow, be radiant with emerald light, or with the

> brightness of stars. Let her countenance emulate dawn: not red, nor yet white – but at once neither of those colours and both. Let her mouth be bright, small in shape – as it were, a half-circle. Let her lips be rounded and full, but moderately so; let them glow, aflame, but with gentle fire. Let her teeth be snowy, regular, all of one size, and her breath like the fragrance of incense. Smoother than polished marble let Nature fashion her chin – Nature, so potent a sculptor. Let her neck be a precious column of milk-white beauty, holding high the perfection of her countenance. From her crystal throat let radiance gleam, to enchant the eye of the viewer and enslave the heart. Let her shoulders, conforming to beauty's law, not slope in unlovely descent, nor jut out with an awkward rise; rather, let them be gracefully straight. Let her arms be a joy to behold, charming in their grace and their length. Let soft and slim loveliness, a form shapely and white, a line long and straight, flow into her slender fingers. Let her beautiful hands take pride in those fingers. Let her breast, the image of snow, show side by side its twin virginal gems. Let her waist be close girt, and so slim that a hand may encircle it. For the other parts I am silent – here the mind's speech is more apt than the tongue's. Let her leg be of graceful length and her wonderfully tiny foot dance with joy at its smallness.
>
> (*Poetria nova,* III; trans. Nims, pp. 36–7)

Now answer the following questions on the above passage.

1. *To what extent is geometry an underlying feature of Geoffrey's design for the woman's beauty?*
2. *In what ways does the subject of the portrait appeal to the senses?*
3. *Exemplify any other principles of ideal female beauty which Geoffrey follows.*
4. *How is Geoffrey's description structured?*

Geoffrey's portrait is an image of perfection, and of geometrical abstraction: Nature, with her compasses, designs the woman by beginning with an ideal shape, a sphere, for the head, adding arch shapes for eyebrows, a half-circle for the mouth, and paying due attention to the interplay of line (nose, shoulders, arms) and curve (head, eyebrows, lips, waist). Balance, proportion and moderation are the underlying principles of the woman's beauty: her nose is to be neither too long nor too short, her mouth moderately rounded, her teeth regular, her complexion neither red nor white but both together. For Nature (like the poet) is an artist, and in particular a 'potent' sculptor, creating a chin which resembles polished marble and a neck which is a 'precious column' of crystal.

Complementing the aesthetic and intellectual appeal of the woman is a sensual one. She is, as Geoffrey indicates, a figure who enchants 'the eye of the viewer' through her dazzling and colourful presence: gold glows in her hair, the eyes are watch-fires 'radiant with emerald light' or bright like the stars, the lips are aflame, the neck also radiant. Proximity to this glamorous idol has a heady, exalting effect: her breath is 'like the fragrance of incense'. The smooth, marble-like texture of her skin, and her slim waist, invite touch. And physical enjoyment of the woman is tentatively suggested through metaphors of food and drink: blackberries for the colour of her eyebrows, milk for the gap which separates them, and for her neck. Geoffrey thus follows his own precepts in striking a balance between the more esoteric aspects of the woman's beauty, and her sexual appeal. She is to be viewed from afar, and displays a considerable hauteur, although she will enslave a man's heart. Geoffrey's sense of decorum is nicely expressed in his reticence over describing certain parts of the woman's body, while at the same time conceding that it is an appropriate topic for the imagination ('here the mind's speech is more apt than the tongue's').

What Geoffrey of Vinsauf is here presenting is a literary convention: the 'top-to-toe' method of describing a beautiful woman. It already enjoyed a long tradition when Geoffrey wrote (he remarks elsewhere that 'the description of beauty is an old and even trite theme'), and it was to endure long after Chaucer's lifetime. Alluding to, while at the same time reversing, the formula, Shakespeare began one sonnet: 'My mistress' eyes are nothing like the sun' (Sonnet 130). The regular occurrence of this and other conventions in the writings of Chaucer and other poets of the period might lead to the conclusion that medieval poetry is derivative and repetitive. Such remarks tend to ignore the extent to which all literature, especially in its popular oral manifestations, is necessarily conventional. To take the analogy of a modern genre like the western: some of its core conventions might be listed as the gunfight, the bar-room brawl, the lynch-mob. Audiences watch cowboy films in the expectation not of seeing something entirely original (which would be unintelligible) but of seeing how the familiar ingredients of a western are recombined to produce a film with new twists and variations. Appreciation and enjoyment of the film lie, to a considerable extent, in the degree to which a viewer is aware both of the conventions and of the ways in which those rules are being manipulated. The same observation applies to medieval literature. The habitual appearance of a convention signals not so much lack of imagination as the existence of a language of conventions which needs to be understood before the true measure of a writer's originality can be gauged.

One way in which a writer (or director) can defamiliarise a long-standing convention is by placing it in an unusual setting. Geoffrey of

Vinsauf's technique of describing a woman implies that she is superior not only in beauty but also in terms of social class. Indeed, the technique tended to be reserved for portraits of aristocratic women. Chaucer uses it as the basis for describing Blanche, the wife of his patron, John of Gaunt, in the *Book of the Duchess*. It comes, therefore, as something of a shock to find elements of the same technique used in the Miller's Tale for representing Alisoun, the wife of a carpenter:

> Fair was this yonge wyf, and therwithal
> As any wezele hir body gent and smal.
> A ceynt she werede, barred al of silk, 3235
> A barmclooth as whit as morne milk
> Upon hir lendes, ful of many a goore.
> Whit was hir smok, and broyden al bifoore
> And eek bihynde, on hir coler aboute,
> Of col-blak silk, withinne and eek withoute. 3240
> The tapes of hir white voluper
> Were of the same suyte of hir coler;
> Hir filet brood of silk, and set ful hye.
> And sikerly she hadde a likerous ye;
> Ful smale ypulled were hire browes two, 3245
> And tho were bent and blake as any sloo.
> She was ful moore blisful on to see
> Than is the newe pere-jonette tree,
> And softer than the wolle is of a wether.
> And by hir girdel heeng a purs of lether, 3250
> Tasseled with silk and perled with latoun.
> In al this world, to seken up and doun,
> There nys no man so wys that koude thenche
> So gay a popelote or swich a wenche.
> Ful brighter was the shynyng of hir hewe 3255
> Than in the Tour the noble yforged newe.
> But of hir song, it was as loude and yerne
> As any swalwe sittynge on a berne.
> Therto she koude skippe and make game,
> As any kyde or calf folwynge his dame. 3260
> Hir mouth was sweete as bragot or the meeth,
> Or hoord of apples leyd in hey or heeth.
> Wynsynge she was, as is a joly colt,
> Long as a mast, and upright as a bolt.
> A brooch she baar upon hir lowe coler, 3265
> As brood as is the boos of a bokeler.
> Hir shoes were laced on hir legges hye.
> She was a prymerole, a piggesnye,
> For any lord to leggen in his bedde,
> Or yet for any good yeman to wedde. 3270
>
> (MillT, 3233–70)

Alisoun's social status, the Miller concludes, need not prevent her from being sexually desired by a lord. His remark, and the passage as a whole, need to be read as part of the Miller's intention to cock a snook at the world of the Knight's Tale, with its remote, idealising appreciation of female beauty. The Miller insists on the sexuality of women – a force to which lords themselves are not immune and which traverses social boundaries (even if it would be for a yeoman, not a lord, actually to marry Alisoun). Now answer the following questions, bearing in mind Geoffrey of Vinsauf's earlier description of ideal female beauty.

1. *To what extent is the portrait of Alisoun a reflection of the Miller's point of view?*
2. *In what ways does Chaucer's description of Alisoun follow the norms of Geoffrey's portrait?*
3. *To what extent does the portrait of Alisoun deviate from those norms?*
4. *Do you detect any common theme in the images used to describe Alisoun's beauty? If so, why do you think the theme is there?*
5. *What effects are achieved through the detailed descriptions of Alisoun's clothes?*

In order to express the Miller's viewpoint, Chaucer has given him a conventional descriptive structure normally reserved for literature reflecting aristocratic values (like the romance of the Knight's Tale). By inserting it into a low-life bawdy narrative (or *fabliau,* to give it its medieval name) he has made it part of the debunking process: not only the sexual values, but also the literary conventions associated with people like the Knight, are held up for inspection if not ridicule. Here is a flesh-and-blood woman, almost (it seems) through an uninhibited description, threatening to burst asunder and render useless the very procedures according to which female beauty of a certain kind was normally represented. The Miller throws aesthetic and moral decorum to the winds, concentrating instead on sexual attractiveness. So the process of subversion is not merely one directed by the Miller at the Knight. It is also directed by Chaucer at the received, 'authoritative' conventions which he inherited, on which he depended, and which were in so many ways inadequate when, say, a woman of Alisoun's ilk was to be described. And here is one of the chief fascinations of the passage: it at once reflects descriptive tradition while making that tradition virtually unrecognisable.

The rhetorical norm, of the sort exemplified in *Poetria nova,* surfaces in familiar details: the 'gent' (delicate) and slender body (3234), milk-white appearance (3236), plucked eyebrows (3245), radiant complexion (3255) and fragrant breath (3261). But, disconcertingly, these are mixed with comparisons which dislocate their received effect. Alisoun's body is 'gent and smal' like a weasel's; it is her apron which is 'as whit as morne milk'; those eyebrows frame 'likerous' eyes; her face shines with the glitter of a newly minted gold coin; and her breath is not like incense but has the fragrance of alcoholic drinks, or the aroma of a hoard of apples stored in hay. Thus Alisoun, and the convention, are brought firmly down to earth (in more senses than one).

The technique of undermining expectations with novel comparisons introduces a range of images which have as their common theme the natural world. Again, their tendency is to counteract the contrived and artificial quality of a portrait such as that by Geoffrey of Vinsauf, as well as, by the Miller's lights, the over-sophisticated attitudes to women found in the Knight's Tale. Alisoun's eyebrows are as black as sloeberries (a variant of Geoffrey's blackberries); her appearance is as pleasing as that of a pear tree in blossom (3247–8); she is softer than a sheep's wool (3249); she sings in an eager and lively way like a swallow (3257–8); she is playful like a kid or calf (3259–60); restive like a colt (3263); she is a primrose or 'pig's eye', ready to be plucked (3268). Alisoun is emphatically a child of Nature, but not Nature the sculptor – instead a Nature who is visible in the countryside in what grows, has vitality, is beautiful, bears fruit. If Chaucer has tipped Geoffrey of Vinsauf's carefully balanced formula in favour of sexuality, he has at the same time escaped his mentor's coyness to associate the female body with the natural world and so secures the legitimacy of sexual attraction. Who can deny the force and the goodness of Nature?

Which is not to say that the portrait of Alisoun does not have an artificial quality, either in its form or its content. The fact that Alisoun is dressed in remarkable clothes lends a considerable sense of enticement and allure to her appearance. Here again there is something of the disorienting doubleness earlier noted: the material repeatedly mentioned, silk, is rich, luxurious, 'aristocratic', but it is annexed to clothes that are themselves unpretentious, homely. Barred silk adorns Alisoun's belt, around a flounced apron (3235–7), her white smock and collar are embroidered with black silk, a detail matched in the ribbons of her cap (3238–42); her broad headband is silk (3243) and her purse has silk tassels (3251). Sensuous as the idea of silk may be, attire is also used to provoke interest in the female body beneath it. The apron covers Alisoun's loins (3237); by her girdle, as an emblem of female sexuality, hangs the silk-tasselled leather purse (3251); a large brooch draws attention to her 'lowe coler' (3265); and her shoes are laced, enticingly, 'on hir legges hye' (3267).

Sensual though the appeal of Alisoun may be – to a much greater degree than Geoffrey of Vinsauf's portrait – through its appeal to texture (silk, wool), appetite and taste (mead, sloe-berries), sound (the swallow) and smell (apples in the hay), it is above all through the sense of sight that Chaucer registers her effects on male desire. Curiously monochrome by the side of her thirteenth-century predecessor, Alisoun is seen through the 'likerous' eye of a man of the Miller's proclivities which (so he would suggest) is representative of the male point of view. In the process, the formal 'head-to-toe' descriptive structure is abandoned in favour of one which more accurately reflects the priorities and vagaries of a sexually interested gaze.

Throughout, the pattern of particular details is punctuated by more generalised statements about Alisoun's attractiveness. The effect is to confirm the fascination and allure of her body. These are centred, for the Miller, at her waist and thighs, which is where he begins his detailed description (3235–7), but which remains the centre of gravity. In an ascending, rather than descending, catalogue of physical charms, he notes the smock, white like her apron, embroidered in black at the collar, suggestively, within as well as without (3238–40). He then notices that the tapes of her 'voluper' or cap are of the same material as the collar, registering the eye's habitual tendency to match and compare appearances and colours. From the cap, the glance falls naturally enough on Alisoun's headband, exposing the forehead in which she takes such a pride. Momentarily the description follows the traditional movement from forehead, to eyes, to eyebrows, but it is the erotic promise of the eyes that receives the emphasis. After some general comments about Alisoun's ripeness and softness, desire again becomes more focused as the Miller's attention is drawn, again, to her waist, with its girdle and tactile purse (3250–1). Further general comments again narrow down to suggestive details: the large brooch and Alisoun's shoes, laced high on her legs and leading back, again, to the Miller's preoccupation.

ii. DOMESTIC DRAMA

By working with the received convention for describing female beauty, Chaucer created character. Alisoun exists as an individual with independent life because she is so different from the model which Chaucer inherited. But the perception of difference depends on an understanding of the norm. So her existence as a literary character is paradoxical: it both depends upon, and rejects, the stereotype. In the gap between what rhetorical precedent leads us to expect, and the disconcerting details which Chaucer provides, is born a sense of Alisoun's personality.

It would be pointless to argue that Chaucer's strategy with a rhetorical model entirely accounts for Alisoun's character. There is more to it than that, and a range of further evidence might be cited: her feeling of being oppressed by the jealousy of her husband (3294–6) – another way in which the Miller's Tale parodies the Knight's Tale; her wily defensiveness in dealing with the sexual approaches of Nicholas (3282–7); her calmness in carrying out Nicholas's plan to dupe John (3408–18); her practical wit in repulsing Absolon (3727–41). Yet all of these features of her character are functions of her primary mode of existence, which is sexual, as established in the Miller's portrait.

To say that Chaucer has created a character in which personal identity is expressed through sexuality is not to accuse him of creative limitation. Rather it is to recognise that the single bold outline, through which a person's essential characteristics are readily recognisable, is more appropriate to a short story like the Miller's Tale than it would be to a more extended narrative. Economy of design is also a feature of his representation of the other characters. Nicholas's individuality is expressed predominantly through his intellectualism, to the point at which, in attempting to trick Absolon a second time, he is too clever for his own good; that of Absolon through his erotic pretensions (and here, at lines 3312–38, Chaucer incongruously uses again the model for describing female beauty, and to devastating effect); and that of John through his doting stupidity. So Chaucer, given the discipline of a tightly organised, fast-paced and brief plot, restricts his delineation of character to essentials. Complexity follows, but through the interaction of clearly differentiated protagonists, rather than through the convolutions of personal psychology. Before proceeding with the rest of this chapter, consider the following questions.

1. *To what extent does the portrait of Alisoun represent her potential or actual energy?*
2. *What images are used to convey her energy?*
3. *Exemplify the ways in which Alisoun energises others.*
4. *What differentiates the response to Alisoun of John, Nicholas and Absolon?*

However much it might be possible to sum up each character of the Miller's Tale in terms of a single, overriding principle, Alisoun, Nicholas, Absolon and John lose nothing of their independence. Sharp differentiation helps, as does their complex situation. Equally important is the care Chaucer takes to follow through the logic of his portraits – to animate them, as it were, according to the principles which he first sets down. For example, Alisoun is unlike the static, statuesque lady of Geoffrey of Vinsauf's imaginings because she is full of potential or actual energy. The opening comparison of her body to that of a weasel suggests lithe, sinuous, quick activity. Later, her nimble feet are likened to those of a kid or calf skipping after its mother. And she is described as skittish and spirited, 'Wynsynge' and 'joly', like a colt. It is altogether appropriate, therefore, and acts as a confirmation of initial impressions, that she springs away from Nicholas's sexual embrace exactly like a colt caught to be shod: 'she sproong as a colt dooth in the trave [*frame*], / And with hir heed she wryed [*twisted*] faste awey' (3282–3).

Restive, and charged with sexual energy, Alisoun is also the source of energy in others, to the point where she might be seen less as an individual, more as a representative of female sexuality. The actions of John, Nicholas and Absolon are all prompted by the desire to keep or possess this woman. Symbolic considerations apart, the fascination which she attracts as a character is sustained and made credible precisely because others, within and without the story, credit her with sexual magnetism, each in his own way. She is in fact subjected to a variety of male points of view. That she suffers not a jot as a consequence is perhaps indicative of the inadequacies of the male attitudes. John, Absolon and Nicholas all endure more or less painful experiences as a result of their desire: John falls from the beams of his house and breaks an arm; Absolon undergoes two unsavoury encounters at Alisoun's shot-window; and Nicholas is severely burned on his backside.

The first male perspective on Alisoun is that of the Miller. Already discussed at some length, it is deeply embedded in the form which her portrait takes, and represents Alisoun as a body promising sexual gratification. It is a point of view shared by Nicholas. Ever 'hende', quick to turn a situation to practical advantage, he seizes the opportunity provided by his landlord's absence to test for himself just how tangible Alisoun is. Soon after the Miller's description, concluding with its assertion that Alisoun is the sort of woman any man would like to get his hands on, 'hende' Nicholas does just that: he grabs her by the crotch (that fulcrum of the Miller's portrait) and 'heeld hire harde by the haunchebones' (3279).

Absolon perceives Alisoun in another way entirely, as an extension of his pretensions as a lover in the aristocratic mode, one who idealises his virtually inaccessible and stand-offish lady. It is as if he has encountered the Miller's description of her, but cannot read it as a parody of a courtly description. Absolon's own pretensions are ludicrous, given the mongrel nature of his social status (parish clerk, part-time solicitor and barber). The travesty of courtly attitudes, expressed through him, bites deepest at the carpenter's shot-window, where Absolon is in the habit of serenading Alisoun in order to express his affections. His pseudo-knightly role, self-selected, is signalled through the vocabulary he adopts in order to represent his predicament: 'love-longynge' (3349), 'curteisie' (3351), 'paramours' (3354), 'gentil' (3360), 'rewe' [*pity*] (3362). These are all words which would give little cause for comment in a chivalric romance like the Knight's Tale. Here, they register the extent of Absolon's delusions. Needless to say, the idol on the pedestal, before which Absolon kneels, behaves in an extremely unexpected and uncouth way. He is cured forever of his courtliness: 'Of paramours he sette nat a kers' (3756).

John also has his share of desire and self-delusion. An old man, he yet imagines that his jealousy of Alisoun will protect her from the designs of younger men. In practice his jealousy, coupled with a superstitious piety, makes him all the more vulnerable. Falling prey to Nicholas's stratagem, he is persuaded to see Alisoun as no less a person than Noah's wife. Impressed by his lodger's supposed prophecy that an apocalyptic flood is imminent, his thought turns immediately to saving his wife's life. Nicholas reminds John of Noah's remedy, and so the hapless carpenter takes on the role of his illustrious predecessor, all the while encouraged by touching vignettes, painted by Nicholas, which appeal to the carpenter's obsessive imagination. When the rain stops, says Nicholas, John and Alisoun will float away in their tubs 'As dooth the white doke after hire drake' (3576). Of course, the chance of John's participating in any of the animalistic activities provoked by Alisoun are exceedingly remote.

Much of the point and humour of John's role is lost unless it is seen in the context of the play of Noah which, when Chaucer wrote, formed part of the cycle of performances representing Christian history, presented each year in cities like Oxford on the June feast of Corpus Christi. Often clever and subtle in their dramatic strategies and verbal dexterity (they were composed by clerks like Nicholas) the plays nevertheless appealed to the popular imagination, both in their content and mode of production. They might include, side by side within a single play, low humour and apocryphal episodes, as well as solemn speeches. They were performed by groups of tradesmen, or guilds – each guild being given a play appropriate to its activity or 'mystery'. The nail-makers, for example, might stage the play of the Crucifixion, or the carpenters the story of Noah and his building of the ark.

That mystery plays are part of the fabric of social life in the Miller's Oxford is clear from a detail given by Absolon: sometimes he played Herod (3384), who was customarily represented as irascible to the point of dementia (good practice for his performance at Alisoun's window). And when Nicholas reminds John of the story of Noah, he refers to an episode which, while not found in the canonical books of the Bible, was traditionally present in the plays: 'The sorwe of Noe with his felaweshipe' (3538–40). In this humorous episode, Noah experiences great difficulty in persuading his rebellious wife to board ship as the flood-waters rise, and their subsequent argument degenerates into slapstick violence. If only, adds Nicholas, imagining further embellishments, Noah had built an additional vessel especially for his wife, then he could have avoided a considerable amount of trouble. The logic of Noah's experience, argues Nicholas, is that John should indeed make provision for separate vessels, one for each of the three of them. Needless to say, the clerk's words, in 'rewriting' the Noah play, are entirely ulterior: such an arrangement will greatly improve the chances of his creeping to bed with Alisoun undetected by her husband.

Nicholas's understanding of John's mentality is flawless: it is predicated on his jealousy and ignorance; appeals to an appropriate level of superstition and popular piety; and exploits an episode in the life of Noah with which John, as another carpenter, is likely to have had close acquaintance. So John slips into a familiar role while (so he thinks) avoiding the worst consequences of the role normally adopted by Mrs Noah, who in his eyes is now reconstituted in the form of Alisoun. But to take the true measure of John's distorted image of Alisoun it is necessary to look in some detail at a representative passage from one of the Noah plays (from the Wakefield cycle), in which God reassures the old man that he enjoys divine protection and will prosper. The task of conveying this information to Mrs Noah is, however, not easy:

NOE:	A, *benedicite!* What art thou that thus	
	Tellys afore that shall be? Thou art full mervelus!	
	Tell me, for charite, thi name so gracius.	
DEUS:	My name is of dignyte, and also full glorius	
	To knowe.	
	I am God most myghty,	
	Oone God in Trynyty,	
	Made the and ich man to be;	*each*
	To luf me well thou awe.	*ought*
NOE:	I thank the, Lord, so dere, that wold vowchsayf	
	Thus low to appere to a symple knafe;	*man*
	Blis us, Lord, here, for charite I hit crafe,	*beg*

The better may we stere the ship that we shall hafe,
Certayn.
DEUS: Noe, to the and to thy fry — *children*
My blyssyng graunt I;
Ye shall wax and multiply,
And fill the erth agane,
When all thise floodis ar past and fully gone away.
NOE: Lord, homward will I hast as fast as that I may;
My wife will I frast what she will say, — *ask*
Exit Deus.
And I am agast that we get som fray
Betwixt us both;
For she is full tethee, — *bad-tempered*
For litill oft angre,
If any thyng wrang be,
Soyne is she wroth. — *soon*
Tunc perget ad uxorem. — *Then shall he go to his wife.*
God spede, dere wife! How fayre ye?
UXOR: Now, as ever myght I thryfe the wars I the see; — *worse*
Do tell me, belife, where has thou thus long be? — *quickly*
To dede may we dryfe, or lif, for the, — *rush*
For want.
When we swete or swynk, — *toil*
Thou dos what thou thynk,
Yit of mete and of drynk
Have we veray skant. — *shortage*
(Wakefield Noah play, lines 163–98; ed. Happé, pp. 103–4)

Now answer the following questions.

1. *Compare and contrast the roles of John and Noah.*
2. *What are the distinguishing features of John's and Noah's piety?*
3. *In what ways is Noah's relationship with his wife similar to, or different from, John's relationship with Alisoun?*

The context of the Noah passage itself indicates the extent to which the Miller's Tale inverts the familiar dramatic episode. God's judgement, expressed in the form of a devastating deluge, is specifically a punishment for the sinfulness of mankind, and especially for sexual promiscuity. Nicholas's invented flood, however, exists precisely to enable a sexual misdemeanour. Further contrasts emerge from the passage itself. If John is a surrogate Noah he is far removed from his role model where devotional matters are concerned. He is prone to superstitious mumbo-jumbo: he regards the sight of a funeral as an omen of bad fortune (3428–30); utters dire warnings of the consequences of enquiring too far into God's secrets (3448–62); and performs a protective ritual, half magic, half devout, on gaining entrance to Nicholas's locked chamber (3477–86). His biblical counterpart, on the other hand, has full and direct access to God's intentions, to the point where he is told of future events. He does not, like John, depend on a false intermediary, with all the opportunities for being misled which that provides. Far from existing as a remote and inscrutable deity, Noah's God speaks in plain language to a man who, unlike the stupid and suspicious John, is genuinely simple-minded, devout, open and trusting. If he is fearful, he is afraid more of communicating with his wife (a relatively insignificant matter) than with God, with whom he is on the best of terms. John's fear is directed at things larger than himself which he cannot understand, when it might indeed be more profitably focused on Alisoun.

Noah's concern for his wife is evident, but it exists within the framework of God's concern for Noah, and is patterned on it. John's besotted devotions have no wider horizon than Alisoun herself who, while as rebellious (if not more so) against the strictures of male control, conceals her hostility to John. Noah's wife is openly cantankerous but, as the water rises, is persuaded to enter the ark and submit to her husband's scheme of things. Alisoun, on the other hand, successfully escapes the jealous keeping of her husband, and asserts female independence by not acceding to male authority unless it suits her own purposes to do so. Those purposes are sexual pleasure, enjoyed for its own sake. On the ark, and in God's reformed world, sexual pleasure exists within the constraints of marriage and for procreative ends: God tells Noah 'Ye shall wax and multiply'.

In a sense, John's perception of Alisoun as a latter-day Noah's wife does not bode well for him since the mystery plays represented her as a type of rebellious woman whose founding mother was Eve herself. On the other hand, were Alisoun to conform to the role model, realising at length the error of her ways, John might have continued to enjoy a trouble-free marriage. But Alisoun is not Noah's wife any more than John, with his pathetic imitation of the ark, is Noah. These roles are laughable fantasies invoked by Nicholas as a convenient fiction under cover of which he can further his own ends and achieve an altogether different resolution of the Noah plot.

Indeed, it might be useful to see the Miller's Tale as a series of narratives within a narrative. In each of these three domestic dramas, Alisoun's character is read somewhat differently (although it is consistently a character based on sexual attractiveness), according to the participants in the narrative and their respective 'authors'. In the 'Noah narrative', invented by Nicholas and endorsed by John, she is from John's point of view Noah's wife. In the 'courtly narrative', authored and enacted by Absolon, she is the unattainable aristocratic lady. In the farce engineered and exuberantly performed by Nicholas she is the means of providing sexual satisfaction.

As is appropriate to an intellectual who understands the imaginative appeal of stories and the functioning of character, ingenious, 'hende' Nicholas is something of a free agent within those narratives. He is able to cross the boundaries between them (and to delineate many of the boundaries in the first place), to create roles, and to manipulate events so that they have, from his standpoint, a happy ending. But even he is unable to foresee the consequences when, as result of humiliating Absolon unnecessarily a second time, the dénouements of the three domestic dramas coincide. He is assaulted by Absolon, wielding a hot plough-blade; shouts 'Water!'; and thereby causes John to cut his moorings in the mistaken belief that the second flood has come. The carpenter crashes to the ground in his tub, so alerting the local community to the unusual state of affairs within his household. In the event, deft Nicholas is able to divert the attention of the neighbours to the folly of John, thus concealing his antics with Alisoun. In doing do, as in playing the crucial second trick on Absolon, he is 'ad-libbing' and in a sense out of character. His role hitherto has been that of an ingenious and imaginative plotter, and all has gone according to plan. Absolon's appearance at the shot-window is a diversion not in the 'script' as originally conceived, but Alisoun deals with it effectively, using her native wit. So admirable is the trick that Nicholas repeats it, unaware that in doing so he is straying into a domestic drama (Absolon's) over which he has no direct control, even if Alisoun does; and that to act spontaneously, rather than deliberately, is not his forte.

Clever though he may be at manipulating character and plot, Nicholas's powers are limited, limited enough for his true character – the seducer of Alisoun – almost to be revealed to the public gaze. In practice, each of the domestic dramas is circumscribed, or at least curtailed and mutually qualified: Absolon's by Alisoun; Nicholas's by Absolon; John's by Nicholas. The Miller's narrative itself 'controls' these others, giving the pilgrim audience access to information denied to the protagonists. But beyond (or behind) the Miller is another author – Chaucer – who provides the possibility of there being one other, extraordinary, domestic drama to which the Miller himself is oblivious. Its outline is faint but complete, and it has the effect of representing Alisoun in a role altogether different from that of sexual lodestar. Nicholas, in addition to his other accomplishments, is a musician. Among the songs he performs on a psaltery, 'So swetely that all the chambre rong' (3215), is *Angelus ad virginem,* a catchy composition about Gabriel's annunciation to Mary of the birth of Christ. Nicholas, certainly, is no angel, however angelic he may appear with his face 'lyk a mayden meke for to see' (3202), but he does go on to perform an annunciation of sorts, when he informs a startled Alisoun of his attachment and intentions.

An illustration of the biblical annunciation to Mary will make some of the parallels clearer (Plate 3). Mary, head raised in astonishment, stands at a lectern within a church interior (rather than within her home). A meek-faced Gabriel, carrying the lilies of chastity which are Mary's emblem, kneels to one side, and holds a scroll bearing his vital message. Through a window, light streams and a dove descends, indicating in symbolic terms her impregnation by the holy spirit. Within and without a 'chamber' above, angels sing in celebration, and play musical instruments. Look carefully at the picture, and answer the following questions.

1. *In what sense does Nicholas perform an 'annunciation' to Alisoun?*
2. *Can you think of a role for John in the biblical narrative of Christ's birth (bearing in mind his occupation)?*
3. *In what respects is Absolon child-like? How does that attribute of his character associate him with the nativity story?*

That it should be possible to see Alisoun as Mary – the very antithesis of that rebellious stereotype, Eve – hardly seems credible. And yet there are other references to the gospel narrative which make the idea difficult to avoid. Joseph, it might be observed, was also a carpenter, like John, and was popularly represented, in the mystery plays and elsewhere, as an old man prone to fits of jealousy over a supposed sexual rival who had made his wife pregnant. The logic of this scenario is that Christ's qualities should, improbable and grotesque as it might seem, be reflected in Absolon. The evidence comes first from his infantile attitude towards Alisoun. His hope of (as well as his disappointment in) pleasure centres on his mouth: it itches in anticipation (3682); he dreams of a feast (3684); he deodorises his breath with cardamon and liquorice (3690); places a sprig of quadrifolia under his tongue (3692); addresses Alisoun as 'hony-comb', 'sweete cynamome' (3698–9); tells her he longs for her like a 'lamb after the tete' (3704); wipes his mouth to await his kiss (3730); kisses her 'naked ers / Ful savourly' (3734–5); feels on his lips 'a thyng al rough and long yherd' (3738); bites his lip for anger (3745); and in disgust rubs his lips with dust, sand, straw, cloth and woodchips (3748). Christ, it will be remembered, was often represented as a baby, sometimes at his mother's breast. And the

Plate 3: Annunciation to Mary.

imagery which Absolon uses is highly suggestive: the reference to himself as a lamb recalls a traditional metaphor for Christ, the innocent victim who was sacrificed for the benefit of others. Finally, when Absolon resolves to take his revenge, weeping 'as dooth a child' (3759), he uses a striking phrase: 'My soule bitake I unto Sathanas' (3750). If his actions are in some way reflecting the Christian drama, then the remark alludes to Christ's descent into hell between his crucifixion and the resurrection. That idea is reinforced by the nature of the place to which Absolon actually does go: a fire-belching blacksmith's shop. Smithies, with their bellows, fires, feverish activity, confusion, and iron instruments, were often associated with hell.

To modern, secularised, tastes, it appears almost blasphemous to think of the world of the Miller's Tale in terms of episodes from Christ's life. We are much more inclined to keep the profane and the sacred in separate compartments. That, in the Middle Ages, comedy could have a significant function in relation to religious narrative, is clear from the play of Noah itself, which moves readily from seriousness to levity. There, comedy is framed by serious events, but in the Miller's Tale it is comedy which encases the thought-provoking references to biblical precedent, almost to the point of obscuring them from view. What are we to conclude from the presence in the Miller's Tale of pious meaning, and of the position which it occupies? It would surely be heavy-handed, and against the spirit of the tale, to insist that there is an overriding biblical domestic drama which 'makes sense' of all the others by providing a spiritual and moral measure against which character and action can be judged. At the same time, however marginalised the position of Christian narrative may be, in another way it occupies a privileged place, being offered to readers or audience – but not to the Miller and the protagonists – as an authoritative and stable reference point against which the antics in John's household seem only the more ludicrous.

iii. DISCUSSION POINTS

Examine closely lines 3312–38, which describe Absolon, and answer the following questions.

1. *To what extent does the portrait of Absolon depend upon a knowledge of conventional ways of describing female beauty?*
2. *What are the effects of describing Absolon in such terms?*
3. *What features of Absolon's character are omitted by using this technique? How are those extra details supplied?*

4. *What are the limitations of the rhetorical convention (as exemplified in the* Poetria nova*) for representing personal beauty?*

The following questions are related more generally to the Miller's Tale.

5. *Describe some of the conventions which occur in a television series with which you are familiar. Then define the term 'convention' and apply your definition to the Miller's Tale in order to exemplify and discuss the uses and effects within it of literary convention.*
6. *In what ways can the Miller's Tale be regarded as a critical commentary upon the Knight's Tale? Consider in particular the portraits and roles of Emelye and Alisoun; the function of windows; the representation of jealousy; the respective values of the tales and their tellers; vocabulary.*
7. *Does the Miller's Tale have a moral? If so, what is it?*
8. *Much of the comedy of the Miller's Tale depends upon a principle of inversion, whereby normal expectations are turned upside-down. Exemplify and discuss this comic mechanism. Can you identify any other devices which Chaucer uses to create comedy?*
9. *By contrast with Alisoun and Absolon, Chaucer provides very little information about the physical appearance of Nicholas. Why might this be? Through what other means does he convey information about the character of John's lodger?*
10. *Explore the ways in which Chaucer establishes Alisoun's character other than through a formal description of her physical appearance.*

iv. FURTHER READING

a. Sources and contexts

Geoffrey of Vinsauf, *Poetria Nova,* trans. Margaret F. Nims (Toronto: Pontifical Institute of Mediaeval Studies, 1967).

Happé, P. (ed.), *English Mystery Plays: A Selection* (Harmondsworth: Penguin, 1975).

b. Selected studies

Atkins, J. W. H., *English Literary Criticism: The Medieval Phase* (Cambridge: Cambridge University Press, 1943).
See ch. 5 for the content and context of Geoffrey of Vinsauf's *Poetria nova.*

Beichner, Paul E., 'Characterization in The Miller's Tale', *Speculum,* 34

(1959), 611–19. Repr. in *Chaucer Criticism,* ed. Richard J. Schoeck and Jerome Taylor, vol. 1, *The Canterbury Tales* (Notre Dame and London: University of Notre Dame Press, 1960), pp. 117–29.

On the characters of Absolon and Nicholas, and their sources of inspiration.

Bennett, J. A. W., *Chaucer at Oxford and at Cambridge* (Oxford: Clarendon Press, 1974).

In ch. 2, details of the Miller's Tale are authenticated from historical records concerning Oxford carpenters, students, domestic architecture, blacksmiths, parish clerks, mystery plays and other social activities.

Bishop, Ian, *The Narrative Art of the Canterbury Tales: A Critical Study of the Major Poems,* Everyman's University Library (London and Melbourne: Dent, 1987).

See the first half of ch. 3 for comparisons between the Miller's Tale and Knight's Tale, and discussion of the values of the Miller's Tale, the portraits of Alisoun, Absolon and Nicholas, and the relation of the tale to play-acting.

Blamires, Alcuin, *The Canterbury Tales,* The Critics Debate (London: Macmillan, 1987). See pp. 15–21 on 'Retrieving literary conventions'.

Brewer, D. S., 'The Ideal of Feminine Beauty in Medieval Literature, Especially "Harley Lyrics", Chaucer and Some Elizabethans', *Modern Language Review,* 50 (1955), 257–69.

Locates source of formal 'head-to-toe' description in classical literature before examining rhetorical examples from the twelfth century, Middle English lyrics and Chaucer's works (including the Miller's Tale).

David, Alfred, *The Strumpet Muse: Art and Mortals in Chaucer's Poetry* (Bloomington and London: Indiana University Press, 1976).

Ch. 6 for the interplay between Knight's Tale and Miller's Tale, the comic inversion of one world by the other, the sexual attractiveness of Alisoun, and the blending of sacred and profane in festive comedy.

Donaldson, E. Talbot, 'Idiom of Popular Poetry in the Miller's Tale', in *English Institute Essays 1950,* ed. A. S. Downer (New York: Columbia University Press, 1951). Repr. in Donaldson, *Speaking of Chaucer* (London: Athlone Press, 1970), pp. 13–29.

On the use of courtly terms (e.g. 'hende', 'gent') in surprising contexts as humorous devices which also parody the Knight's Tale and contribute to the characters of Nicholas, Absolon and Alisoun.

Gallo, Ernest, *The 'Poetria Nova' and Its Sources in Early Rhetorical*

Doctrine, De Proprietatibus Litterarum, series maior, 10 (The Hague: Mouton, 1971).
Pages 181–7 on the 'top-to-toe' tradition of describing female beauty.

Harder, Kelsie B., 'Chaucer's Use of the Mystery Plays in the *Miller's Tale*', *Modern Language Quarterly*, 17 (1956), 193–8.
The Miller's Tale parodies the mystery plays, e.g. in modelling Absolon on Herod, and in basing the plot on that of a Noah play.

Kaske, R. E., 'The *Canticum Canticorum* in the *Miller's Tale*', *Studies in Philology*, 59 (1962), 479–500.
Absolon's speech to Alisoun beneath her shot-window includes excerpts from the *Song of Songs*, traditionally interpreted as a dialogue between Christ and his beloved (Mary, the human soul, or the church).

Kiernan, Kevin S., 'The Art of the Descending Catalogue and a Fresh Look at Alisoun,' *Chaucer Review*, 10 (1975–6), 1–16.
On the positive qualities of rhetorical conventions, and the creative possibilities of the 'head-to-toe' model of female beauty, with reference to a wide variety of examples from Chaucer and medieval English literature.

Kolve, V. A., *The Play Called Corpus Christi* (London: Arnold, 1966).
See especially chs 6 and 7 on the place and purpose of laughter in religious contexts, including the play of Noah.

Muscatine, Charles, *Chaucer and the French Tradition: A Study in Style and Meaning* (Berkeley and Los Angeles: University of California Press, 1957).
Chs 2 and 3 examine the respective styles characteristic of romance (e.g. Knight's Tale) and fabliau (e.g. Miller's Tale), while pp. 222–30 discuss the mixing of styles in the Miller's Tale.

Prior, Sandra Pierson, 'Parodying Typology and the Mystery Plays in the Miller's Tale', *Journal of Medieval and Renaissance Studies*, 16 (1986), 57–73.
References to the mystery plays in the Miller's Tale add up to a parody of the representation of biblical figures and events in popular religious drama.

Richardson, Janette, *Blameth Nat Me: A Study of Imagery in Chaucer's Fabliaux*, Studies in English Literature, vol. 58 (The Hague and Paris: Mouton, 1970).
Ch. 9 on the images used to animate the characters of Alisoun, Nicholas, Absolon and John.

Rowland, Beryl, 'Chaucer's Blasphemous Churl: A New Interpretation of the Miller's Tale', in *Chaucer and Middle English*

Studies in Honour of Rossell Hope Robbins, ed. Rowland (London: George Allen and Unwin, 1974), pp. 43–55.
On the blasphemous features of the Miller's Tale, with particular reference to the mystery plays as they concern John as a burlesque of Joseph, Nicholas as the angel of the annunciation, Alisoun as Mary and Absolon as Christ.

Rowland, Beryl, 'The Play of the Miller's Tale: A Game within a Game', *Chaucer Review*, 5 (1970–71), 140–6.
On allusions to the mystery plays within the Miller's Tale, especially the plays of Noah, and of Joseph.

CHAPTER FOUR

The Wife of Bath's Prologue and Tale

i. INVENTING THE WIFE OF BATH

The previous chapters have drawn attention to the crucial importance of literary convention and stereotype in the construction of character. Whether the received image be that of Mirth, or of Geoffrey of Vinsauf's ideal woman, or a mystery play representation of Mrs Noah, it is not possible to take the true measure of Chaucer's creations without considering the interplay between model and innovation. The same holds true for another woman who, to an even greater extent than her counterpart in the Miller's Tale, has been hailed as one of Chaucer's most enduring and realistic characters.

It is the Wife of Bath herself who identifies the stereotype by virtue of which she exists when she says:

> Deceite, wepyng, spynnyng God hath yive
> To wommen kyndely, whil that they may lyve.
>
> (WBP, 401–2)

In other words, it is in women's nature ('kyndely') to be deceitful, to experience much sorrow ('wepyng') and to work arduously ('spynnyng'). It is their God-given destiny. The received image is essentially that of Eve. No less than Mrs Noah, Dame Alys belongs to the lineage of Eve. According to the teachings of the medieval church, Eve was the first cause of man's sinfulness. It was she who, in the garden of Eden, rebelled against God by listening to the blandishments of the serpent, and so ate from the tree of knowledge of good and evil, before passing the forbidden fruit on to Adam. Hence her deceitfulness. As a result of their disobedience, God condemned Eve to pain and sorrow, especially in childbirth; made her subservient to Adam; decreed that Adam would endure endless, difficult work; and banished them both from paradise (Genesis 3: 16–24). Now look carefully at the illustration on page 104 (Plate 4) and answer these questions.

1. *Identify the subject of the scene. Where is it located?*
2. *What kinds of activity are shown and what is their significance?*
3. *How does the picture convey ideas of suffering and self-awareness?*

This drawing of the exiled pair, done within a few years of Chaucer's death in 1400, shows Adam and Eve both working, for only by following God's ordinance was there to be any chance of salvation. Eve sits, spinning thread laboriously from her distaff. At her side is a cradle, with its tiny occupant, a testimony to the 'wepyng' of childbirth. To the right, Adam digs the ground with a spade. Both figures are clothed, the awareness of nakedness and sexuality being one of the consequences of eating from the tree of knowledge. As if in recollection of that crucial event, trees flourish in the background.

The story of what happened in the garden of Eden, Eve's key role in it, and the subsequent interpretations of theologians, help to explain the hostility expressed towards women and marriage in some quarters (especially clerical ones) throughout the middle ages. The Genesis narrative, together with other biblical passages, provided male commentators with evidence and justification for their hostile views. One of the most learned, revered and influential of the church fathers in this respect was St Jerome (*c.* 342–420). In his thirties he had lived the life of a scholar hermit in the desert east of Antioch, before becoming secretary to Pope Damasus at Rome. At the pope's request, he undertook a revision of the Bible, a task which lasted more than thirty years, involving as it did extensive translation into Latin from Hebrew and Greek. The result, generally known as the 'vulgate Bible', is still in use and is the achievement for which Jerome is chiefly remembered.

But Jerome was anything but a self-effacing scholar, quietly producing his magnum opus. He had strong views on celibacy, and on the virtues of the monastic life in general – views which he put into effect. In Rome he became the leader of a group of widows who were attracted to the self-denying life of religious study. Following the death of Pope Damasus in 384, Jerome established with them, and with their financial help, a religious community at Bethlehem for men and women. From there, as well as continuing his work on the Bible, Jerome engaged in fierce controversy on theological matters. Among his polemical writings is one known as the *Epistle against Jovinian* (393),

Plate 4: Eve spinning and Adam digging.

which became a popular source of views hostile to women and marriage. Jerome wrote it to refute the argument of a monk named Jovinian that, in the sight of God, a virgin is no better than a wife. Jerome, while not opposed to marriage as such, argued for the supremacy of virginity. In doing so he deployed biblical quotations critical of women, such as the following one from the book of Proverbs (27:15):

> 'A Continual dropping on a wintry day' turns a man out of doors, and so will a contentious woman drive a man from his own house. She floods his house with her constant nagging and daily chatter, and ousts him from his own home, that is, the Church ...
>
> (*Epistle against Jovinian,* I, 28; trans. Fremantle, in Miller (ed.), p. 427)

Jerome's views on women and marriage were widespread and influential. Chaucer was well acquainted with them, both directly and through the writings of other poets such as Jean de Meun (the continuator of the *Romance of the Rose*) and Chaucer's contemporary, Eustache Deschamps. Thus, the biblical stereotype identified by the Wife of Bath was sustained and elaborated by other writers, so enduring as a powerful encoder of meaning about the nature of women.

And yet, the Wife of Bath does not read simply as an example of a medieval stereotype. Most readers agree in finding her character various and complex. How has Chaucer performed this conjuring trick, of creating the illusion of personality out of such bare essentials? The passage just quoted from Jerome may strike a familiar note because a version of it appears in the Wife of Bath's Prologue:

> Thow seyst that droppyng houses, and eek smoke,
> And chidyng wyves maken men to flee
> Out of hir owene houses ... (WBP, 278-80)

Compare the passage by St Jerome, just cited, with the Wife of Bath's version of the same words and then answer the following questions.

1. *Consider the context of what Dame Alys says, as it occurs within her prologue, and discuss how that context compares with the circumstances which gave rise to Jerome's words.*
2. *Identify and discuss the different tones of voice found in the two passages.*
3. *What intention lies behind the Wife of Bath's use of Jerome's words, and how is that intention achieved?*

As we have seen, Dame Alys's words derive from a tradition of writing hostile to women, but their function here, as well as their context, is radically altered. Chaucer has put the revered words into the mouth of a woman, and one who is not inclined to believe that they represent the truth. The Wife of Bath's use of these words occurs within a longer passage in which she exemplifies the kind of remark she endured from her first three husbands, and how she dealt with their verbal attacks. So Jerome's words are domesticated, are made to have more local, less sonorous effects, by becoming part of a supposed dialogue between husband and wife. At the same time, the view the husband endorses is spurned and rejected. The Wife of Bath finishes her 'quotation'; by saying 'a benedicitee! / What eyleth swich an old man for to chide?' (280–1). So the effect of antifeminist views is reversed: they are put by Chaucer into the mouth of a woman reporting her husband, and used to attack men.

The new context in which Chaucer places hostility towards women points towards a second means whereby he constructs the Wife of Bath's character. Unlike her stereotype, she appears to have a point of view, a mind of her own, and refuses to accept the traditional attitudes which are latent in the received image of Eve. Here it is important not to jump to the conclusion that Dame Alys arose spontaneously from Chaucer's imagination as a fully fledged, three-dimensional character to cut a swathe through the reductive and reprehensible male image of the shrew. The idea of there being an alternative point of view, opposed to male church orthodoxy, is fully present in Jerome's *Epistle against Jovinian,* which is in part cast in the form of a dialogue between representatives of opposing standpoints. Jerome, of course, ensures that the dialogue demonstrates the superiority of his opinions. For example:

> ... you will say: 'If everybody were a virgin, what would become of the human race?' Like shall here beget like. If everyone were a widow, or continent in marriage, how will mortal men be propagated? Upon this principle there will be nothing at all for fear that something else may cease to exist. To put a case: if all men were philosophers there would be no husbandmen. Why speak of husbandmen? there would be no orators, no lawyers, no teachers of the other professions. If all men were leaders, what would become of the soldiers? If all were the head, whose head would they be called, when there were no other members? You are afraid that if the desire for virginity were general there would be no prostitutes, no adulteresses, no wailing infants in town and country. Every day the blood of adulterers is shed, adulterers are condemned, and lust is raging and rampant in the very presence of the laws and the symbols of authority and the courts of justice. Be not afraid that all will become virgins: virginity is a hard matter, and therefore rare, because it is hard: 'Many are called, few chosen.' Many begin, few persevere. And so the reward is great for those who have persevered. If all were able to be virgins, our Lord would never have said: 'He that is able to receive it, let him receive it': and the Apostle would not have hesitated to give his

advice: 'Now concerning virgins I have no commandment of the Lord.'
(*Jerome against Jovinian,* I, 36; trans. Fremantle, in Miller (ed.), p. 428)

This is the Wife of Bath's version of the same debate:

Wher can ye seye, in any manere age,
That hye God defended mariage 60
By expres word? I pray yow, telleth me.
Or where comanded he virginitee?
I woot as wel as ye, it is no drede,
Th'apostel, whan he speketh of maydenhede,
He seyde that precept therof hadde he noon. 65
Men may conseille a womman to been oon,
But conseillyng is no comandement.
He putte it in oure owene juggement;
For hadde God comanded maydenhede,
Thanne hadde he dampned weddyng with the dede. 70
And certes, if ther were no seed ysowe,
Virginitee, thanne whereof sholde it growe?
Poul dorste nat comanden, atte leeste.
A thyng of which his maister yaf noon heeste.
The dart is set up for virginitee; 75
Cacche whoso may, who renneth best lat see.

(WBP, 59–76)

Now answer the following questions.

1. *Compare and contrast the use which Jerome and Chaucer make of dramatised voices engaged in dialogue.*
2. *Comment on the use which each speaker makes of biblical authority.*
3. *Although they use similar material, Jerome and the Wife of Bath reach radically different conclusions. How do they?*

In using the *Epistle against Jovinian,* Chaucer animates the dialogue, and alters its bias in favour of a position opposed to Jerome's. The effect is to provide the Wife of Bath with the semblance of intellectual autonomy, to create the impression that she is endowed with mental acuity. In the manner of a Jerome, the Wife of Bath weighs the textual evidence of the Bible, observing that Christ nowhere commanded virginity, while accepting that St Paul did advise Christians to follow the path of chastity. But advice is not binding: 'conseillyng is no comandement' (67), and the individual is therefore allowed to exercise discretion as to the best path to follow. In any case, obligatory virtue would hardly sit well with marriage, which Christ certainly condoned. The final absurdity of universal chastity would be the depopulation of the world, and the drying up of the supply of those people who might choose to become virgins: 'if ther were no seed ysowe, / Virginitee, thanne wherof sholde it growe?' (71–2).

Jerome had countered this order of argument (if somewhat cynically) by pointing out that with lechery so rampant in human society there is little danger of everyone becoming chaste: 'Be not afraid that all will become virgins: virginity is a hard matter, and therefore rare, because it is hard: "Many are called, few chosen".' He therefore reaches a position similar to that later adopted by the Wife of Bath: 'The dart is set up for virginitee; / Cacche whoso may ...' (75–6). It is remarkable what relatively minor changes in voice, context and emphasis can achieve in promoting the illusion of character.

If the Wife of Bath's Prologue were little more than a debate, deriving from Jerome and subsequent writers, on the pros and cons of being a woman, that would hardly account for the sense of vitality which the Wife of Bath conveys. Chaucer has, however, done much more than rehearse, in disguised form, the arguments for and against the negative female stereotype. Crucially, he embodies and dramatises them in the persons of Alys and her fifth husband, Jankyn. One particular episode illustrates the process better than any other.

Jankyn is – as Jerome was – a scholar, a student, a man of books, those repositories of words under male control which had been, and which still are, instrumental in perpetuating the traditional image of woman as Eve. In fact, Jankyn possesses a volume, his Book of Wicked Wives, which in its content is a boiled down version of the whole legacy of misogyny. It is a collection of excerpts from classical authors like Ovid, from the Bible, and from Jerome, on the evil known as woman. It is an anthology of authorities – authority in this sense meaning both a 'respected point of view' and 'what is written down by an author'. Significantly, it includes first the story of Eve and its devastating consequence:

> Of Eva first, that for hir wikkednesse 715
> Was al mankynde broght to wrecchednesse,
> For which that Jhesu Crist hymself was slayn,
> That boghte us with his herte blood agayn.
> Lo, heere expres of womman may ye fynde
> That womman was the los of al mankynde. 720
>
> (WBP, 715–20)

Jankyn takes mischievous pleasure in goading his wife by reading such passages to her. However playful his intentions, the role of antifeminist cleric is enabled by the writings he possesses and the attitudes they express. One famous night, the play suddenly becomes deadly serious. Losing patience as Jankyn trots out the stories of Eve, Delilah, Xantippe, and others, Alys rips three leaves from his book and clouts her husband so hard that he falls backwards into the fire. Singed and angry, he fells his wife with a mighty blow. Jankyn fears that he has killed Alys and, as if at death's door, she murmurs a few words. He apologises profusely and, taking her chance, Alys again clouts Jankyn. After some debate the two of them reach an agreement: Alys is to take control of their marital affairs: have 'governance of hous and lond, / And of his tonge, and of his hond also' (814–15); and Jankyn is to burn his book. Subsequently, they live a life of affection and harmony, in which the traditional roles of berating male and shrewish wife are abandoned in favour of a relationship altogether more mutual and fulfilling. Their fight and reconciliation articulate the conflict between authorised stereotype (whether of male attitudes or female behaviour) and the altogether more complex matter of subjective experience.

But Chaucer's revision of the received image of woman as Eve goes further: he systematically reverses the Wife of Bath's three descriptive terms: 'deceite, wepyng, spynnyng'. Now consider the following questions.

1. *In what ways does the Wife of Bath practise deceit?*
2. *To what extent is 'wepyng', or sorrow, a feature of the Wife of Bath's marriages, and who experiences it?*
3. *How do the Wife of Bath's professional and commercial activities colour her attitude towards men?*
4. *In what ways, other than those just described, does Chaucer dramatise the debate on the nature of women?*

The Wife of Bath's deceitfulness can hardly be denied. Alys is a superb instance of a woman who unashamedly deceives, ensnares and schemes against men. She glories in her capacity to dupe her husbands, seeing it as an essential part of a woman's role and something of which to be proud: 'For half so boldely kan ther no man / Swere and lyen, as a womman kan' (227–8). For example, she controls her husbands in part by making false accusations, declaring that whoever speaks words of complaint first is likely to win the argument. As a result of this tactic, her husbands end by apologising for things they have actually never done (379–94). Again, when courting Jankyn she pretends that he has enchanted her, to the point of inventing a dream which seems to betoken their future union (575–84). In short, the Wife of Bath is an embodiment of precisely what male writers on women and marriage inveigh against. She might be seen as the very fulfilment and justification of Jerome's warnings who, through her very exuberance in deceiving men, and exaggerated conduct, disarms criticism.

According to the next term in the Wife of Bath's formula, 'wepyng', or suffering, is part of her lot as a descendant of Eve. Indeed the Wife of Bath's Prologue contains a considerable amount of information about suffering. But the suffering in question is not experienced by Alys. Instead it is *caused* by her, and those who undergo it are her unfortunate husbands. Thus an expectation raised by the stereotype is confounded. The grumbling and railing, the invented accusations, the constant nagging – all these, the Wife asserts, cause her partners much 'peyne ... and ... wo' (384). The Wife is even audacious enough to make a virtue out of the suffering she causes. Once she has subdued her husbands into exasperated silence, she taunts them with the virtue of patient suffering by reminding them of the biblical story of Job, who was a man sorely tried by his wife. Men, claims the Wife of Bath, are forever preaching about the merits of patience and the advantages of having a patient and submissive wife. They should practise, and experience, what they preach:

> Ye sholde been al pacient and meke,
> And han a sweete spiced conscience,
> Sith ye so preche of Jobes pacience.
>
> (WBP, 434–6)

Alys admits that she made the life of her fourth husband so miserable that his earthly suffering and punishment, which were like the pains of purgatory, surely deserve reward in heaven (489–90). With tongue in cheek, she suggests that marriage to her (although it entails a reversal of orthodox roles) is far from being spiritually destructive. Suffering – supposedly her lot – is transferred to the man, but this, in the light of Christian teaching about the spiritual benefits of sorrow and suffering, can only be to the advantage of the man's soul.

Chaucer's final modification to the stereotype of Eve concerns the professional activities of the Wife of Bath. The traditional expectation is that the work appropriate to her, as a woman, is spinning. Chaucer identifies Alys in the General Prologue as someone involved in the practice of 'clooth-makyng' (GP, 447) to the point of being a nonpareil. She stands comparison with other European representatives of cloth-making famed for the excellence of their products – the weavers of Ypres and Ghent. The introduction of this idea, namely that cloth-making is an international industry, conducted according to commercial principles, represents a marked break with the image of a woman who spins in token of the judgement passed on her and Adam after the Fall. For the significance of women as producers, and the importance of their place in the economic world, are credited. To the extent that commercial activity is accepted as natural and desirable, the old image of 'woman as spinner', the demeaning result of a God-given ordinance, loses much of its power. What, one might ask, is its relevance in a world where female labour is so much to their (and everyone else's) advantage?

If commercial attitudes seem to be naturalised in the Wife of Bath's Prologue, having become so much the order of the day that the traditional, theological image of 'women's work' is almost lost, it is in large part due to the care which Chaucer has taken to show how Alys evaluates her experience in terms of work (or effort), profit and loss. In acquiring husbands she has an eye to gain, being drawn to those who are old and rich, therefore easy to master and most likely to die within a short space, their wealth bequeathed to her (197). Relations between men and women are represented as market-place exchanges, with the woman trying harder to attract the 'buyer' the more he appears uninterested in what she has to offer (515–24). Even sex itself is seen as a commodity transaction: her old husbands work hard for their reward of pleasure, and might have to pay – in gifts of money – before the Wife will respond to their approaches (407–17).

This attempt to provide an account of how Chaucer incorporates and manipulates a dominant image of woman – through the medium of words and through the medium of behaviour – allows us to imagine Chaucer in his 'workshop', the character of the Wife of Bath taking shape as he finds new ways of breathing life into the old image of woman as Eve. Even so, the analysis is far from complete. There are several other ways in which Chaucer promotes the illusion of the Wife's existence: through a sense of place, a sense of time, and a sense of self. First, Alys is thoroughly integrated with contemporary urban life. Her prologue provides a vivid impression of its network of gossips, its processions, sermons, miracle plays and, last but not least, its funerals, courtship practices, and weddings (543–62). Dame Alys lives in such a setting; her experiences grow from it; she is in part conditioned by the place where she lives, its inhabitants, and social activities. For example, she gives her heart to Jankyn, the clerk, on seeing his shapely legs and feet as he follows in procession the bier of her fourth husband. Second, the recollections of the Wife of Bath as she reviews her past life – 'whan that it remembreth me / Upon my yowthe, and on my jolitee' (469–70) – the occasional regret and nostalgia, her hopes for the future, give her a location in time, or rather give her a sense of time which is highly personal, being located in her individual experience. Finally, she is aware of her own identity, of the image of Eve according to which others might perceive her. With this image, as we have seen, she takes issue and so persuades us that she is independent of it.

ii. THE QUEST FOR *GENTILLESSE*

The character of the Wife of Bath may be said to exist in a state of tension between the claims of personal, subjective awareness and those of impersonal, institutionalised knowledge or, to use her own terms, between 'experience' and 'auctoritee'. If her character is to some considerable extent defined in opposition to the stereotype of woman as Eve, it is nevertheless dependent upon it: no stereotype, no character. But however ancient and notorious the ancestry of the Wife of Bath, and however radical her attack upon the image by virtue of which she exists, the tenor of the debate remains playful, the Wife of Bath's autobiography a comedy. It is therefore easy enough to argue that the issues which Chaucer explores through the medium of her character are not to be taken seriously.

That impression changes with the Wife of Bath's Tale, in which the detrimental effect of stereotypes, and the value of personal, inner, qualities are treated with the utmost seriousness, and allied to the example of Christ himself. Before proceeding any further, try to answer the following questions.

1. *To what extent is the hero of the Wife's tale a stereotype?*
2. *What evidence is there that he perceives others in terms of stereotypes?*
3. *Does the knight's attitude change? If so, how, and with what consequences?*

The knight of Arthur's court, whose adventure is described, can initially perceive women only in terms of male clichés, to such an extent that he himself is devoid of inner complexity. He sees a vulnerable, unprotected young woman and, using his innate physical mastery, rapes her: she is for him nothing more than a means of providing sexual gratification. Similarly, when faced with the prospect of spending the night with an old hag he recoils in disgust because he can think only in preconditioned terms: young, lusty knights should have young, attractive, noble wives. But he is pressured by the old hag to look inwards, to consider the principle of courtesy which he, as a knight, is supposed to uphold, thereby treating all as equals with respect not for their riches or beauty (outer value) but for their inner qualities and virtues.

The knight yields superiority to his wife's wisdom and then the miracle happens: she changes into the woman of his dreams. The stereotypes dissolve, showing that the young woman is implicit in the old, at the moment when the knight's perceptions go deeper than surface appearances, at the moment when he is prepared to abandon the traditional role of authoritative decisive husband, and allow his wife to determine their future. Like the Wife of Bath's Prologue, then, her tale is about the reductiveness and cruelty of stereotypes, about the limitations which they arbitrarily place on the perception of self and others unless one is prepared to look beyond, think through, the reflex attitudes and relationships which familiar and unquestioned images provoke.

Central to the old hag's argument is her speech on *gentillesse,* or true nobility. It is not found in other medieval versions of the story, although the knight's attitude – common to comparable narratives – raises the issue of *gentillesse* naturally enough. What appears to have fed Chaucer's thought at this point is an already existing debate such as is found in Boethius, Jean de Meun's continuation of the *Romance of the Rose* (*c.*1275), Dante's *Il Convivio* (*The Banquet*) of 1304–8, and contemporary writings on the spiritual reformation of society. Within that debate, Chaucer found a number of features which tallied with his intentions for the Wife of Bath's Tale. As well as blending material from different sources, as we have already seen him do on a number of occasions, we should recognise that in this case Chaucer is also contributing to a well established and continuing theoretical discussion, the central question of which was: What is the basis of true nobility? By examining Jean de Meun's and Dante's handling of that question we can see both the terms of the debate and its usefulness to Chaucer before going on to consider his own points of emphasis.

Jean de Meun gives the task of expounding true nobility to Nature, an unquestionably authoritative figure whose attributes include the principle of procreation. She declares herself opposed to falsely based social divisions founded in specious claims to nobility. No one, be he of noble birth or a labourer, can be considered truly noble unless he practise virtue:

> And if anyone who boasts of his nobility dares contradict me and say that noblemen – those whom people call noblemen – are, through their nobility of birth, of better standing than those who cultivate the earth or live by their labor, then I reply that no one is noble unless he is intent on virtue, and no man is base except because of his vices, which make him appear unbridled and stupid.
>
> Nobility comes from a good heart, for nobility of ancestry is not the nobility of true worth when it lacks goodness of heart. For this reason a nobleman must display the prowess of his ancestors, by means of the

great labor that they gave to it. When they passed from the world, they carried all their virtues with them and left their possessions to their heirs, who could have nothing more of them. They have the possessions, but nothing else is theirs, not nobility or valor, unless they act so that they may be noble through the sense and the virtues that they themselves possess.

Romance of the Rose lines 18607–34; trans. Dahlberg)

Now answer the following questions.

1. *What are the moral implications of Jean de Meun's discussion of nobility?*
2. *In what ways is nobility a social as well as a moral issue?*
3. *What are the outward manifestations of (a) true nobility, and (b) false nobility?*

From the outset, the discussion of nobility is essentially a moral debate. True nobility cannot be inherited. It is available to all, and here (Nature goes on to insist) clerks have special obligations. Since they have access to the books in which virtue is expounded and exemplified, they have a responsibility themselves to cultivate nobility. Failing to do so, given their opportunities, is particularly reprehensible. But for all that Nature appears to be advocating a democracy of the spirit, it is clear that nobility in the fullest sense is for her a social as well as a moral category: she continues by saying that 'whoever turns his desire towards nobility must guard against pride and laziness, must give himself to arms and to study and must empty himself of baseness' (18681–4). It would therefore seem to be a quality more expected of the aristocracy, or fighting class, than of others. Its components are humility, courtesy and gentleness towards all people (except enemies). Ladies and girls should be honoured. Since nobility is a quality which manifests itself through behaviour, it is a virtue which, in order to be credited to an individual, must be publicly recognised. Praise, esteem and a blameless reputation are essential.

Inherited nobility, based on wealth and status, is easily squandered by vicious living. True nobility is more difficult to retain, although the example of precursors can act as a guide. Above all, the outward trappings of nobility (reputation, noble birth, costly life-style) should not be confused with its actuality. Riches are in themselves base, and those who found their claims to nobility on wealth, or the status of their forbears, are in reality 'villanous vassals' (18865), the very opposite of what they claim to be. True nobility is based on natural freedom, or a conscious decision to be virtuous. This freedom is God-given. Those who neglect it bring shame to themselves, and the shame is all the greater if opportunities of birth, wealth and education have provided them with the means to practise virtue and models to follow.

Dante's discussion of nobility occurs at the beginning of the third canzone of *Il Convivio*. In substance and direction the argument is similar to that covered by Jean de Meun, with some important modifications. The context is one of sexual love in crisis: the poet has temporarily abandoned 'tender rhymes of love' (III, 1) because of the scornful attitude of his lady, to talk instead about the quality which makes a person truly noble, and particularly in order to refute the idea that nobility derives from the possession of riches. Thus the ensuing discussion again has the stamp of authority, but it is that of the poet's own voice. To that extent the argument which follows is more intimate in tone, more domestic, than the utterances of Nature. Dante, one feels, is encountering the problems at a personal level, rather than listening to *ex cathedra* pronouncements.

Like Jean de Meun, Dante gives the impression of working against the grain of received ideas: ancestry, no less than the accumulation of wealth is not, as is commonly thought, the source of nobility. Instead, that source is found in the attainment and maintenance of virtue, and no virtue is the exclusive preserve of any particular social order. Therefore, the possession of true nobility is not restricted to the high-born: 'Nobility resides wherever virtue is, / But virtue not wherever there's nobility' (III. 6). Insofar as virtue, the cause of true happiness, derives from God, nobility is a God-given quality and not simply to be achieved through social position. Dante goes on to identify the various qualities through which the virtuous soul finds expression in the different ages of life. In that the soul is characterised as female, these qualities are by implication 'feminine' in nature (though not for that reason inaccessible to men):

> The soul which this goodness adorns
> Does not keep it concealed,
> For this, from the time she is wed to the body,
> She displays till the moment of death.
> Obedient, pleasant, and full of shame
> Is she in life's first interval,
> And she adorns her body with the beauty
> That derives from parts well harmonized.
> In maturity she's strong and self-restrained
> And full of love and courteous praise,
> And takes her sole delight in acting honestly.
> In old age she's just and prudent
> And is renowned for her generosity,
> And in herself is gratified
> To hear and speak of others' worth.
> And then in the fourth phase of life

She is married once again to God,
Reflecting on the end awaiting her
While blessing all the times gone by.

(*Convivio*, III, 7; trans. Lansing)

At death, therefore, the soul is united with God in a 'marriage' which represents an ideal relationship of female to male. Thus Dante returns to his original theme of love, although the sexual aspect has now been supplanted by a spiritual one.

In the Wife of Bath's Tale the discussion of nobility takes place in the unpromising context of a pillow talk by the hag:

But, for ye speken of swich gentillesse
As is descended out of old richesse, 1110
That therfore sholden ye be gentil men,
Swich arrogance is nat worth an hen.
Looke who that is moost vertuous alway,
Pryvee and apert, and moost entendeth ay
To do the gentil dedes that he kan; 1115
Taak hym for the grettest gentil man.
Crist wole we clayme of hym oure gentillesse,
Nat of oure eldres for hire old richesse.
For thogh they yeve us al hir heritage,
For which we clayme to been of heigh parage, 1120
Yet may they nat biquethe for no thyng
To noon of us hir vertuous lyvyng,
That made hem gentil men ycalled be,
And bad us folwen hem in swich degree.
Wel kan the wise poete of Florence, 1125
That highte Dant, speken in this sentence.
Lo, in swich maner rym is Dantes tale:
'Ful selde up riseth by his branches smale
Prowesse of man, for God, of his goodnesse,
Wole that of hym we clayme oure gentillesse'; 1130
For of oure eldres may we no thyng clayme
But temporel thyng, that man may hurte and mayme.

(WBT, 1109-32)

Now answer the following questions.

1. *Is the tone of this passage closer to the tone of the* Convivio *or to that of the* Romance of the Rose?
2. *To what extent does the hag modify the ideas of Jean de Meun and Dante?*
3. *What is the relevance of the hag's speech to the former and future behaviour of the knight?*
4. *To what extent are the ideal 'female' qualities of Dante's soul reflected in, or contradicted by, (a) the Wife of Bath, and (b) the old hag?*

The hag hardly commands the authority of Nature; nor is she necessarily voicing Chaucer's opinion. Nevertheless, he takes pains to indicate that what she says is meant to be taken extremely seriously. Respectful reference is made not only to Dante, 'the wise poete of Florence' (1125), but also to the Roman authors Valerius Maximus and Seneca and to Boethius, whose *Consolation of Philosophy* Chaucer translated. By buttressing the hag's speech with the names of revered authors, Chaucer is indicating its importance and significance. He is also demonstrating his affiliations with certain kinds of authoritative discourse, however much, elsewhere in the Wife of Bath's Prologue and Tale, he may question and reject others.

The cue for the hag's speech is the knight's disparaging remark about her social status. Not only is she old and ugly but also, unlike him, 'comen of so lough a kynde' (1101). The aim of her riposte is to detach *gentillesse* from the province of a single social class (that of the nobility), as if it were their prerogative. In doing so she is seeking a basic change in the knight's attitude: 'I koude amende al this ... / ... er it were dayes thre, / So wel ye myghte bere yow unto me' (1106–8). Her initial objection is to the unquestioned assumption of the knight's moral superiority: that *gentillesse* follows from aristocratic birth. The carapace of this received idea the hag pierces with the dismissive remark that it is sheer arrogance. *Gentillesse,* to be valid, must be perpetually practised and reaffirmed through *gentil,* which is to say, virtuous, actions. In this respect the only true ancestor and model is Christ himself: 'Crist wole we clayme of hym oure gentillesse, / Nat of oure eldres for hire old richesse' (1117–18). *Gentillesse* is therefore accessible to all. It cannot be bequeathed: the 'vertuous lyvyng' (1122) of our forebears, however socially elevated they may have been, can at best act as an example. From 'oure eldres' we may inherit material benefits, but *gentillesse* (like fire) is an abstract quality existing independently of the vehicles through which it finds temporary expression.

Gentillesse, then, cannot be transmitted along with inherited wealth, 'annexed to possessioun' (1147). If that were the case, then the members of a given family would be virtuous in perpetuity. In practice, the inheritors of nobility are not immune from vice (as the knight has amply demonstrated): 'men may wel often fynde / A lordes sone do shame and vileynye' (1150–1). Reprehensible behaviour cancels true *gentillesse,* whatever the social status of the person in question: 'He nys nat gentil, be he duc or erl, / For vileyns synful dedes make a cherl' (1157–8). *Gentillesse* derives from God and his grace. It has nothing to do with social position, and is the province of the poor as much as of the rich, for 'he is gentil that dooth gentil dedis' (1170). The hag, therefore, whatever the nature of her ancestry, may claim to be *gentil* and therefore worthy of the knight from the moment 'that I bigynne / To lyven vertuously and weyve synne' (1175–6).

By this, and by what follows on the virtues of poverty, the knight stands reproved. The hag has, after all, saved his life, and done little more than insist on the keeping of a promise. She has committed no offence against the knight, and yet she is treated as being guilty (1096). Her only faults are ones over which (apparently) she has no control: her ugliness, great age, and low birth. The knight is therefore represented as responding not to the governing principle of *gentillesse,* which should cause him to express gratitude and appreciation, but to superficial values of appearance, status and male authority. Once he abandons these, resigning control to his wife, he enters into an altogether different order of existence, one that is immeasurably richer and more complex since it is based on mutual understanding.

iii. DISCUSSION POINTS

Read the opening of the Wife of Bath's Prologue (lines 1-24), and then answer the following questions.

1. *To what extent are these lines representative of the Wife of Bath's mode of arguing?*
2. *How does Chaucer here begin to create the illusion of Dame Alys's character?*
3. *What is the dramatic potential of this passage?*
4. *To what extent are 'experience' and 'authority' misleading categories for what follows?*
5. *Are there any aspects of this passage which prepare the reader for the Wife of Bath's Tale?*

The following questions are more generally related to the Wife of Bath's Prologue and Tale.

6. *To what extent does the Wife of Bath's credibility as a character depend upon her integration with urban life?*
7. *What would Jean de Meun's Nature have thought of Jankyn the clerk?*
8. *Consider the extent to which the Wife of Bath has a sense of past time, and how this might contribute to the representation of her character.*
9. *What connections do you perceive between the advent of self-awareness, as*

expressed in the Genesis myth of the Fall, and the character of the Wife of Bath?

10. *In the Wife of Bath's Prologue and Tale, what qualities are identified as distinctively 'mannish', what qualities as distinctively feminine? Are these qualities necessarily restricted to men and women respectively? If not, discuss the ways in which women might adopt 'male' attitudes (and why) and the ways in which men might adopt 'female' attitudes (and why).*
11. *Devise an argument to refute the idea that the Wife of Bath's character is solely invented from antifeminist models.*
12. *The Wife of Bath's Prologue and Tale suggest that only on rare occasions, and in special circumstances, can men and women come to a mutually beneficial understanding. Do you agree with this perspective on male–female relations?*
13. *Identify some modern stereotypes of men and women – for example, in advertisements. Do they enhance or degrade an individual's sense of identity? Who or what 'authorises' and sustains such stereotypes, and for what reasons?*

iv. FURTHER READING

a. Sources and contexts

Blamires, Alcuin, with Karen Pratt and C. W. Marx, *Woman Defamed and Woman Defended: An Anthology of Medieval Texts* (Oxford: Clarendon Press, 1992).

A new and wide-ranging compilation of antifeminist texts and ripostes, a number of which are here translated for the first time. Includes selections from classical authors, the scriptures and church fathers, with much of relevance to the Wife of Bath.

Dante, *Il Convivio (The Banquet)*, trans. Richard H. Lansing, Garland Library of Medieval Literature, series B, vol. 65 (New York and London: Garland, 1990).

Guillaume de Lorris and Jean de Meun, *The Romance of the Rose,* trans. Charles Dahlberg (Princeton, NJ: Princeton University Press, 1971).

Miller, Robert P. (ed.), *Chaucer Sources and Backgrounds* (New York: Oxford University Press, 1977).

St Jerome, *The Principal Works of St Jerome,* trans. W. H. Fremantle, A Select Library of Nicene and Post-Nicene Fathers of the Christian Church, 2nd series, vol. 6 (Oxford: Parker; New York: Christian Literature Co., 1893).

Pages 346–416 for a full version of *Epistle against Jovinian*. Excerpts in Blamires and Miller.

b. Selected studies

Aers, David, *Chaucer, Langland and the Creative Imagination* (London: Routledge and Kegan Paul, 1980).
Ch. 6 on the oppression of women by men in medieval marriage; the collusion of the church; and the effects of Christian ideology on the Wife of Bath (who both conforms and rebels), the Merchant's Tale and Franklin's Tale.

Amsler, Mark, 'The Wife of Bath and Women's Power', *Assays,* 4 (1987), 67–83.
On the functions of the Wife of Bath's character, her power (e.g. economic, political) and critique of women's autonomy.

Boren, James L., 'Alysoun of Bath and the Vulgate "Perfect Wife"', *Neuphilologische Mitteilungen,* 76 (1975), 247–56.
The influence of the biblical book of Proverbs on Chaucer's portrayal of the Wife of Bath.

David, Alfred, *The Strumpet Muse: Art and Morals in Chaucer's Poetry* (Bloomington and London: Indiana University Press, 1976).
Ch. 9 on the clash of experience and authority in the character of the Wife of Bath (a persona for Chaucer) and on the *sentence* and *solaas* of her tale.

Delany, Sheila, 'Sexual Economics, Chaucer's Wife of Bath, and *The Book of Margery Kempe*' (1975), in her *Writing Woman: Women Writers and Women in Literature, Medieval to Modern* (New York: Schocken Books, 1983), pp. 76–92.
How the Wife of Bath's trade as a cloth-maker commercialises her attitude towards sex.

Knapp, Peggy A., 'Alisoun Weaves a Text', *Philological Quarterly,* 65 (1986), 387–401.
Uses genre (apologia and confession) and characterisation (through the manipulation of types: entrepreneur, feminist, Eve, sociopath) as 'horizons of expectation' in reading the Wife of Bath's Prologue and Tale; the result is a 'closely woven' text.

Leicester, H. Marshall, Jr, 'Of a Fire in the Dark: Public and Private Feminism in the *Wife of Bath's Tale*', *Women's Studies,* 11 (1984), 157–78.
The fire imagery in the hag's speech on *gentillesse* is linked by the Wife to sexuality, self-assertion and independence – a private form of

feminism somewhat at odds with the public variety she articulates more directly.

Lowes, John Livingston, 'Chaucer and Dante's *Convivio*', *Modern Philology,* 13 (1915–16), 19–33.

Chaucer draws on Jean de Meun and Boethius, as well as Dante, in dealing with the topic of *gentillesse*.

Mann, Jill, *Geoffrey Chaucer,* Feminist Readings (London: Harvester Wheatsheaf, 1991).

A book-length study of Chaucer's representation of women and female values, including extensive passages on the Wife of Bath, e.g. her derivation from antifeminist authorities (pp. 70–86) and the surrender of *maistrye* in her tale (pp. 87–94).

Matthews, William. 'The Wife of Bath and All Her Sect', *Viator,* 5 (1974), 413–43.

Precedents in European medieval literature for the old woman skilled in the arts of love.

Murphy, Ann B., 'The Process of Personality in Chaucer's *Wife of Bath's Tale*', *Centennial Review,* 28 (1984), 204–22.

Chaucer blends a complex array of literary and cultural conventions with idiosyncratic detail to create the illusion of character.

Pratt, Robert A.,'The Development of the Wife of Bath', in *Studies in Medieval Literature in Honor of Professor Albert Croll Baugh,* ed. MacEdward Leach (Philadelphia: University of Philadelphia Press; London: Oxford University Press, 1961), pp. 45–79.

Chaucer's conception of the Wife of Bath developed in response to the influence of antifeminist materials.

Pratt, Robert A., 'Jankyn's Book of Wikked Wyves: Medieval Antimatrimonial Propaganda in the Universities', *Annuale Medievale,* 3 (1962), 5–27.

Reconstructs Jankyn's Book of Wicked Wives and in so doing reviews, with detailed discussions, examples of clerical misogyny from Jerome to Oxford theologians of the fourteenth century.

Robertson, D. W., Jr. '"And for My Land Thus Hastow Mordred Me?": Land Tenure, the Cloth Industry, and the Wife of Bath', *Chaucer Review,* 14 (1979–80), 403–80.

On the nature of the Wife of Bath's involvement in the cloth-making industry.

Roppolo, Joseph P., 'The Converted Knight in Chaucer's "Wife of Bath's Tale"', *College English,* 12 (1950–51), 263–9.

The tale is as much about a radical change in the knight's attitudes (in which the hag's speech on *gentillesse* is crucial) as it is about the transformation of the hag into a beautiful woman.

Rowland, Beryl, 'Chaucer's Working Wife: The Unraveling of a Yarn-Spinner', in *Chaucer in the Eighties,* ed. Julian N. Wasserman and Robert J. Blanch (Syracuse, NY: Syracuse University Press, 1986), pp. 137–49.

Dame Alys's involvement in the wool trade; her association with traditional images of weaving women, including Eve; her sexual attitudes.

Shumaker, Wayne, 'Alisoun in Wander-Land: A Study in Chaucer's Mind and Literary Method', *English Literary History,* 18 (1951), 77–89.

On the extent to which the character of the Wife of Bath is 'sketched from life' as the portrait of an individual, and how far this is a literary contrivance or artifice expressing general ideas about women.

Spisak, James, 'Anti-Feminism Bridled: Two Rhetorical Contexts', *Neuphilologische Mitteilungen,* 81 (1980), 150–60.

Chaucer uses Jerome's *Epistle against Jovinian* to comic ends by putting it into the mouth of a woman Jerome would have despised, and by opposing the extremes of Jerome's arguments with common sense.

Walker, Denis, 'The Psychological Realism of Fictional Characters', *Neuphilologische Mitteilungen,* 86 (1985), 337–42.

Characters are verbal constructs, not real people – with reference to the Wife of Bath.

Weissman, Hope Phyllis, 'Antifeminism and Chaucer's Characterization of Women', in *Geoffrey Chaucer: A Collection of Original Articles,* ed. George D. Economou (New York: McGraw-Hill, 1975), pp. 93–110.

Examines tradition of antifeminist satire and Chaucer's manipulations of the received images of women in the Knight's Tale, Miller's Tale and Wife of Bath's Prologue.

Wurtele, Douglas J., 'Chaucer's Wife of Bath and Her Distorted Arthurian Motifs', *Arthurian Interpretations,* 2 (1987), 47–61.

Compares the Wife's tale with other versions of the same story, concentrating on the issue of realism.

Wurtele, Douglas J., 'The Predicament of Chaucer's Wife of Bath: St Jerome on Virginity', *Florilegium,* 5 (1983), 208–36.

On Chaucer's extensive use of *Epistle against Jovinian* and other writings by Jerome, all of which are summarised at length.

CHAPTER FIVE

The Merchant's Tale

i. WHAT'S IN A NAME?

Character is one of the most accessible features of Chaucer's narratives but, as we have seen, it is not an end in itself. Character is, rather, a literary device by means of which Chaucer explores and articulates the central preoccupations of his work. Alisoun of the Miller's Tale, for example, reflects various differing male points of view, all of them more or less distorted. The figure identified as the Wife of Bath is an arena within which struggle the rivals known as authority and experience. Thus character is, to a considerable extent, determined by its function within the thematic scheme. As we have seen, character is also predicated on models, on stereotypes. If we scrape beneath the surface of character, and its obvious attractions, we discover – as an archaeologist might – that Chaucer's constructions are in fact façades concealing other creations of great antiquity: a rhetorical ideal of feminine beauty in the case of Alisoun, the figure of Eve in the case of Dame Alice.

The same observations hold true for the character of January in the Merchant's Tale. It is a relatively straightforward matter to describe the prominent trait in his personality: blindness, fostered by immoderate lust, intellectual pride and jealousy. When the old man becomes physically blind, it seems but a natural extension of his inner condition. In the manner of the other characters which have been discussed January is, therefore, the expression of a body of ideas. But, as in their cases, that is only half the story.

January's character as an expression of the theme of blindness is a point of entry to the Merchant's Tale with which few modern readers will have difficulty. No doubt it was also a point of entry for Chaucer's contemporaries. But counterbalancing it and providing another, equally intriguing, access route would have been the associations and expectations raised by the name of the duke of Pavia. These are not now immediately obvious, and have to be consciously regained. January is, of course, the name of a month, but to Chaucer's audience it was also the name of a man who personified the month. Visual representations of January were widespread, and were typically found in the calendar (giving saints' days and other useful information) which prefixed devotional books such as psalters and books of hours. An early fifteenth-century example will identify some of the salient features of the familiar image (Plate 5). Now look at the following picture and answer these questions.

1. *Describe the contents of the left-hand side of the picture.*
2. *Can you identify the subject of the right-hand side of the picture?*
3. *What connections exist between the two halves of the composition?*

The right half of the design represents the zodiac sign of Aquarius, the water carrier, which is dominant during the month of January. As is appropriate to the time of year, the ground is devoid of flowers and the trees are bare. Contrasting with the external scene is a no less seasonal one set in an interior. A trestle table is laden with food. Behind it a man, whose dress and demeanour suggest prosperity and power, is feasting. He holds food in one hand and drink in the other. His two heads allow

Plate 5: The month of January.

him to look simultaneously to right and to left. With his bearded, older-looking, face, he gazes at a doorway which frames an attendant, also bearded, who is carrying a vessel associated with the feast. With his younger, clean-shaven, face, he looks towards an opposite doorway where another attendant waits.

The medieval calendar figure of January is a development of the classical image of Janus, the two-faced god of beginnings who, at the turning of the year, looks to both past and future. As the image evolved within Christian contexts, he became domesticated as a two-faced man indulging in those activities typical of the time of year: eating and drinking. The medieval January is sometimes shown as an old man – suggesting the state of the waning year – warming himself by a fire. Not infrequently, he is associated with doors, signifying the entry of the new year and the exit of the old. (*Janus* literally means *doorway,* and is the root of the modern word *janitor.*) By the late fourteenth century, the tendency is to represent January feasting in the manner of a lord at his table. It is always an interior scene. Now answer the following questions.

1. *Are there any ways in which January's personal appearance reflects aspects of the calendar representation of the month after which he is named?*
2. *In what ways might January's attitudes be called 'two-faced'?*
3. *To what extent does January, like his namesake, look upon his experiences in terms of the consumption of food?*

With this calendrical information in mind it becomes clear that Chaucer's portrait of January depends to a considerable extent on traditional motifs. First, his appearance is seasonal: he is all white on top, like a tree in winter, although he feels as vital as the evergreen laurel (1461–6). Second, there is his sense of age. At sixty or more, 'olde Januarie' (1956 and 2042) is acutely conscious of his advanced years. He feels that time is running out, and refers to his 'dayes olde' (1394). Intending to stem the onrush of death he wants to marry 'in al the haste I kan' (1406), with the hope of heavenly reward and of begetting an heir. Third, his attitude is appropriate to his name. He looks in two directions at once: backwards to his single life, and forward to marriage and the possibility of offspring; backwards to an earthly paradise framed as a garden, forward to a heavenly one; backwards to his mis-spent past and forward to the possibility of damnation after death.

Fourth, January – like his calendar counterpart – experiences life as if it were one huge feast. He 'folwed ay his bodily delyt / On wommen, ther as was his appetyt' (1249–50), and thinks of marriage as 'honysweete' (1396). Anticipating the young, tender flesh of his future bride, January seems to lick his lips in delectation (1418–20). Images of food come readily to his lips: he would rather be eaten by hounds than not have an heir (1438–40); he would not give a basketful of herbs for the observations of Justinus on marriage (1568–9). Not only in his imagination, but also in practice, January does what the calendar tradition shows him doing. Before his own wedding-night he eats and drinks aphrodisiac wines and spices (1807–12), and takes another 'sop in fyn clarree' (1843) when the day dawns. It is ironic that May's alleged appetite for pears – a craving which January might well appreciate, and which he helps her to satisfy – is what heralds his own cuckolding.

Fifth, January's natural habitat is indoors. Whether at the wedding feast or afterwards, he customarily sits 'In halle' with his wife (1895). After the onset of blindness he tries to restrict May's activities by containing *her* (2088–91), although he soon loses control of her out of doors. Finally, there is plenty of coming and going through doorways: from hall to chamber to Damian's room, to hall again, to chamber, to the critical threshold of the garden – a doorway which this god of entries tries in vain to control (2116–24 and 2149–55).

The occasion on which January most resembles his calendar counterpart is at the feast, described at some length, which follows his marriage to May. He sits with her and other 'worthy folk' upon the dais, dining on the finest delicacies. The servers come and go with the different courses. January is in his element:

> Thus been they wedded with solempnitee,
> And at the feeste sitteth he and she 1710
> With othere worthy folk upon the deys.
> Al ful of joye and blisse is the paleys,
> And ful of instrumentz and of vitaille,
> The mooste deyntevous of al Ytaille.
> Biforn hem stoode instrumentz of swich soun 1715
> That Orpheus, ne of Thebes Amphioun,
> Ne maden nevere swich a melodye.
> At every cours thanne cam loud mynstralcye
> That nevere tromped Joab for to heere,
> Nor he Theodomas, yet half so cleere 1720
> At Thebes whan the citee was in doute.
> Bacus the wyn hem shynketh al aboute,
> And Venus laugheth upon every wight,
> For Januarie was bicome hir knyght
> And wolde bothe assayen his corage 1725
> In libertee, and eek in mariage;
> And with hire fyrbrond in hire hand aboute
> Daunceth biforn the bryde and al the route.
> And certeinly, I dar right wel seyn this,

Ymeneus, that god of weddyng is, 1730
Saugh nevere his lyf so myrie a wedded man.
Hoold thou thy pees, thou poete Marcian,
That writest us that ilke weddyng murie
Of hire Philologie and hym Mercurie,
And of the songes that the Muses songe! 1735
To smal is bothe thy penne, and eek thy tonge,
For to descryven of this mariage.
Whan tendre youthe hath wedded stoupyng age,
Ther is swich myrthe that it may nat be writen.
Assayeth it youreself; thanne may ye writen 1740
If that I lye or noon in this matiere.
 Mayus, that sit with so benyngne a chiere,
Hire to biholde it semed fayerye.
Queene Ester looked nevere with swich an ye
On Assuer, so meke a look hath she. 1745
I may yow nat devyse al hir beautee.
But thus muche of hire beautee telle I may,
That she was lyk the brighte morwe of May,
Fulfild of alle beautee and plesaunce.

(MerchT, 1709–49)

Now answer the following questions.

1. *Compare and contrast the calendar image with Chaucer's description of January's wedding feast.*
2. *To what extent does the festive atmosphere at January's wedding celebrations include a note of threat and foreboding?*
3. *Considering the calendrical associations of their names, is May an appropriate choice of mate for January?*

However much January's celebrations might have reminded members of a medieval audience of the image of the month, they would also have registered some significant alterations. Most obvious is that January's traditional feasting has been incorporated within an aristocratic wedding feast represented in terms which Chaucer's audience would have recognised: it is crowded, festive and hierarchical. Thus a symbolic image is embedded within a realistic one. The sense of animation and atmosphere of celebration are supported by the music. The palace, 'ful of instrumentz' (1713), is exceptionally noisy: each course is accompanied by 'loud mynstralcye' (1718). In fact, the 'joye and blisse' (1712) are almost too good to be true, for the music also carries a note of menace: the players are better than Orpheus (who lost his wife), or the musicians who played before the city of Thebes (which was destroyed).

On closer inspection, the entire passage elicits a series of 'double takes': things are not what they seem at January's court. He is both the duke of Pavia celebrating his marriage and a seasonal figure behaving characteristically; while the music both promotes festivity and threatens disaster. The same doubleness pervades the references to Bacchus and Venus. Their pagan energies are released by a wedding which – if only in outward form – is a Christian union (1700–8). Exuberantly, the god of wine pours drinks, while Venus laughs and dances with her phallic firebrand before the bride and guests. These classical figures might be understood as costumed actors performing a pageant as part of the wedding festivities at a Christian court. That does not dispel their incongruous effect. Their presence and activities raise questions about the motives of January's wedding and create the impression that matters are now beyond January's control. Until this point, he has carefully argued for, planned and executed his marriage as a Christian union, ensuring that it is 'siker ynogh with hoolynesse' (1708). But his desire for May – the true driving force behind his apparently pious attitudes and actions – has unwittingly released pagan (or sexual) powers over which he has no jurisdiction and which the mere form of marriage is unlikely to contain: he is likely to become their victim, rather than their manipulator.

The idea that events are at a turning-point for January is conveyed through the ambivalence of the mirth which his wedding occasions. Ostensibly, the feast prompts joy and laughter because it is a festive event. But the mirth is double-edged, so that January's marriage is not so much celebrated as mocked. Thus, an ambiguous tone lies behind the laughter of Venus (1723) at the thought that January, not content with proving his sexual prowess as a bachelor, now intends to demonstrate it as an old married man as well. A similar irony colours the rhetorical address to 'Marcian', whose encomium on the marriage between Philology and Mercury is, we are told, inadequate as a model for describing January's marriage. The inadequacy is not all on one side: January is a self-styled intellectual and false philologist prone to twist the meaning of words (like 'paradys') until they suit his own desires. And in case there is any doubt about the ludicrous nature of January's wedding, Chaucer generalises the situation so that he and May become examples of an inevitable, time-honoured, almost inexpressible cause of mockery: 'Whan tendre youthe hath wedded stoupyng age, / Ther is swich myrthe that it may nat be writen' (1738–9).

The most incongruous feature of the entire scene is the presence of May on the dais with January. It is not only their ages which contrast, and provoke mirth, it is also their names and the associations of their names. On this occasion Chaucer is careful to remind his audience that May, no less than January, is the name of a month with its own visual associations: 'she was lyk the brighte morwe of May, / Fulfild of alle beautee and plesaunce' (1748-9). The calendar image for May bears out these details. It is always located out of doors, set with flowers and trees in full leaf. Sometimes the central figure is a young man on horseback, carrying a hawk – a squire like Damian. Or the scenes may be of love and courtship which take place in a garden or 'plesaunce'.

Just as elements in January's character can be plotted on the basis of the calendar image for that month, so can aspects of May's character and behaviour. But what is of present interest is the deliberate juxtaposition of these two characters, rooted as they are in opposite kinds of seasonal image. Their union is, at one level, unnatural, likely to lead to contention, and bodes ill for January: it is as inevitable that May will triumph over January as it is inevitable that spring will succeed in overcoming winter. For such an interpretation there is ample evidence in medieval verse, which boasts an entire genre of lyric poetry in which the personified force of winter attempts to repress a resurgent spring. Needless to say, winter always fails. Now answer the following questions.

1. *What can be said for and against interpreting the Merchant's Tale as a myth of the seasons?*
2. *How does the story of Pluto and Proserpina relate to that of January and May?*
3. *What effect does a knowledge of the seasonal background to the Merchant's Tale have on its moral content?*

It is not necessary to go too far afield to substantiate the proposition that the Merchant's Tale, whatever else it may do, incorporates a nature myth in the relationship between January and May. The tale itself includes extensive reference to a seminal story about the origins of springtime, through the presence of Pluto and Proserpina, figures who are absent from previous versions of the story. They happen to appear in January's garden just before Damian's seduction of May. Pluto sympathises with January's predicament, and Proserpina takes May's part. From their intervention follow the extraordinary events at the end of the tale. It is highly appropriate that they should act as the mythical counterparts to the story of January and May. As Chaucer reminds us, Proserpina was forcibly abducted by Pluto, king of the dark underworld (2225-36). According to Ovid, from whom Chaucer probably knew the story, Proserpina was the daughter of Ceres. She inhabited a place where it was always springtime. One day, as Proserpina gathered flowers, she was seen by Pluto, who raped her and carried her off to the underworld. Ceres searched the world for her daughter and, failing to find her, cursed the earth, causing crops to die. In other words she created the seasons, and particularly winter. Ceres eventually discovered that her daughter had become Pluto's queen. At length he agreed to let his wife spend a certain period on earth each year. At that time the ground would become fruitful again because Ceres would be happy. It would be spring.

This myth of the seasons, and how they began, underpins the story of January and May. January thinks of making love with May in terms of a rape (1750–9). Like Proserpina, May escapes from her husband's control at a time of year when conditions are especially favourable to her (2132–3). Her natural surroundings, in which January is out of place and relatively impotent are – like Proserpina's – a bright, green, flowering garden. Here *she* is in her element and able to exert control over January. Pluto dwells in darkness, like January, who is blind. So the mythology of the tale's closing section casts a particular light (or shadow) on the story of January and May: May's infidelity is as predictable as the arrival of a resurgent spring after a retentive winter.

ii. JANUARY'S GARDEN

To read the Merchant's Tale as a nature myth deprives the protagonists of independence of action and of moral responsibility. That does not square very easily with what is seen of January and May. They appear to be – or think themselves – in control of their own thoughts and actions. The extended debate at court on the merits and pitfalls of marriage, however specious January's own contribution, reveals the existence of his vigorous intellectual life. The act of choosing a bride is, again, the result of January's conscious decisions and certain (overheated) thought processes. He appears to be in every respect his own man, and capable of ensuring that his will is put into effect. Similarly May, however passive she may at first seem as the unwilling bride of January, has a mind of her own. The narrator hazards a guess (no doubt accurate) as to what she thought 'in her herte' at the sight of a mangy January crowing on the edge of their bed after a night of love-making. And, to say the very least, she connives with some enthusiasm at Damian's pursuit of her, concealing a love-letter, stealing a key, and deceiving January through verbal sleights. In spite of all that January can do, it is she who takes control.

But however autonomous January and May are, their room for

independent manoeuvre exists within constraints determined by their associations with the months. Successful as they may be in engineering congenial forms of existence, the outcome is to a considerable degree fated. So in looking at them and their behaviour we are in effect considering two levels of reality. The first level might be called that of personal existence. It is expressed through the self-consciousness of January and May and through their confidence that it is they who manipulate their own lives and those of others. The second level is of a type explored in the first part of this chapter. It is symbolic in its form of expression, but no less real for that, dealing as it does with the interrelationship of natural forces. At this level, which is accessible to the reader but beyond the awareness of the protagonists, roles are prescribed and determined by inherited patterns of meaning. An even more complex structure of 'layered' reality surrounds the garden which January builds. Now consider the following questions.

1. *In what senses is January's garden a garden of love?*
2. *What affinities does May herself have with January's garden?*
3. *Can you identify any other associations which January's garden has?*

In the mind of its creator, the garden is a place for erotic pleasure, a place where 'he wolde paye his wyf hir dette' (2048), and one blessed with energising powers, for 'thynges whiche that were nat doon abedde, / He in the gardyn parfourned hem and spedde' (2051–2). As the Merchant reminds us it is of a kind with the garden described in the *Romance of the Rose* (2031–3), dedicated to the pursuit of sexual pleasure. Appropriately enough, the pagan Priapus is invoked as a god who might bear testimony to the excellence of January's construction (2034–7). Called here the 'god of gardyns', Priapus was also remembered as the god who was ridiculed when he was discovered naked in one such place, attempting to seduce a nymph and sporting an erect penis.

The second layer of reality corresponds to the calendrical level previously identified. It is not part of January's intention, but in making his garden he is in effect creating an environment in which May herself is likely to be naturally dominant for, as has been noted, the month after which she is named was habitually imaged as a garden. Within that setting one would expect to find not an old man but a young squire engaged in amorous pursuits. In this respect, Damian plays the appropriate role at the appropriate time. In a garden representing the season of May, with its flowers, sunny warmth, bright blue sky and fresh, green appearance (2219–36), he and the 'fresshe May, that is so bright and sheene' (2328) form a seasonal tableau.

An altogether different transformation in the meaning of the garden occurs when January invites May to it with these words:

> 'Rys up, my wyf, my love, my lady free!
> The turtles voys is herd, my dowve sweete;
> The wynter is goon with alle his reynes weete. 2140
> Com forth now, with thyne eyen columbyn!
> How fairer been thy brestes than is wyn!
> The gardyn is enclosed al aboute;
> Com forth, my white spouse! Out of doute
> Thou hast me wounded in myn herte, O wyf! 2145
> No spot of thee ne knew I al my lyf.
> Com forth, and lat us taken oure disport;
> I chees thee for my wyf and my confort.'
>
> (MerchT, 2138–48)

January's words recall verses from the biblical Canticle of Canticles (or Song of Songs), attributed to Solomon. Lines 2138–40 echo Canticles 2: 10–12:

> Behold, my beloved speaketh to me: Arise, make haste, my love, my dove, my beautiful one, and come:
> For winter is now past, the rain is over and gone.
> The flowers have appeared in our land: the time of pruning is come: the voice of the turtle is heard in our land ...

Line 2142 quotes from chapter 4, verse 10:

> How beautiful are thy breasts, my sister, my spouse! thy breasts are more beautiful than wine, and the sweet smell of thy ointments above all aromatical spices.

The following line recalls verse 12 of the same chapter:

> My sister, my spouse, is a garden enclosed, a fountain sealed up.

Line 2146 uses the same image as that found in verse 7 of chapter 4:

> Thou art all fair, O my love, and there is not a spot in thee.

The biblical poem was known to Chaucer's audience as an allegory of the love that existed between Christ and the church, expressed historically through his love for Mary and spiritually through his love for the human soul. Within this range of meaning lay the Christian reality of the text. That January is blind to the possible application of his words is clear from the line with which Chaucer concludes the pastiche: 'Swiche olde lewed wordes used he' (2149), where 'lewed' may mean both 'ignorant' and 'lecherous'. In other words, he can see no further than the literal level of meaning; he cannot get beyond the erotic content of the sacred text. Now answer the following questions.

1. *In what ways is the garden of the Canticle like or unlike January's garden?*
2. *Evaluate the relative authority which attaches to each 'transformation' of January's garden.*
3. *Do the various gardens to which the poem alludes share any common features?*
4. *To what extent do January, May and the reader have different understandings of the way in which the Merchant's Tale ends?*

That the Canticle of Canticles – whatever else it may be – is about sexual love, is impossible to deny. Sexual anticipation and arousal are rendered in terms of the sensual and natural appeal of the garden. Here, the poem has much in common with the *Romance of the Rose,* and with the Merchant's Tale itself. For example, the female speaker of the Canticle is represented as a 'garden enclosed' waiting to be 'unlocked' by her lover: 'My beloved put his hand through the key-hole, and my bowels were moved at his touch ... I opened the bolt of my door to my beloved' (Canticles 5: 4 and 6). This order of imaging helps to identify another layer of reality in the representation of January's garden. It, no less than its biblical counterpart, functions as a topographical version of May's body. She is associated with stone, the material out of which the garden wall is built (1818 and 1990). The wall is penetrated by a gate, a 'smale wyket' (2045), to which January alone has the key until Damian counterfeits one, so gaining secret entry to the garden. In a similar way, January has exclusive access to May's body until Damian finds a way of gaining entry: 'in he throng' (2353).

What therefore unites the different levels of reality, as far as January's garden is concerned, is the common theme of human sexuality. Each level offers a different slant on the uses and abuses of erotic love. In the *Rose* garden sexual pleasure is a good in itself. In the May garden it is part of the natural order. In the Canticles garden it is sanctified by association with Christ and the church. The final level of reality endorses such an interpretation, for it reconstitutes the original moment when an awareness of sexuality was born. As has often been said, the closing scene of the Merchant's Tale travesties events in the garden of Eden. For this there is some preparation. January compares marriage with 'paradys' (1265), a word that is later equated with May herself (1822). The origins of wives are traced by the Merchant, somewhat caustically, to the creation of Eve, a wife supposedly being man's 'helpe and ... confort' and his 'paradys terrestre' (1331–2). Having chosen May for his wife, January worries if the possession of 'hevene in erthe' (1647) won't limit his chances of attaining heavenly bliss. What promotes his enjoyment of an earthly paradise is, of course, the building of his own Eden in the form of a walled garden. With expectations raised and the scene set, it is all but inevitable that events within the garden should follow those in the first paradise. And so it transpires. A tree is the focus of activity, the desire for fruit the immediate occasion of May's fall, the cause her own consent and the presence of a demon (Damian) who is like a snake, 'the naddre' (1786).

Identifying the garden's different levels of reality does not solve the problem of moral responsibility. Their parodic Fall over, January and May remain sublimely ignorant of the larger significance of where they are, what they have done, and the consequences of their attitudes and actions. Indeed it might be said that, as far as they are concerned, the story ends happily: May has satisfied her desire for Damian; and January, contentedly patting his wife's belly, can look forward to an heir of sorts. For readers it is otherwise. There is by this time an immense distance between the limited self-awareness (or devoted self-interest) of January and May, and the relatively expansive overview which Chaucer has made accessible to his audience through – among other things – the calendrical conduct of January and May, and his polyvalent representation of the garden. The sense of discrepancy between what the protagonists understand of themselves, and what we might understand about them, has led many a reader to regard the tale as an exercise in black comedy (with a happy ending that inverts the usual expectations of that convention), or just downright cynical.

For the ending calls into question the validity of all those high-falutin ramifications of meaning which it is possible to elicit from the names of January and May, and from January's garden. They are evidently irrelevant to the continued existence and happiness of January and May in their world of politicised sexuality. But to deny the reality of the received interpretation of the Canticles garden (for example) was not an option open to members of Chaucer's culture. It was presumed truth, a starting-point, and standard of measurement. A contemporary reader would therefore have been challenged, but also obliged, to form some sort of moral, or spiritual, estimate of the behaviour of January and May, however successful they might seem to be in evading the responsibilities or consequences of their own actions.

It nevertheless remains true that Chaucer does not propel his readers or listeners in the direction of a particular interpretation. Instead he enables judgement to be made by providing access to a range of contexts, or levels, which raise moral or spiritual questions. If January and May dodge their obligations in this respect the issues cannot so easily be dodged by an audience, but they are left with the freedom to make up their own minds (within certain parameters) about January and May.

iii. DISCUSSION POINTS

Read carefully the description of January's wedding night at lines 1795–1865 and then answer the following questions.

1. *To what extent does Chaucer show that the activities of January and May are determined by natural forces?*
2. *What elements of the calendar image of January are found here?*
3. *How does this passage demonstrate that January is, metaphorically speaking, blind?*
4. *Does this passage anticipate in any ways the ideas later explored through the representation of January's garden?*
5. *In what ways does Chaucer contrast the behaviour, point of view and experience of January and May?*
6. *Identify the frequency of words associated with work, and discuss their immediate and wider contexts.*

The following questions are related more generally to the Merchant's Tale.

7. *Explore the character of January as an expression of intellectual blindness.*
8. *To what extent is January blinded by lust?*
9. *How significant is jealousy as a force which distorts January's perception of May?*
10. *To what extent and in what ways is January responsible for the misfortunes which befall him?*
11. *Can May's behaviour be excused?*
12. *Do you think that the narrator's description of Damian as a 'naddre' is appropriate?*

iv. FURTHER READING

a. Sources and contexts

The Holy Bible: Douay Version 1609, translated from the Latin Vulgate (Douay, A.D. 1609; Rheims, A.D. 1582) (London: Catholic Truth Society, 1956.)

b. Selected studies

Adams, John F., 'The Janus Symbolism in "The Merchant's Tale"', *Studies in Medieval Culture,* 4 (1974), 446–51.

Explores the mythological, astrological and seasonal implications of January's name, and their relation to the tale's realism and moral issues.

Bleeth, Kenneth A., 'The Image of Paradise in the *Merchant's Tale',* in *The Learned and the Lewed: Studies in Chaucer and Medieval Literature,* ed. Larry D. Benson, Harvard English Studies 5, (Cambridge, MA: Harvard University Press, 1974), pp. 45–60.

Explores the parodic references to the biblical paradise in the first part of the tale.

Burrow, J. A., 'Irony in the Merchant's Tale', *Anglia,* 75 (1957), 199–208.

The unrelenting, ironical scrutiny of January and the other characters makes the Merchant's tale a medieval *Madame Bovary,* a quality tempered by the poem's tendency towards allegory (as, for example, in representing January's garden), which counters irony with pathos and with a widening frame of significance and reference.

Brown, Emerson, Jr, 'Chaucer and a Proper Name: January in *The Merchant's Tale', Names,* 31 (1983), 79–87.

On the implications of January's name (especially its derivation from Janus) for the thematic development of the Merchant's Tale.

Donovan, Mortimer J., 'The Image of Pluto and Proserpine in the Merchant's Tale', *Philological Quarterly,* 36 (1957), 49–60.

Parallels between the story and characteristics of Pluto and Proserpine, and those of January and May.

Kee, Kenneth, 'Two Chaucerian Gardens', *Medieval Studies,* 23 (1961), 154–62.

Classical models and the biblical idea of an earthly paradise fuse, but with different emphases, in Chaucer's representation of January's garden, and the garden of the Franklin's Tale.

Olson, Paul A., 'Chaucer's Merchant and January's "Hevene in Erthe Heere"', *English Literary History,* 28 (1961), 203–14.

On January's morally ambivalent perceptions of paradise and on Chaucer's representation of his blindness and garden.

Stock, Lorraine K., '"Making It" in the Merchant's Tale: Chaucer's Signs of January's Fall', *Semiotica,* 63 (1987), 171–83.

On the various meanings of January's garden.

Tuve, Rosemond, *Seasons and Months: Studies in a Tradition of Middle English Poetry* (Paris: Librairie Universitaire, 1933; repr. Cambridge: Brewer, 1974).

Pages 122–91 on traditions in the medieval visual arts of representing seasonal activities, months and the zodiac.

Wimsatt, James I., 'Chaucer and the Canticle of Canticles', in *Chaucer the Love Poet,* ed. Jerome Mitchell and William Provost (Athens: University of Georgia Press, 1973), pp. 66–90.

On the traditional spiritual meanings of the erotic poem and its influence on religious and secular writing, including the Miller's Tale and Merchant's Tale.

Wurtele, Douglas, 'The Blasphemy of Chaucer's Merchant', *Annuale Medievale,* 21 (1981), 91–110.

The implication of January's parody of the Song of Songs, and that of other features of the tale, is that May is a travesty of the virgin Mary.

CHAPTER SIX

The Franklin's Tale

i. THE VIRTUES OF PATIENCE

So far, this book has concentrated on ways in which Chaucer conveys meaning through character and through image. Occasionally, as in the Wife of Bath's Tale, he opts for a more direct statement or discussion of ideas which elsewhere are mediated through a January or through a prison. The more direct method of working is the subject of the first part of the present chapter, which considers the treatment of patience in the Franklin's Tale, and particularly in the opening lines of the narrative. Strictly speaking, the statement made there about patience is not unmediated at all: it is uttered by the Franklin in the context of an account of a fictional marriage. Nevertheless, the speaking is so direct, and is so much an appeal to first principles, that the immediate circumstances which have prompted it seem secondary. As with the unadorned treatment of *gentillesse* in the Wife of Bath's Tale, it is as if Chaucer is addressing a topic close to his heart.

That patience was a subject which gave him pause for thought is clear from the Clerk's Tale, where it characterises the conduct of the heroine, Griselde, in spite of all the hardship she suffers at the hands of her husband. In the Merchant's incredulous response to the Clerk's Tale, with its unfavourable comparisons between Griselde and his own wife, as well as through the Wife of Bath's revolt against the idea of the submissive wife, Chaucer recognised that the practice of patience (within marriage or elsewhere) was difficult and contentious. But Chaucer was not alone in identifying patience as a key issue for members of his society. For his contemporary, William Langland, the author of *Piers Plowman,* it is a recurrent theme; and another poet of the period, the unknown author of *Sir Gawain and the Green Knight,* devotes an entire work to it. His *Patience,* written in north-western dialect, begins with the following lines:

> Pacience is a poynt, thagh hit displese ofte. 1
> When hevy herttes ben hurt wyth hethyng other elles,
> Suffraunce may aswagen hem and the swelme lethe,
> For ho quelles uche a qued and quenches malyce.
>
> For quo-so suffer cowthe syt, sele wolde folwe, 5
> And quo for thro may noght thole, the thikker he sufferes.
> Then is better to abyde the bur umbestoundes
> Then ay throw forth my thro, thagh me thynk ylle.
>
> (*Patience,* lines 1–8; ed. Cawley and Anderson)

Paraphrased, the passage reads as follows. Patience is a virtue ('poynt'), even though practising it may lead to some personal discomfort. When the downhearted are treated with contempt ('hethyng') or similarly abused, then patient endurance ('Suffraunce') is a consoling and healing antidote, taking the heat out of suffering ('the swelme lethe'). Patience destroys everything bad ('quelles uche a qued') and defeats malice. Whoever knows how to endure suffering is assured of happiness ('sele'), but whoever through anger ('thro') cannot endure, then his suffering will only intensify. Hence it is better sometimes to succumb to blows, rather than to react with resentment, even if to do so goes against the grain ('thagh me thynk ylle'). Now answer the following questions.

1. *Summarise what the practice of patience entails according to the* Gawain-*poet.*
2. *What are the rewards of patience?*
3. *What are the social implications of the practice of patience?*

Patience, then, entails suffering, pain and submission, endurance, the suppression of resentment, passivity in the face of misfortune and an internalising of the aggression of others. Its eventual rewards are happiness, and the overcoming of personal difficulties. The poet goes on to connect patience with poverty – a condition in which trials and tribulations come thick and fast – and with the biblical story of Jonah, which occupies the bulk of the poem. A brief examination of the *Patience* narrative and its significance will help to provide a frame of reference for the subject of patience as it occurs in the Franklin's Tale.

A resident of Judea or Galilee, Jonah is told by God to go and prophesy to the people of a non-Jewish community at Nineveh. Jonah is not enamoured of the idea when he thinks of what the citizens of Nineveh might do to him if he stands up in their city to preach against the errors of their ways. He decides instead to rebel against God's directive, and so embarks at Joppa on a ship travelling in the opposite direction from Nineveh, towards Tarsis. Jonah feels pleased with himself, but the poet warns that he is foolish to think that he can escape the creator of the world: those who refuse to suffer only increase their eventual distress.

God now sends a storm – one that terrifies the entire ship. The mariners and voyagers pray to their different gods, but all to no avail. The wisest among them assert that there must be someone aboard who has offended his god, and they decide to identify the culprit. Eventually Jonah is discovered, oblivious to the storm, having fled from it in terror to fall asleep in the bottom of the boat. Kicked awake, he is brought up on deck, lots are cast, and Jonah is revealed as the cause of the tempest. He explains that he has attempted to escape God's demands. The others resolve to throw him overboard in an act of appeasement. At that moment a whale rises from the deep, opens its jaws, and swallows Jonah whole. The storm ceases.

In the muck and mire of the whale's belly, Jonah comes to his senses, prays to God for deliverance, and submits to his will. After three days he is vomited up at the very city to which God wanted him to go. Asked a second time if he is prepared to preach to the citizens of Nineveh, Jonah agrees. So he prophesies that the city will be destroyed within forty days. His words are effective in producing an immediate transformation in the lives of the inhabitants. To express their penitence for past sins they put on sackcloth and ashes. God therefore decides to be merciful towards the people of Nineveh and not destroy them or their city.

Jonah is exasperated at this turn of events, saying that he has gone through hell and high water to fulfil God's command, only to see his efforts come to nothing. He might just as well have stayed at home. Having retired to a place outside Nineveh in order to watch what will happen, Jonah now builds himself a bower to protect himself from the sun. God causes a woodbine to grow to increase the shade, and Jonah is extremely pleased with this stroke of luck. But on the next day God makes the plant wither and Jonah is exposed to blazing heat and a burning wind. Jonah is angry, but God has intended his experience as a lesson: if he was glad at the existence of the plant, and grieved at its loss, should not God be glad at the continued existence of the people of Nineveh and not, like Jonah, resentful at their survival? Now answer the following questions.

1. *In what ways does the biblical story of Jonah exemplify the advantages of patience?*

2. *What does Jonah's story teach about the ways of God?*
3. *What are the consequences of rebelling against God's will?*
4. *Do you perceive any similarities between the story of Jonah and that of Christ?*

The story of Jonah provides a highly effective means of exemplifying the virtue of patience. Patience, as Jonah learnt, entails the tempering of irascible, wilful and rebellious tendencies; the recognition that the ways of God are unpredictable; that he is all-powerful; that failure to be patiently submissive will only result in further tribulations; but that the practice of patience leads to an enlarged and beneficial spiritual knowledge of the nature of God. Traditionally, patience was allied with the virtue of charity – 'Charity is patient', said St Paul (I Corinthians 13:4) – and was associated with God, one of whose attributes is forbearance in dealing with rebellious human nature (Psalm 102: 8–9). As a moral quality it was considered an antidote to the vice of anger.

Jonah's tale, as it appears in *Patience,* is part of an effective homily on a virtue which seems to have preoccupied English poets in the later fourteenth century. But it is more than that: the Old Testament story is represented as an anticipation of Christ's suffering. There are a number of general correspondences: Christ was, like Jonah, a resident of Galilee, a prophet who faced the possibility (and actuality) of physical suffering and who, before his crucifixion, manifested a reluctance to be the instrument of God's will. *Patience,* however, urges more specific comparisons. Jonah's entry into the whale's belly is described as if it were a descent into hell. The place 'stank as the devil', and 'savoured as helle' (274–5). While there, Jonah prays to God from 'hellen wombe' (306). Since the entry to hell was traditionally represented as the mouth of a great beast, the connection is secure. Now the words of anguish which Jonah utters from his whale-cum-hell are a paraphrase of Psalm 68 ('Save me O God, for the waters are come in even unto my soul'), itself often illuminated with a picture of Jonah being swallowed by the whale, and a psalm which medieval theologians interpreted as being a foretaste of the voice of Christ in his passion declaring the excessiveness of his sufferings and the malice of his persecutors. The subject of the psalm is, appropriately enough, patient submission to trial and tribulation.

Again, the *Gawain*-poet reiterates from the Bible the fact that Jonah stayed in the belly of the whale for three days and three nights. This parallels the experience of Christ, who was crucified and rose from the dead on the third day following. Between his death and resurrection he descended into hell to release the virtuous people, like Adam and the prophets, who were awaiting the redemptive life and patient suffering of Christ. So Jonah, the man thrown overboard into the mouth of a great beast, signifies Christ descending into hell, a necessary part of his redeeming, sin-conquering actions, and an act made possible by patient submission to God's will to the point of death itself. Similarly, the resurrection of Christ is figured by the return of Jonah to dry land on the third day. Matthew himself reports Christ as saying: 'as Jonas was in the whale's belly three days and three nights; so shall the Son of man be in the heart of the earth three days and three nights' (Matthew 12:40).

The virtue of patience therefore boasts an impressive pedigree of champions. Expressed through the story of Jonah (as also through the story of Job), its chief exemplar is Christ himself. This inheritance is inescapable, and although the opening lines of the Franklin's Tale do not invoke the names of Christ or his precursors, their association with patience was presumed. The immediate context of the lines is, however, the nature of the marriage between Dorigen and Arveragus, which is designed to promote and preserve their mutual love:

For o thyng, sires, saufly dar I seye,
That freendes everych oother moot obeye,
If they wol longe holden compaignye.
Love wol nat been constreyned by maistrye.
Whan maistrie comth, the God of Love anon 765
Beteth his wynges, and farewel, he is gon!
Love is a thyng as any spirit free.
Wommen, of kynde, desiren libertee,
And nat to been constreyned as a thral;
And so doon men, if I sooth seyen shal. 770
Looke who that is moost pacient in love,
He is at his avantage al above.
Pacience is an heigh vertu, certeyn,
For it venquysseth, as thise clerkes seyn,
Thynges that rigour sholde never atteyne. 775
For every word men may nat chide or pleyne.
Lerneth to suffre, or elles, so moot I goon,
Ye shul it lerne, wher so ye wole or noon;
For in this world, certein, ther no wight is
That he ne dooth or seith somtyme amys. 780
Ire, siknesse, or constellacioun,
Wyn, wo, or chaungynge of complexioun
Causeth ful ofte to doon amys or speken.
On every wrong a man may nat be wreken.
After the tyme moste be temperaunce 785
To every wight that kan on governaunce.
And therfore hath this wise, worthy knyght,
To lyve in ese, suffrance hire bihight,

And she to hym ful wisly gan to swere
That nevere sholde ther be defaute in here. 790
(FrankT, 761–90)

Now answer the following questions.

1. *What are the connections between patience and married love?*
2. *How is patience an antidote to 'maistrye'?*
3. *Is patience anything more than the practice of common sense?*

The passage begins with words that are both intimate and authoritative. The narrator addresses the members of his audience directly as 'sires', and appears to take them into his confidence on an issue which is for him a matter of personal conviction – 'saufly dar I saye'. The next two lines sum up the content of the speech which follows. If amity is to be preserved (whether expressed through friendship or married love) then submission to each others' will is vital: 'everych oother moot obeye' (762). Patience is therefore identified as a virtue with social applications: it sustains 'compaignye' (763), a word itself used of the pilgrim fellowship.

The mutuality of patience is crucial. Outright dominance by one partner destroys affection, for it 'wol nat been constreyned by maistrye' (764). This is because 'maistrye', or the constraint imposed by dominance, is opposite to the natural element in which love in its various forms can thrive: freedom. Men, no less than women, therefore hate to feel that they are restricted, 'constreyned as a thral' (769). The key to preserving love (and therefore social bonds in general) is patience. As a virtue, it brings its own spiritual rewards, 'avantage al above' (772). Here, the Franklin alludes to the traditional status of patience in theological discourse. It is a 'heigh vertu', and according to the theologians, or 'clerkes', it overcomes what sheer force of will ('rigour') never can (773–4).

The exercise of patience is, after all, a matter of common sense. One cannot continually take exception at every slight misdemeanour: 'For every word men may nat chide or pleyne' (776). To learn to suffer is also an imperative because failing to do so at appropriate times will only increase the intensity of suffering at a later date. (The Franklin and the author of *Patience* would have understood each other.) Everyone is at some time guilty of causing offence, in spite of themselves, and for reasons beyond their immediate control, whether through anger, sickness, the stars, drinking, sorrow or mood. Given that this is the human condition it must be patiently tolerated, without thought of redress: 'On every wrong a man may nat be wreken' (784). Those who profess self-control, 'governaunce' (786), should respond to the effects of others' actions with temperance. In understanding the causes of their behaviour, and its circumstances, its consequences can be neutralised.

Arveragus is identified as one of those wise and tolerant people who practise patience. He promises forbearance, 'suffrance', as far as his wife Dorigen is concerned, thereby ensuring his happiness, 'To lyve in ese' (787–8). The arrangement, however, is not mutual. Dorigen herself does not promise to be patient in her dealings with Arveragus. Instead, she undertakes not to give him cause for complaint: 'she to hym ful wisly gan to swere / That never sholde ther be defaute in here' (789–90). However good her intentions, the absence of any reference to patience in Dorigen's disposition does not augur well. According to the passage itself, and to the tradition of thought which lies behind it, if she does not know how to face difficulties with patient endurance then her suffering will only increase and the lesson of patience will have to be learnt the hard way.

ii. DORIGEN'S ROCKS

No sooner is the Franklin's discussion of patience ended than the happiness of Dorigen also ends. Arveragus departs for England, to do what is expected of a knight in his position: 'To seke in armes worshipe and honour' (811). Dorigen is therefore presented with a major test to her powers of forbearance. She does indeed act in an exemplary manner, but as an *im*patient heroine.

The Franklin appears to link this attribute to her aristocratic status, thereby implying that patience is not often found, and perhaps not often needed, among those whose word is others' command. With a complete absence of philosophical resignation 'wepeth she and siketh, / As doon thise noble wyves whan hem liketh' (817–18). Her grief is extreme: she mourns, cannot sleep, wails, does not eat, utters complaints (819). She is afflicted to the point of despair and suicide but (which makes her behaviour absurd as well as poignant) it is without good cause and to no good effect: 'causeless she sleeth hirself, allas!' (825). Now answer the following questions.

1. *To what extent do the attitude and behaviour of Arveragus embody the practice of patience?*
2. *What are the symptoms and consequences of Dorigen's impatience?*
3. *How does Chaucer account for, and represent, Dorigen's social and emotional isolation?*

Impervious at first to the approaches of friends who are anxious about her condition, and who attempt to comfort and distract her, Dorigen at length accepts some consolation. Her sorrow and passionate grief, or 'rage' (836) – the very opposite of patience – are thereby assuaged. What also helps are the letters of Arveragus, bringing her news of his 'welfare' (838), and of his plans to return. These, too, counteract the more lethal consequences of Dorigen's sorrow.

Throughout this episode it is notable that Dorigen's 'rage', or inability to tolerate her situation, is isolating. Separated from Arveragus, it deprives her also of that 'compaignye' (843) of friends in which she might have found some more immediate support. It is only on their insistence that she recovers some measure of social integration. Her friends are in fact practising a kind of redemptive patience as far as she is concerned, demonstrating through their actions what the Franklin has maintained in theory: that the practice of patience is vital to the maintenance of social bonds.

What is also notable is that the application of patience and comfort to Dorigen's condition – whether through her friends or through Arveragus – is entirely from without. She has no inner resources of tolerance with which to accommodate the hardship of her husband's long absence. But there is hope, even if the education of Dorigen in this respect is a slow process. Her eventual acceptance of some comfort, at her friends' patient insistence, is likened to the gradual imprinting of a recognisable form in a stone after the long work of an engraver (829–36).

Dorigen, indeed, has a particular affinity with stone and rocks. They figure her obdurate resistance to the virtue of patience. It is as if she recognises a feature of her own inner landscape when, looking out to sea, and longing for the return of Arveragus, her eye is caught by some 'grisly rokkes blake' (859):

> Another tyme ther wolde she sitte and thynke,
> And caste hir eyen dounward fro the brynke.
> But whan she saugh the grisly rokkes blake,
> For verray feere so wolde hir herte quake 860
> That on hire feet she myghte hire noght sustene.
> Thanne wolde she sitte adoun upon the grene,
> And pitously into the see biholde,
> And seyn right thus, with sorweful sikes colde:
> 'Eterne God, that thurgh thy purveiaunce 865
> Ledest the world by certein governaunce,
> In ydel, as men seyn, ye no thyng make.

But, Lord, thise grisly feendly rokkes blake,
That semen rather a foul confusion
Of werk than any fair creacion 870
Of swich a parfit wys God and a stable,
Why han ye wroght this werk unresonable?
For by this werk, south, north, ne west, ne eest,
Ther nys yfostred man, ne bryd, ne beest;
It dooth no good, to my wit, but anoyeth. 875
Se ye nat, Lord, how mankynde it destroyeth?
An hundred thousand bodyes of mankynde
Han rokkes slayn, al be they nat in mynde,
Which mankynde is so fair part of thy werk
That thou it madest lyk to thyn owene merk. 880
Thanne semed it ye hadde a greet chiertee
Toward mankynde; but how thanne may it bee
That ye swiche meenes make it to destroyen,
Whiche meenes do no good, but evere anoyen?
I woot wel clerkes wol seyn as hem leste, 885
By argumentz, that al is for the beste,
Though I ne kan the causes nat yknowe.
But thilke God that made wynd to blowe
As kepe my lord! This my conclusion.
To clerkes lete I al disputison. 890
But wolde God that alle thise rokkes blake
Were sonken into helle for his sake!
Thise rokkes sleen myn herte for the feere.'
Thus wolde she seyn, with many a pitous teere.

(FrankT, 857–94)

Now answer the following questions.

1. *What similarities exist between Dorigen's psychological state and the rocks?*
2. *What questions do the rocks raise about the nature of God and his universe?*
3. *To what extent is Dorigen experiencing a 'loss of faith'?*

That Dorigen is looking inwards at the moment when the image of the rocks strikes her with such force is clear from the opening line: she sits and thinks, looking downwards after having scanned the open sea for her husband's ship. She is at this juncture on a high outcrop of land, 'upon the bank an heigh' (849). The description of it as a 'brynke' (858) causes a vertiginous impression: the rocks far below are a dizzying and fearsome sight. Significantly, their sight affects Dorigen's heart, petrified 'For verray feere' (860). But 'brynke' suggests more than that. In her melancholic, suggestible state, Dorigen is on the verge of psychological breakdown: the 'void with rocks' into which she stares, having stonily resisted consolation, is the void of her own identity, threatened as it is by an impatient and uncontrolled response to Arveragus' absence.

Inwardly oppressed, 'with sorweful sikes colde' (864), and looking into the rocky sea, Dorigen projects her loss of self-governance on to the world outside and its creator. What evidence is there for a universe ordered by the 'purveiaunce' and 'certein governaunce' of God when such rocks exist? Their presence testifies to confusion, a lack of plan, an absence of stability and reason. Why would God want to make anything so out of kilter with his otherwise 'fair creacion'? They benefit neither man, bird, nor beast, and do nothing but threaten and destroy on a huge scale: 'An hundred thousand bodyes of mankynde' (877). Since God made man in his own image, it would seem virtually self-destructive to create also the means of man's death. Why should rocks exist in a universe created according to principles of order, beauty and the sustenance of life? (Which is another way of asking why Arveragus' absence should threaten Dorigen's happiness to the point where she considers suicide.)

True to form, Dorigen soon abandons to 'clerkes' the theological problems she has raised, admitting that the issues are too great for her – 'To clerkes lete I al disputison' (890) – and attempting to suppress, rather than resolve, the image of the rocks, their associated problems, and their power to focus her preoccupations: ' … wolde God that all thise rokkes blake / Were sonken into helle for his sake!' (891–2). But Dorigen's soliloquy has been enough to set her personal impatience within a much wider context. The self-governance which patience enables has been connected with the governance of God, as it was earlier associated with the governance of society. And the loss of patience has been implicitly linked to a loss of faith, not only in the self, but in God as well. The 'brynke' on which Dorigen stands is therefore that of an abysm of self-doubt and despair which leads in due course to thoughts of suicide, but which at the same time images a world without God, in which chaos and destruction hold sway. The state which Dorigen is experiencing, and which she imagines having wider effects, is a hellish one. Hell is traditionally a place of confusion, a godless place 'down there' threatening human life, and Chaucer leaves us in no doubt that the rocks, whatever else their function may be, are also meant to suggest the abode of Satan. They are black, the colour of evil (as well as of melancholy); 'feendly' (868), as if devils lurk there; and seem properly to belong in hell (891–2). Thus in questioning the place of rocks within God's fair creation, Dorigen is implicitly raising the question of the place of hell and evil in a universe governed by a good God. She is on the brink of hell itself. Now examine Plate 6 carefully and answer the following questions.

1. *What connections can you make between Dorigen's experience and the image of hell?*
2. *In what ways does this image recall the story of Jonah?*
3. *In what senses is Dorigen in need of liberation, and what form does her liberation take?*

'Clerkes' familiar with the idea of hell, and with its forms of representation, would have been quick to supply an answer to Dorigen's fundamental questioning. That hell is a rocky place is clear from the illustration opposite. Entry to it is figured, as it is in *Patience,* as the mouth of a huge beast. Here, Christ is undertaking the act which Jonah's experience foretold: after the crucifixion (of which the marks are visible), he descends into hell to release the virtuous souls of such people as Adam and the prophets (including Job and Jonah) and, as shown in the drawing, other saints (the words above read: 'Sancti liberantur de inferno' – 'The saints are freed from hell'). Their long endurance of hell is a testimony to their patience, which is rewarded with liberation and heaven. But their release by Christ also dramatises the triumph of good over evil and the enthralling of Satan by one who is the supreme example of suffering patience.

Thus the 'clerkly' answer to Dorigen's predicament is that evil has its place in the world as a realm vanquished by Christ. Nevertheless, it still has fatal powers over those who fail to register and absorb the significance of his example. Dorigen, indeed, contrives to be oblivious to it. Rather than face through suffering patience the existence of the rocks, and thereby the cause of her personal distress in Arveragus' absence, she enters into a promise which conflicts directly with her commitment to her husband. It is a promise, perhaps, only half-heartedly made, but which underlies the extent to which Dorigen wants wish-fulfilment rather than a true answer to the problem she faces. Thus she undertakes to become the mistress of her husband's squire if he (Aurelius) will make the rocks disappear.

When, by magic, the rocks do appear to have gone, Dorigen is propelled further into crisis, to the point where she considers suicide. At last she is driven to confess everything to Arveragus, who has by now returned and who reacts in a manner not unlike God in his dealings with Jonah: unpredictably, and exasperatingly from Dorigen's point of view, he insists that she keep to the terms of her agreement with

Plate 6: Christ frees the saints from hell.

Aurelius. To say as much costs him dearly: he weeps in testimony to his suffering and his patience (1480). True to the terms and the spirit of his marriage he is steadfastly not taking offence at his wife's misdemeanour.

With hesitating steps, Dorigen sets out for her tryst with Aurelius. She has become, at last, the figure of someone who is internalising her difficulties and who can no longer depend on the agency of others to resolve them. Meeting Aurelius unexpectedly she explains what has happened. Aurelius is so impressed by Arveragus' integrity, and by the suffering which Dorigen now endures, that he releases her from her promise. In so doing, he causes further suffering to himself by shouldering a large debt to the clerk-magician of Orleans which he has now incurred to no avail. But the example of patience spreads like a contagion, and the clerk cancels the debt. Arveragus, Dorigen, Aurelius, clerk, all act with forbearance towards people against whom otherwise they might have had cause for redress. The practice of patience reforms and enlarges them as individuals (they have an inner autonomy and freedom which delivers them from oppression, lust and greed), and it creates a more harmonious social order. The fabric of Arveragus' society was on the brink of disintegration, but it has been brought back from the abyss. In achieving this, the practice of patience has been crucial.

iii. DISCUSSION POINTS

Read carefully lines 1499–1556 of the Franklin's Tale and answer the following questions on the final meeting of Dorigen and Aurelius.

1. *Compare and contrast the place in which Aurelius meets Dorigen with the place in which he first speaks to her (lines 901–1020).*
2. *Comment on the use of the word 'trouthe' in this passage and relate it to other uses of the same word.*
3. *How is Aurelius' attitude to Dorigen different from his previous attitudes, and what accounts for this change of heart?*
4. *Compare and contrast the emotional states of Dorigen and Aurelius.*
5. *To what extent is* gentillesse *a key concept in this passage and for the tale as a whole?*
6. *What importance is attached to promises here and elsewhere in the Franklin's Tale, and why?*
7. *Is the marital relationship of Dorigen and Arveragus at the end of the story essentially the same as it was at the beginning, or not?*

The following questions are related more generally to the Franklin's Tale.

8. *What connections do you perceive between the biblical story of Job (as told by the* Patience *poet) and the Franklin's Tale?*
9. *In what ways does the Franklin's Tale show that the practice of patience is vital to the maintenance of stable human relationships?*
10. *To what extent can lines 857–94 be seen as a passage in which the key issues of the Franklin's Tale meet?*
11. *In what respects does Aurelius develop as a character as the tale progresses?*
12. *How important is the role of Arveragus to the development of the Franklin's Tale?*
13. *Comment on the treatment of 'illusion' within the Franklin's Tale.*

iv. FURTHER READING

a. Sources and contexts

Cawley, A. C., and J. J. Anderson, (eds), *Pearl, Cleanness, Patience, Sir Gawain and the Green Knight* (rev. edn, London: Dent, 1976).

b. Selected studies

Andrew, Malcolm, 'Jonah and Christ in *Patience*', *Modern Philology,* 70 (1972–73), 230–3.

Jonah's experiences anticipate, and contrast with, Christ's.

Mann, Jill, 'Chaucerian Themes and Style in the *Franklin's Tale*', in *Medieval Literature: Chaucer and the Alliterative Tradition,* ed. Boris Ford, The New Pelican Guide to English Literature, vol. 1, pt 1 (Harmondsworth: Penguin, 1982), pp. 133–53.

On the treatment of patience, time and change, and the bearing of the Franklin's Tale on the *Canterbury Tales* as a whole.

Owen, Charles A., Jr, 'The Crucial Passages in Five of the *Canterbury Tales:* A Study in Irony and Symbol', *Journal of English and Germanic Philology,* 52 (1953), 294–311. Repr. in *Chaucer: Modern Essays in Criticism,* ed. Edward Wagenknecht (London: Oxford University Press, 1959), pp. 251–70.

The rocks reinforce the theme of appearance and reality by functioning as a symbolic image which changes meaning in Dorigen's eyes from love menaced to love made permanent (pp. 252–5).

CHAPTER SEVEN
The Pardoner's Prologue and Tale

i. THE PORTRAIT OF HYPOCRISY

The 'clerkes' to whom Dorigen refers in the Franklin's Tale, those who studied, advanced, debated and upheld interpretations of the Bible, were in positions of great responsibility. Deferred to by lay people (like Dorigen) as authorities, they exerted considerable influence. Their activities were, of course, regulated by the church itself, which policed its own intellectuals to ensure that unorthodox views, and especially ones hostile to its own institutional power, were not broadcast. The biblical text itself was embedded in the time-honoured interpretations of the church fathers (like Jerome) and other scholars. As may be imagined, there existed by Chaucer's lifetime a vast accretion of approved commentaries on the Bible. It was a text thoroughly mediated by ecclesiastical authority.

To those who could not read Latin – the majority of the lay population – the Bible was a closed book, known only through the agency of clerics acting as interpreters and translators within the context of a church service or of open-air preaching. During Chaucer's lifetime, however, literacy in English was increasing. It was prompted in part by mercantile people (represented by members of his own family) who needed the skills of writing and reading for the conduct of business. Consequently the demand for literature in English grew. Much of the material produced for the expanding numbers of English readers was of a devotional nature, and it did not exclude translations of the Bible and versions of biblical commentaries.

One relatively early example is a translation of the Psalms by the mystical writer and hermit, Richard Rolle, completed before 1349. Although undertaken for a nun associated with Rolle's own abbey of Hampole, his English psalter subsequently enjoyed wide circulation. Copies of it were owned by devout lay people as well as by clerics. It included a commentary based on a revered author, Peter Lombard, whose *Sentences* were required reading for anyone wishing to make a serious study of the Bible.

As an example of Rolle's translation of the Psalms – an example the relevance of which will gradually become clear – consider his version of Psalm 13, which begins, 'The fool said in his heart: There is no God'. Towards the end of the third verse the psalmist elaborates on God-denying fools:

> A byriel openyng is the throte of them. With her tungis triccherously thei wrought; venym of snakis undir the lippis of hem. Whos mouth is ful of cursyng and bittirnesse: swifte ben her feett to spille blood. Soruwe and unhap in the weyes of hem: and the weye of pees thei knewe not, the dreede of god is not bifore the eyen of hem. Ne shal thei not knowe all that worchith wikkednesse: the whiche deuourith my folk as mete of breed. God thei in callide not: ther thei qwoke for drede whar dreede was not. For oure lord is in ryghtwis getyng: the counceyl of helplees you shamed, for oure lord is the hope of hym.
>
> (Psalm 13: 3–6, trans. Rolle, ed. Bramley)

A modern biblical version reads:

> … Their throat is an open sepulchre: with their tongues they acted deceitfully; the poison of asps is under their lips.
>
> Their mouth is full of cursing and bitterness: their feet are swift to shed blood.
>
> Destruction and unhappiness in their ways; and the way of peace they have not known: there is no fear of God before their eyes.
>
> Shall not all they know that work iniquity, who devour my people as they eat bread?
>
> They have not called upon the Lord; there have they trembled for fear where there was no fear.
>
> For the Lord is in the just generation; you have confounded the counsel of the poor man: but the Lord is his hope.
>
> (Psalm 13: 3–6; Douay-Rheims version)

In certain circumstances, the translation of the Bible into English might become a political issue. For the sacred text and its interpretation thereby escape the control of the church and its officers and become instead directly accessible to literate lay people. The political dimension of vernacular biblical translation in the later fourteenth and early fifteenth centuries is clear from the activities of the Oxford clerical reformer John Wyclif (*c.*1330–84) and his followers. They initiated a translation of the entire Bible into English, while at the same time criticising abuses and corruption within the established church. Not infrequently, they used the biblical text itself as a means of attacking their targets. A Wycliffite commentary on Psalm 13, for example, launches an assault on gluttony and clerical hypocrisy:

> Truly, wicked men corrupt their neighbours because their mouth is like an open sepulchre, killing men through evil air, and swallowing them. Thus they kill those who incline to listen, through their wicked denial of God's wishes, in vicious and over-delicate living ... they are buried in obstinacy, condemned to live in sinfulness until their lives' end. The 'open grave' also signifies gluttony, which wastes both physical and spiritual goods ... 'Poison of asps' means the incorrigible malice under the tongues of those whom, because their hearts are set on vainglory of the world, God's love and fear cannot affect ... Their mouths are always ready to abuse and reprove and threaten boastfully by virtue of their own authority and greed, not charitably and meekly to amend sin for Christ's sake ... They 'devour my people' – that is, they greedily eat and waste their goods, by which the people should be sustained, as they do who come falsely to the offices of holy church in order to win riches and honour of men and not to heal man's soul: not to praise God but to devour God's folk, eating luxuriously ... stealing goods from simple, undeserving men ... their asking and taking is unjust robbery resulting in their own damnation, for proud, covetous men are not called by God. 'They have not called upon the Lord': here the prophet speaks of covetous men coming into the church more for pleasure and to acquire riches than for the love of God ... for however meek they might seem to the people, they are, through false living and greedy taking of goods, ravishing wolves ... therefore they 'trembled for fear when there was no fear', because in name they are men of holy church ... and should not dread the wrath of God ... 'For the Lord is in the just generation' ... that is in those who are truly in good conversation and true teaching of God's law, giving to God also the tithes and offerings which are his true part ... But in untrue getting and giving is not God, but the devil ... Priests who through pride and covetousness despise on earth to follow Christ in humility and wilful poverty shall be shamed by God.
>
> (Unpublished Wycliffite commentary on Psalm 13, modernised from British Library MS, Royal 18 D.I)

Now answer the following questions.

1. *How does the Wycliffite commentator use the text of Psalm 13 to make his points?*
2. *What forms do 'sins of the mouth' take, what images are used to describe them, and with what effects?*
3. *In what respects is the Wycliffite commentary relevant to the Pardoner?*

Much of what the Wycliffite polemicist writes applies to the Pardoner. His abuse of authority, devotion to greed and the pleasures of the alehouse, reckless exploitation of the poor and ignorant, refusal to live in poverty, and obstinate rejection of virtuous living, spring to mind. But it is his account of preaching techniques which brings him especially close to the Wycliffite portrait:

> I stonde lyk a clerk in my pulpet,
> And whan the lewed peple is doun yset,
> I preche so as ye han herd bifoore
> And telle an hundred false japes moore.
> Thanne peyne I me to strecche forth the nekke, 395
> And est and west upon the peple I bekke,
> As dooth a dowve sittynge on a berne.
> Myne handes and my tonge goon so yerne
> That it is joye to se my bisynesse.
> Of avarice and of swich cursednesse 400
> Is al my prechyng, for to make hem free
> To yeven hir pens, and namely unto me.
> For myn entente is nat but for to wynne,
> And nothyng for correccioun of synne.
> I rekke nevere, whan that they been beryed, 405
> Though that hir soules goon a-blakeberyed!
> For certes, many a predicacioun
> Comth ofte tyme of yvel entencioun;
> Som for plesance of folk and flaterye,
> To been avaunced by ypocrisye, 410
> And som for veyne glorie, and som for hate.
> For whan I dar noon oother weyes debate,
> Thanne wol I stynge hym with my tonge smerte
> In prechyng, so that he shal nat asterte
> To been defamed falsly, if that he 415
> Hath trespased to my bretheren or to me.
> For though I telle noght his propre name,
> Men shal wel knowe that it is the same,
> By signes, and by othere circumstances.
> Thus quyte I folk that doon us displesances; 420
> Thus spitte I out my venym under hewe
> Of hoolynesse, to semen hooly and trewe.
>
> (PardP, 391–422)

Now answer the following questions.

1. *What similarities and differences do you detect between the above passage and the Wycliffite commentary on Psalm 13?*
2. *To what extent is the Pardoner a hypocrite in Wycliffite terms?*
3. *In this passage, how does the Pardoner disarm criticism?*

The hypocritical nature of the Pardoner's performance is signalled in the first line: he is 'lyk a clerk' – a comparison which raises the question of whether or not he is a true clerk. But since to all appearances, standing in his pulpit and accentuating his words with oratorical gestures, he *is* a clerk, he is in a strong position to exercise authority and control, especially when the members of the congregation are uninformed and impressionable, or 'lewed', relying on him for spiritual guidance. The less ignorant among Chaucer's own audience might have had pause for thought at the Pardoner's second simile: his nodding at listeners from right to left, like a dove sitting on a barn. It is a homely image appropriate to the rural origins of the people whom he usually addresses, but it is also a disturbing one, since the dove was inevitably read as a sign for the holy spirit. Whatever he may seem to be, it would be difficult to imagine an individual less spiritual than the Pardoner. He is not what he seems.

As the Pardoner goes on to explain, his objective is to raise consciousness about the sin of avarice, sensitising his audience to the point where they are prepared to give away their money – not to the church as part of its sanctioned collecting of tithes and offerings, but to the Pardoner himself. His intention is only financial gain, not the curing of souls. In claiming such a motive, he allies himself with the target of Wycliffite polemic, which highlights the corrosive effects of clerics who, through self-interest, care little for the souls of the faithful. The Wycliffite writer would hardly have agreed with the Pardoner that good can come of such 'yvel entencioun', but he would readily have recognised the nature of those intentions. For they are the same as those identified in the biblical commentary: the desire to please, a love of flattery, the lure of professional or social advancement, vanity or 'veyne glorie' (411), and vindictiveness.

In view of the emphasis placed by the Wycliffite author on the venomous loquacity of false clerics, it is interesting that the Pardoner makes special mention of his own verbal assaults. When debate fails, he launches a stinging attack on his opponent from the safety of the pulpit. False defamation is for him a justifiable weapon if anyone has been so presumptuous as to attack either him or his brethren. His all-devouring mouth thus becomes the open sepulchre of the psalmist. His vengeance is achieved from a place (the church pulpit) which should be a forum for the display of exemplary virtue. Standing there, the Pardoner represents instead malicious clerical hypocrisy, and he fixes the image with words that recall the Middle English words of Psalm 13: 'With her tungis triccherously thei wrought; venym of snakis undir the lippis of hem': 'Thus spitte I out my venym under hewe / Of hoolynesse, to semen hooly and trewe' (421–2). The Pardoner is more truly a serpent, the agent of the devil, than a dove, the messenger of God.

In considering a Wycliffite psalm and commentary as texts which inform the Pardoner's Prologue, what kind of exercise are we engaged in? It would be claiming too much for the Wycliffite material to say that it was, in the conventional sense, a source of Chaucer's composition. What it does point to, however, is the existence – independent of Chaucer's writings – of a discourse sharply critical of certain kinds of clerical hypocrisy, and linked to the idea of the God-denying fool as expressed in the Psalms. Whether the Wycliffites originated that discourse, or whether they adopted and developed an established one, is a moot point. What is certain is that Chaucer is drawing on, and engaging with, an established language of anticlerical satire, the evidence for which also surfaces in Wycliffite writings.

ii. DICING WITH DEATH

One symptom of foolishness is wilful ignorance. The Pardoner, for all that he professes to know the significance of poverty and humility within Christian teaching, fails to apply that knowledge to himself. The rioters of his tale are in a similar plight and, towards the end of their violent lives, they participate in a tableau which vividly expresses their blindness to spiritual truth. Before doing so, they are given an opportunity to reject their sinful ways, but choose to ignore it. They meet at a stile a mysterious old man who in appearance and manner is a reproach to their form of life and a challenge to renounce it. Being old and poor, where they are young and hungry for wealth, he deserves considerate treatment. Instead, the rioters are overbearing; but the old man meets their bullying ways with humility and self-effacing modesty. It soon emerges that they also see death in opposite ways: the rioters want to vanquish it in revenge for the death of their friend; the old man, however, wants nothing so much as to be overcome by death. In all this, the dialogue is itself a measure of the distance between opposing attitudes. The old man returns loud insults and uncontrolled blasphemy with quiet protest and a scattering of heartfelt blessings and biblical allusions. But neither what he says, nor what he is, has any effect on the rioters' headlong rush to their own destruction. At last, the scene for the tableau where they meet death is set as he directs them to their desired destination:

> 'Now, sires,' quod he, 'if that yow be so leef 760
> To fynde Deeth, turne up this croked wey,
> For in that grove I lafte hym, by my fey,
> Under a tree, and there he wolde abyde;
> Noght for youre boost he wolde hym no thyng hyde.

> Se ye that ook? Right there ye shal hym fynde. 765
> God save yow, that boghte agayn mankynde,
> And yow amende!' Thus seyde this olde man;
> And everich of thise riotoures ran
> Til he cam to that tree, and ther they founde
> Of floryns fyne of gold ycoyned rounde 770
> Wel ny an eighte busshels, as hem thoughte.
> No lenger thanne after Deeth they soughte,
> But ech of hem so glad was of that sighte,
> For that the floryns been so faire and brighte,
> That doun they sette hem by this precious hoord. 775
> (PardT, 760–75)

Now answer the following questions.

1. *Describe the differences in attitude of the old man and the rioters.*
2. *What are the dominant features of the landscape in this scene, and what do those features signify?*
3. *Who or what is responsible for the rioters' deaths?*

The old man's words are a test of perceptiveness as much for the reader as for the rioters. They are hell-bent on finding death, believing him to be an individual who has slain their companion, whom they in turn will kill. Such literalism pervades their attitudes. But the old man offers another perspective, one which diminishes the drunken blustering of the rioters to self-destructive folly. We, but not they, might therefore catch the note of incredulity and regret in the old man's 'if': 'if that yow be so leef / To fynde Deeth, turne up this croked wey' (760–1).

Even the landscape, in this haunting episode, has a double value. For the rioters it is no more than the terrain they must cross to track down their quarry. But 'croked wey' has another resonance. It recalls the path of sin, the opposite of the straight and narrow path of virtue. Metaphorically speaking, the rioters (or 'anti-pilgrims') are already well advanced along the crooked way by the time that they reach the stile, having dedicated their lives to greed, gluttony and blasphemy. What lies at the end of the crooked path? Death, in a grove, under a tree. What the rioters first find there, of course, is a fabulous horde of gold, the sight of which whips them into a frenzy of divisive avarice, and which thereby causes their own destruction. This is the inexorable logic of inveterate sin: it blots out the spiritual world and destroys its practitioners. But even as the inevitable drama unfolds, an alternative view of human existence forms a backdrop to the action. To a Christian audience, the old man's reference to death, under a tree, would unavoidably recall an image of the crucifixion. It was by first dying on a tree that Christ did indeed overcome death, and rose from the grave. The idea was sometimes expressed pictorially by showing a skull at the foot of the cross. (Christ was crucified at Golgotha, the place of skulls, and on the spot – so legend had it – of Adam's burial.) The juxtaposition of Christ's victory with the pitiful bragging of the rioters, that they will kill Death, only increases the sense of their utter perdition and the depths of their ignorant blasphemy. As if to bring the image of the crucifixion into sharper focus, the old man at this point makes a specific allusion to Christ's sacrifice: 'God save yow, that boghte agayn mankynde' (766). Again, the value put here on the idea of spiritual, redemptive purchase is altogether different from its value in the minds of the rioters, whose obsession is entirely with gold, the 'floryns ... faire and brighte' (774), the sight of which they find so elating, so blinding.

The tableau, then, is complete: at the foot of the tree, in a grove which lies at the end of a crooked path, the three rioters exult in their new-found riches. Unknown to them, they have found Death. Equally unknown to them in their folly, they are enacting a parody of a crucifixion scene. The tree with death at its foot acts as an emblem of the cross, and they themselves have a role prefigured in the biblical story. For the rioters, whatever else they may be, are gamblers, viewing life itself as a game of chance. The treasure which they have discovered is a gift of Fortune (779); they draw lots to decide who should go to town for bread and wine, those potent symbols of Christ's body and blood (793–805); and as rich men the two who remain look forward to lives of perpetual 'hasardrye': 'Thanne may we bothe oure luste all fulfille, / And pleye at dees right at oure owene wille' (833–4). At the crucifixion itself soldiers, failing to recognise the divinity of Christ, cast lots for his clothes. St John's gospel includes the story of Christ's seamless coat:

> 23. The soldiers, therefore, when they had crucified him, took his garments (and they made four parts, to every soldier a part) and also his coat. Now the coat was without seam, woven from the top throughout.
> 24. They said then one to another: Let us not cut it, but let us cast lots for it, whose it shall be; that the scripture might be fulfilled, saying: They have parted my garments among them, and upon my vesture have they cast lots. And the soldiers indeed did these things.
>
> (John 19: 23–4)

Now look carefully at the next picture (Plate 7), and answer the following questions.

1. *To what extent does the picture (a) illustrate, (b) elaborate the biblical passage?*
2. *'The picture, like the Pardoner's Tale, includes two levels of*

Plate 7: The crucifixion, with soliders dicing.

understanding of Christ's sacrifice: the literal and the symbolic.' Discuss.

3. *In what ways does an examination of this picture enhance your understanding of the Pardoner's Prologue and Tale?*

The biblical episode is well represented in this French missal of the late fifteenth century. Two soldiers, eyes downcast, watching nothing but the fall of dice, oblivious to the profound importance of the scene in which they act, gamble for Christ's coat. It is a painting which captures well the kind of double perception explored in the Pardoner's Tale. Behind the dicers stand two other soldiers, looking upwards towards Christ as if recognising him as God's son. Unconsciously, and to signal their realisation, the staves of the weapons which they carry form a crucifix. The extremes of perception are rendered more obviously in the group at the foot of the cross: Mary Magdalene kneels with a pot of ointment at her feet; Christ's mother swoons and is comforted by John and her other companion. Two women pray. Each member of this group, like Christ himself, has a halo. They share his light. But in the gloomy background a soldier taunts and rails; others march away, their job of execution done; and scribes and pharisees watch the events with some satisfaction.

Some attention to the imagery of the crucifixion, and of dicing in particular, allows us to place the rioters more securely in relation to Christian ideology. In retrospect, the wider significance of dicing has been in play, directly and indirectly, throughout the Pardoner's Prologue and Tale. Thus one rioter refers to the tools of the gambler's trade, in a typically foul-mouthed way, as 'The bicched bones two' (656). But other bones are the occasion for cursing and blasphemy, notably 'Goddes digne bones' (695), by which is meant the bones of Christ. With this is introduced the idea of holy relics, and so one is led back to the narrator himself and the worthless relics – pigs' bones – which he himself carries. Such is the insistence of the prologue and tale, however, on evaluation, on setting the claims of the material world against those of the spiritual world, that the matter cannot be left there. The Pardoner's relics may be impotent, but does it follow that all holy relics are thereby rendered useless? Are the bones of Christ to be treated with similar contempt? Are not the pilgrims themselves on their way to a shrine which contained the bones of a saint, Thomas Becket, which were considered to have miraculous qualities?

iii. DISCUSSION POINTS

Read carefully lines 661–701 of the Pardoner's Tale, which describe the rioters in a tavern, and answer the following questions.

1. *In what ways is this episode a turning-point in the narrative?*
2. *Describe the atmosphere of this passage and discuss the ways in which that atmosphere is evoked.*
3. *Compare and contrast the attitudes to death of the knave and the taverner on the one hand and the rioter on the other.*
4. *Is the setting of the scene significant?*
5. *What resonance does the blaspheming of the rioter have for the tale as a whole?*
6. *Visualise and describe the appearance, activities and effects of Death.*

The following questions are related more generally to the Pardoner's Prologue and Tale.

7. *In what respects can the Pardoner be said to be a 'fool'?*
8. *What sins hold the key to the Pardoner's hypocrisy?*
9. *To what extent are Chaucer's sympathies with the illiterate people whom the Pardoner dupes?*
10. *What evidence is there to support the view that the rioters are blind to spiritual truth?*
11. *Consider how the image of the crucifixion has been suggested* before *the rioters reach the grove, through references to the body and blood of Christ.*
12. *In what ways does the Pardoner challenge the motives of Chaucer's pilgrims in travelling to Canterbury?*

iv. FURTHER READING

a. Sources and contexts

Bramley, H. R. (ed.), *The Psalter or Psalms of David ...*, trans. Richard Rolle (Oxford: Clarendon Press, 1884).

b. Selected studies

Brown, Peter, and Andrew Butcher, *The Age of Saturn: Literature and History in the Canterbury Tales* (Oxford: Blackwell, 1991).
Ch. 3 for a more elaborate account of the argument found in this chapter.

Delasanta, Rodney, '"Sacrament and Sacrifice" in the *Pardoner's Tale*', *Annuale Medievale*, 14 (1973), 43–52.
The rioters' meal, as well as their slighting references to Christ's body and blood, travesty the Mass, in which Christ's sacrificial death is commemorated through the symbolic use of bread and wine.

Hudson, Anne, *The Premature Reformation: Wycliffite Texts and Lollard History* (Oxford: Clarendon Press, 1988).
Authoritative study of the origins of the Wycliffite movement, its development into 'Lollard' forms (social, educational, scholarly), and its impact as a vehicle for reform.

Jordan, Robert M., *Chaucer's Poetics and the Modern Reader* (Berkeley, Los Angeles and London: University of California Press, 1987).
Pages 127–36 on the difficulties of interpreting the Pardoner's Tale as the expression of an individual personality.

Lawton, David, *Chaucer's Narrators*, Chaucer Studies 13 (Cambridge: Brewer, 1985).
Ch. 2 explores the implications of the mismatch between corrupt teller and moral tale, and resists a psychological interpretation of the Pardoner's character: he is a disturbing and challenging 'grotesque'.

Pittock, Malcolm, 'The *Pardoner's Tale* and the Quest for Death', *Essays in Criticism*, 24 (1974), 107–23.
The relationship between the spiritual death and actual death of the rioters, their literalist understanding of the world and encounter with the old man: the tale explores the difference between substantial or emotional awareness of the significance of death and notional or intellectual awareness.

Steadman, John M., 'Old Age and *Contemptus Mundi* in the Pardoner's Tale', *Medium Aevum*, 33 (1964), 121–30.
On the contrasts (in age and moral and spiritual attitudes) between the old man and the rioters.

CHAPTER EIGHT
The Nun's Priest's Tale

i. THE PLAY OF LANGUAGE

The previous chapters have revealed a Chaucer who worked with a considerable degree of self-consciousness about the process of literary composition. Whether remodelling a source, manipulating a convention, or drawing on contemporary discourse, there is always present an active intelligence with its own priorities and criteria. Chaucer selects, re-emphasises, places in new contexts, his raw materials, aware all the time of the kind of activity in which he is engaged.

This is not a hermetic activity. Chaucer is not to be imagined as an isolated writer, merely deriving aesthetic pleasure from his transformations of old stories and old forms. His writing is an act of communication, of engagement with an audience about matters of mutual interest and concern. To an unusual degree, he generally allows the reader wide scope for interpretation. Characteristically, the reader's space is opened up by Chaucer's refusal to adopt an authoritative voice. He prefers instead to be a ventriloquist, speaking at one or several removes through narrators who themselves wear masks: the Wife of Bath imitating the chiding of one of her husbands, for example. Just as crucial, however, is Chaucer's preference for debate at the expense of resolution. He is not very good at endings, or at the very least his endings invite further speculation. What he excels at is the articulation of problems (marital relations, chivalric honour, the nature of freedom) and their expression within a dramatic and narrative context.

One important result of these strategies (or predilections) is that Chaucer's texts support a wide variety of meanings. In the absence of an authoritative author, and stimulated by a continuing debate, the reader or critic soon discovers a need to express his or her own opinion of the matter in hand, and to become the absent authority. In such ways, Chaucer includes his audience in the process of realising his intentions. But there are dangers in this procedure, not least the likelihood that, on account of the critical largesse which he dispenses, interpretations of his writings will be far removed from the scope of his original purposes. It therefore becomes part of Chaucer's literary project to raise his audience's awareness of the literary activities in which *they* are engaged: to show that the most authoritative-seeming explanation of a text is, at best, relatively true; and that some interpretations are, quite simply, absurd. One result is Chaucer's most slippery narrative, the Nun's Priest's Tale.

The reader of the Nun's Priest's Tale is never on firm ground. Its style fluctuates from homely description – 'A povre wydwe, somdeel stape in age' (2821) – to rhetorical flights of the most bombastic kind. There is a medley of voices, each clamouring for attention; the narrator's tone shifts with the style: now he appears to be direct, now sardonic, now profound, now light-hearted. In this respect, matters are not eased by the narrative vehicle, in which animals take on human roles (or do humans take on animal roles?). Throughout, there is a strong sense of satirical intention, but the precise target of the satire is not clear. Is it pride and vanity, as exhibited by Chauntecleer? Or the tendency of the narrator (a tendency shared by critics) to overburden a simple tale with solemn and learned meanings? Now answer the following questions from what you already know about the Nun's Priest's Tale.

1. *To what extent does the telling of the Nun's Priest's Tale expose the means and techniques whereby it was created?*
2. *Provide some examples of the ways in which a reader of the tale is allowed room for interpretation.*
3. *Identify three different voices used by Chaucer for the tale and discuss their distinctive qualities and uses.*

One way of confronting the peculiar problems of the Nun's Priest's Tale, if only to describe them more accurately, is by examining ways in which a particular passage parodies its source. An invitation to compare and contrast copy and 'original' (such comparisons being the mainspring of parody) occurs at the moment when Chauntecleer is seized by the fox. The narrator invokes an author, 'Gaufred', or Geoffrey of Vinsauf, whose handbook on the art of writing poetry *(Poetria nova)* has already been discussed in relation to the description of

Alisoun in the Miller's Tale. This time Chaucer, through the Nun's Priest, is quite specific in his flattering reference to a master of rhetoric, whom he addresses as 'deere maister soverayn' (3347), and to the passage he has in mind – a passage impressive enough to have circulated independently of the main treatise. It is Geoffrey's complaint on the death of Richard I, who was accidentally slain in 1199 by one of his own soldiers:

> In time of grief, express your grief with these words:
>
> Once defended by King Richard's shield, now undefended, O England, bear witness to your woe in the gestures of sorrow. Let your eyes flood with tears, and pale grief waste your features. Let writhing anguish twist your fingers, and woe make your heart within bleed. Let your cry strike the heavens. Your whole being dies in his death; the death was not his but yours. Death's rise was not in one place only but general. O tearful day of Venus! O bitter star! That day was your night; and that Venus your venom. That day inflicted the wound; but the worst of all days was that other – the day after the eleventh – which, cruel stepfather to life, destroyed life. Either day, with strange tyranny, was a murderer. The besieged one pierced the besieger; the sheltered one, him without cover; the cautious one pierced the incautious; the well-equipped soldier pierced an unarmed man – his own king! O soldier, why, treacherous soldier, soldier of treachery, shame of the world and sole dishonour of welfare; O soldier, his own army's creature, why did you dare this giant against him? Why did you dare this crime, this hideous crime? O sorrow! O greater than sorrow! O death! O truculent death! Would you were dead, O death! Bold agent of a deed so vile, how dare you recall it? You were pleased to remove our sun, and condemn day to darkness. Do you realize whom you snatched from us? To our eyes he was light; to our ears, melody; to our minds an amazement. Do you realize, impious death, whom you snatched from us? He was the lord of warriors, the glory of kings, the delight of the world. Nature knew not how to add any further perfection; he was the utmost she could achieve.
>
> (*Poetria nova,* III; trans. Nims, pp. 29–30)

Now answer the following questions.

1. *Comment on the success or failure of this passage in communicating a range of emotions.*
2. *What claims does Geoffrey make, either directly or indirectly, for the role and power of poetic or rhetorical utterance on the occasion of this national tragedy?*
3. *To what extent does Geoffrey perceive irony in the circumstances of Richard's death?*

The context of Geoffrey's lamentation is significant. However effective, it is a text-book example of how grief might be expressed. It is not a poet's direct response to a national tragedy, it is an exercise in eloquence; it uses that tragedy as a convenient occasion for displaying apostrophe, a rhetorical technique for amplifying a given theme by addressing something absent or inanimate as if it were capable of hearing and understanding. Another appropriate occasion would have served equally well. There is thus a certain coldness and detachment in what Geoffrey says, in spite of the passion with which he expresses himself, an awareness both of the need to give vent to powerful emotion, and the technical procedures to be followed.

The grief which he expresses is not merely personal. He projects his poet's role as one of discharging the grief felt by an entire country for a matter of general concern. England is thus personified, and imagined in a posture which expresses deep sorrow and mourning, to the point where the body of the king is identified with the body of the state: 'the death was not his but yours'. Geoffrey therefore pitches his claim for the power of poetic utterance extremely high: it encompasses all, speaks for all, consoles all, and provides some kind of explanation for what has happened. By berating in turn fate, the murder, and death itself, he attempts to lessen their effects.

Maintaining for the time being his privileged, omniscient control of such elements as 'England' and 'king', Geoffrey now includes fate itself, operating through the planets, in his perspective. Since Richard's death was thought to have occurred on a Friday, Venus – whose day it is – had a hand in the tragedy. Faced with the inexplicability of sudden death, Geoffrey explores its ironic contradictions: a powerful king was subject to the tyranny of fate; a soldier who served him was the cause of his murder. Geoffrey thus effects a transition from the general to the particular, and now focuses on the individual who was the immediate cause of Richard's death, heaping on him terms of opprobrium which are the very opposites of those ideals to which a knight aspires: treachery and shame. At this, the note of extreme exasperation is transferred to death itself – death, which turns upside-down the familiar world: joy becomes sorrow; light becomes darkness; possession becomes loss. In this case, possession was particularly dear: Richard was universally admired as an exemplary warrior and king, and as Nature's darling.

Geoffrey's mode of utterance, in the high style, is entirely suited to his content. His subject is a genuine, national tragedy within which an apostrophe to Friday is quite acceptable, however artificial the trope may sound to modern ears. If one looks for comparable tragic moments in the *Canterbury Tales,* the death of Arcite in the Knight's Tale comes to mind as an occasion of great sorrow and solemnity. But there, Chaucer concentrates his emotional effects in the speech of the dying man, full of the pathos of bewilderment in its evocation of a knightly ideal that has destroyed one of its chief exponents. There the language, though formal, is direct and undeniably heartfelt. Instead, Chaucer reserved the most elevated Vinsaufian rhetoric for a trivial and mundane incident in a farmyard, in which a fox does what foxes do (seize chickens), in which there is no death, and which is connected tenuously to Richard's death-wound by the coincidence that both events supposedly happened on a Friday. Why did he use the *Poetria nova* in this way?

> This Chauntecleer stood hye upon his toos,
> Strecchynge his nekke, and heeld his eyen cloos,
> And gan to crowe loud for the nones.
> And daun Russell the fox stirte up atones,
> And by the gargat hente Chauntecleer, 3335
> And on his bak toward the wode hym beer,
> For yet ne was ther no man that hym sewed.
> O destinee, that mayst nat been eschewed!
> Allas, that Chauntecleer fleigh fro the bemes!
> Allas, his wyf ne roghte nat of dremes! 3340
> And on a Friday fil al this meschaunce.
> O Venus, that art goddesse of plesaunce,
> Syn that thy servant was this Chauntecleer,
> And in thy servyce dide al his poweer,
> Moore for delit than world to multiplye, 3345
> Why woldestow suffre hym on thy day to dye?
> O Gaufred, deere maister soverayn,
> That whan thy worthy kyng Richard was slayn
> With shot, compleynedest his deeth so soore,
> Why ne hadde I now thy sentence and thy loore, 3350
> The Friday for to chide, as diden ye?
> For on a Friday, soothly, slayn was he.
> Thanne wolde I shewe yow how that I koude pleyne
> For Chauntecleres drede and for his peyne.
>
> (NPT, 3331–54)

Now answer the following questions.

1. *Identify and discuss the two styles of writing in this passage and comment on their different functions.*
2. *Compare and contrast the circumstances which give rise to (a) the passage by Geoffrey of Vinsauf quoted above, and (b) the passage spoken by the Nun's Priest. What effects do those circumstances have on the reader's reponse to the two passages?*
3. *To what extent might the Nun's Priest be seen as critical of the kind of rhetoric advocated by Geoffrey of Vinsauf?*

The lines which echo *Poetria nova* are prefaced by some direct, plain description which forms a counterpoint and frame for the rhetorical excursus that follows. (After the apostrophe to Geoffrey of Vinsauf there are some equally inflated lines on Pertelote's sorrow, before the narrator turns again, at line 3375, to his direct style: 'This sely wydwe and eek hir doghtres two'.) Plain, colloquial language is used to advance the action, and give essential information. Rather like January in the Merchant's Tale, who stretches his scrawny neck and 'crows' the morning after his wedding night, Chauntecleer stands on tiptoe, with his eyes closed, the very image of unsuspecting pride, and begins to display his prowess in crowing. Within three lines the fox has quickly pounced, seized Chauntecleer by that outstretched neck, and carried him off to the wood. The opportunist – 'For yet ne was ther no man that hym sewed [*followed*]' (3337) – has for the time being triumphed over the self-engrossed. The scene now goes into suspended animation, and the language changes accordingly, as the Nun's Priest delivers himself of his observations on what has transpired.

It is with the mention of destiny that Geoffrey of Vinsauf's passage first comes into play. The narrator bewails the patterning of events much as Geoffrey lamented the circumstances of Richard's death. If only Chauntecleer had not flown from his perch, and had listened to his wife's views on dreams ... If only Richard's soldier had not been where he was when he was ... Similarly, the Nun's Priest takes on the role of representative mourner, expressing and channelling grief, but to ludicrous effect: it is not clear whom he represents, he is presumptuous in his mourning, and the incident is, on the scale of human (or even animal) suffering, insignificant. Undeterred, he continues sententiously with the profound, but inconsequential, pronouncement: 'And on a Friday fil al this meschaunce' (3341). Here, apparently, is the key to the obscure workings of destiny.

At this point Chaucer exploits an advantage over his mentor. Friday is ruled by Venus, the goddess of love and, since Chauntecleer is dedicated to amorous exploits, 'Moore for delit than world to multiplye', he can address Venus – as Geoffrey could not – with the question of why she might let her servant die on the very day over which she exerts maximum control. Again, the question is so much hot air, produced on the wings of rhetoric, and entirely premature. It is as if the narrator has found an opening for a sonorous set-piece and is not going to be denied the exercise of his eloquence, even if it means incorporating a grossly exaggerated account of Chauntecleer's death.

There may be more than a hint of truth in the confession of inadequacy which follows, as the Nun's Priest substitutes Geoffrey of

Vinsauf's sustained clamour against the injustice of arbitrary death with an apostrophe to Geoffrey himself. But the confession of inadequacy – 'Why ne hadde I now thy sentence and thy loore ...?' (3350) – is itself a cunning rhetorical device, allowing the narrator, with the 'Why ...?' repeated from his similar address to Venus (3346), to intensify his sense of helplessness in the face of overwhelming sorrow. More than this, it allows him to add dignity and authority to his lament by invoking an acknowledged master of the art, and an event (Richard's death) of unquestionable seriousness.

And yet there is also a sense in which the narrator is cocking a snook at Geoffrey of Vinsauf. His response to Richard's death was 'The Friday for to chide'. To that extent it trivialised the king's death, reducing it to an occasion for a rhetorical exercise. The invocation of Geoffrey and his high style to embellish a farmyard incident is therefore entirely in keeping with the trivialising pattern set by Geoffrey himself. The uselessness of his kind of eloquence on demand is indicated by the dead end to which it leads. The narrator, having twice before stated that his hero faced death on a Friday (3341 and 3346), can derive no more sentence and solace from the great Geoffrey of Vinsauf than the reassurance that Richard I, too, supposedly received his fatal wound on the same day: 'on a Friday, soothly, slayn was he' (3352).

Some of the functions of Chaucer's passage – so unnecessary to the development of the plot, so in keeping with the tone of the tale – are now becoming clearer. It puts on conspicuous display the learning of the Nun's Priest, who is as dangerously self-absorbed in his rhetorical voice as Chauntecleer is in his own vocal skills. It sustains comic effects of a mock-heroic kind, whereby humdrum actions are inflated beyond recognition by means of comparisons and language usually associated with momentous events. It highlights the underlying absurdity, bordering on cynicism, of a rhetorical proficiency (like Geoffrey of Vinsauf's) which is adrift either from the structures and pressures of continuous narrative, or from content, or from both. And it mocks the idea of tragedy (here surfacing in the story of Richard's death) with its opposite, comedy (the story of Chauntecleer and the fox, which ends happily, without fatality). It therefore helps to fulfil the Nun's Priest's commission, as defined by Harry Bailly at the outset of the tale, to counteract the dreary tragedies of the Monk with 'swich thyng as may oure hertes glade' (NPP, 2811).

ii. TAKING THE MORAL

Tragedy and comedy, to the medieval way of thinking, were opposite sides of the same coin. Failure to appreciate this accounts for the motion sickness which some readers suffer as the Nun's Priest takes his roller-coaster ride from high seriousness to low comedy and back again. For the effects of both tragedy and comedy were to create an inverted world, the opposite of the status quo. For Geoffrey of Vinsauf, lamenting Richard's death, day has become night, a soldier has attacked his own king. Chaucer, on the other hand, turns the world upside-down by bestowing human characteristics on animals.

The original tragic hero was, from the Christian point of view, and as the Monk himself reminds us, Adam:

> ... he for mysgovernaunce
> Was dryven out of hys hye prosperitee
> To labour, and to helle, and to meschaunce.
>
> (MkT, 2013–15)

Now answer the following questions.

1. *What other references to the story of Adam and Eve can you find within the Nun's Prist's Tale?*
2. *In what ways can Pertelote's role be matched with that of Eve?*
3. *How is our understanding of Chauntecleer's faults affected by reference to Adam's story?*

There are sufficient allusions to Adam's story in the Nun's Priest's Tale to be sure that it is a source of significance, providing one of the tale's many morals. The location of the action, in 'A yeerd ... enclosed al aboute' (2847), is not unlike the paradisal garden, traditionally represented with an encircling wall, in which Adam and Eve enacted their downfall. The time of Chauntecleer's downfall is even more suggestive of the Genesis story. It is as if the Nun's Priest is going out of his way to include the reference. The fox comes into the yard

> Whan that the month in which the world bigan,
> That highte March, whan God first maked man,
> Was compleet, and passed were also,
> Syn March was gon, thritty days and two . . .
>
> (NPT, 3187–90)

The main protagonists, like their counterparts in Eden, are three in number: a male and a female who enjoy sovereignty over their little world, and a usurper, a wily deceiver, intent on destroying the harmony of 'the garden'. The fox is, indeed, represented as devilish both in his appearance and in his ways. In Chauntecleer's dream, which prefigures the fox's appearance, he is a menacing reddish beast with black-tipped tail and ears, a 'snowte smal, with glowynge eyen tweye' (2905), and a terrifying look. 'Ful of sly iniquitee' and the agent of a higher power (3215-17), the fox describes himself, if ironically, as 'worse than a feend' (3286).

The female's role in Chauntecleer's downfall is crucial, as it was in Adam's. Taunted by Pertelote – 'I kan nat love a coward, by my feith!' (2911) – the Nun's Priest is not slow to make the connection between his own narrative and the biblical one. His tale, he says, 'is of a cok ... / That tok his conseil of his wyf, with sorwe' (3252–3), and he draws the inevitable lesson:

> Wommannes conseil broghte us first to wo
> And made Adam fro Paradys to go,
> Ther as he was ful myrie and wel at ese.
>
> (NPT, 3257–9)

The 'sin' which Chauntecleer goes on to commit is precisely that associated with the Genesis story – pride – whether expressed through sexual temptation (3160–2) and excess – 'He fethered Pertelote twenty tyme, / And trad hire eke as ofte, er it was pryme' (3177–8) – or through intellectual arrogance. At great length Chauntecleer attempts to refute Pertelote's theory that dreams are caused by bad digestion, and argues instead that they foretell the future. So determined is he to exert dominance over his wife that he will neglect the lesson of his own dream, and allow himself to be seized by a reddish beast who, provoking again Chauntecleer's self-admiration (this time as a singer) asks, as if half-thinking of Adam, the father of mankind: 'konne ye youre fader countrefete?' (3321). Chauntecleer concludes his discourse with a memorable Latin tag, wilfully mistranslated as 'Womman is mannes joye and al his blis' (3166), which itself points back to the beginning of it all: *'In principio, / Mulier est hominis confusio'* (3163–4).

Now answer the following questions.

1. *Plate 8 shows simultaneous representations of the events of the Fall. What are the crucial actions, and what is their significance?*
2. *To what extent does the picture use posture to convey meaning?*
3. *Relate the design of Eden, and the events which happened there, to the Nun's Priest's Tale.*

Such is the frequency of reference to the fall of Adam and Eve that it is as well to have a vivid idea of how Chaucer's readers might have imagined the biblical episode. The example overleaf, from a Bible illustrated in the middle of the fourteenth century, conveniently superimposes the crucial actions. Within a walled garden, Eve accepts fruit from a serpent (with a female face) coiled around the tree of knowledge, from which God has forbidden the pair to eat. With her other, extended, arm she passes the apple to Adam, who in turn eats it. This transaction completed, Adam and Eve are ejected from the garden by an angel, brandishing a sword. Their cowering postures, contrasting with their former, upright, demeanours, suggest remorse and humiliation. In order to signify their initiation into sexual awareness and shame, they hold leaves over their genitals.

That being said, the farmyard enclosure where Chauntecleer and Pertelote dwell is a strange Eden. Long before catastrophe overtakes them, they have lost their innocence and sense of peaceful co-existence in dissension, rivalry over the authority which knowledge confers, and the display of sexual attractiveness and prowess. Even if one were to ignore the fallen state of Chauntecleer and Pertelote, and take the Edenic references at face value – no easy matter when they refer to a cock and a fox – their import does not exactly square with traditional interpretations of Adam's fall. The Nun's Priest's parodic, upside-down, version of that event, apportions as much blame, if not more, to the man as to the woman. Rather like the Wife of Bath's Prologue, it questions the relevance of a long-established myth (or rather, particular interpretations of it) to individual experience.

One way of accommodating a satiric version of the Fall is to invoke, again, the idea of Christian comedy. If comedy is defined as a story with a happy ending, then the story of Christ, the second Adam who remedied the sins of the first, is the supreme comedy. Even death, the nemesis faced by many a tragic hero, was overturned by him. With this expansive context, the light-hearted, or revisionary, treatment of revered truths, becomes tolerable, because in the end all works out for the best. Christ redeems the sins of Adam and Eve, and Chauntecleer, too, escapes from the jaws of death. Thus the comic 'sacrilegious' perspective of the Nun's Priest's Tale makes the tragic 'orthodox' perspective of the Monk's Tale, based as it is on the pagan idea of the revolutions of Fortune's wheel, look two-dimensional and utterly inadequate.

The closing lines of the Nun's Priest's Tale are sufficient warning against solemn speculations on the nature of comedy:

> But ye that holden this tale a folye,
> As of a fox, or of a cok and hen,
> Taketh the moralite, goode men. 3440

Plate 8: The temptation of Adam and Eve and their expulsion from the garden of Eden.

For Seint Paul seith that al that writen is,
To oure doctrine it is ywrite, ywis;
Taketh the fruyt, and lat the chaf be stille.

(NPT, 3438–43)

That the tale has a moral (or morals) is unavoidably clear. What precisely it or they may be is deliberately left open to debate, to the continuing and changing engagement of audience with text. No reader of the Nun's Priest's Tale can be sure of not becoming a victim of his or her own pontificating, or falling victim to presumed knowledge, or being seized by the 'gargat' by a much more wily writer. Certain it is that one of the practical morals of the narrative is 'keep your mouth shut and your eyes open' – one which both Chauntecleer and the fox learn to their cost, and which the present writer is now resolved to take to heart.

iii. DISCUSSION POINTS

Read carefully the opening lines (2821–81) of the Nun's Priest's Tale, and then answer the following questions.

1. *How important is the setting of the tale to its subsequent effects and meanings?*
2. *How would you describe the language used in this passage, and what passage would you choose from the remainder of the tale as a contrast?*
3. *Compare and contrast the values, attitudes and activities of the poor widow with those of Chauntecleer.*
4. *Comment on the use made of colour in this passage.*
5 *How would you describe the mood of this opening passage? How is it created? What is its purpose?*

The following questions are related more generally to the Nun's Priest's Tale.

6. *What parallels exist between the identities of Chauntecleer and the narrator of his tale, and what are the implications of those parallels?*
7. *To what extent can the moral of the Nun's Priests's Tale be summed up in the words 'pride must have its fall'?*
8. *Exemplify and discuss the use of parody in the Nun's Priest's Tale.*
9. *'The Nun's Priest's Tale explores the links between comedy and tragedy.' Discuss.*
10. *In what ways does the Nun's Priest's Tale either endorse* or *refute orthodox ideas about the responsibility of women for the sinfulness of men?*
11. *'Chauntecleer is a victim of his own loquacity.' Discuss.*

iv. FURTHER READING

a. Sources and contexts

Geoffrey of Vinsauf, *Poetria nova,* trans. Margaret F. Nims (Toronto: Pontifical Institute of Mediaeval Studies, 1967).

b. Selected studies

Bishop, Ian, *The Narrative Art of the 'Canterbury Tales': A Critical Study of the Major Poems,* Everyman's University Library (London and Melbourne: Dent, 1987).
Explores the relationship of tale to the various strands of the university curriculum, especially Dialectic – the art of establishing truth through logical argument.

Corsa, Helen Storm, *Chaucer: Poet of Mirth and Morality* (Notre Dame, IN: University of Notre Dame Press, 1964).
Pages 211–20 on the various morals which the tale makes possible, including the triumph of comedy over tragedy.

Donovan, Mortimer J., 'The *Moralite* of the Nun's Priest's Sermon', *Journal of English and Germanic Philology,* 52 (1953), 498-508.
On the various ways in which the fox signifies the devil.

Hieatt, Constance B., 'The Moral of *"The Nun's Priest's Tale"*', *Studia Neophilologica,* 42 (1970), 3–8.
Stresses the predominance of the Adam and Eve story among the many morals which the tale provides.

Muscatine, Charles, *Chaucer and the French Tradition: A Study in Style and Meaning* (Berkeley and Los Angeles: University of California Press, 1957).
The meaning of the tale should not be taken too seriously: for any one interpretation evidence can be found from the poem to undercut it: the poem constantly shifts focus and offers a 'multiple perspective' (pp. 237–43).

Pearsall, Derek, 'Chaucer, the Nun's Priest's Tale, and the Modern Reader', *Dutch Quarterly Review,* 10 (1980), 164–74.
Lively survey of critical approaches.

Pearsall, Derek, (ed.), *The Nun's Priest's Tale,* A Variorum Edition of the Works of Geoffrey Chaucer, vol. 2: *The Canterbury Tales,* pt 9 (Norman: University of Oklahoma Press, 1984).
Pages 8–82 for a feisty, comprehensive and detailed review of source studies and criticism.

Scheps, Walter, 'Chaucer's Anti-Fable: *Reductio ad Absurdum* in the

Nun's Priest's Tale', *Leeds Studies in English*, ns 4 (1970), 1–10.
The tale blurs the distinction between humans and animals to the point where the whole idea of fable (i.e. an animal story with a human moral) as a genre is ridiculed.

Shallers, Paul A., 'The "Nun's Priest's Tale": An Ironic Exemplum', *English Literary History*, 42 (1975), 319–37.
Chaucer blends beast fable and moralised sermon story to make a hybrid which both offers morals and questions human ability to act morally.

Speirs, John, *Chaucer the Maker* (London: Faber, 1951).
Pages 185–93 on mock-heroic elements of the poem, the theme of pride and the Fall of man.

Watson, Charles S., 'The Relationship of the "Monk's Tale" and the "Nun's Priest's Tale"', *Studies in Short Fiction*, 1 (1963–64), 277–88.
Detailed comparisons and contrasts show the extent to which the two tales are deliberately linked (e.g. in their treatment of Fortune, tragedy and comedy, and clerical outlook).

Index